PRIVATE LAW, SOCIAL LIFE

AN INTRODUCTION

Second Edition

Logan Atkinson
B.A., LL.B., M.Phil., M.A., LL.D.
Department of Law, Carleton University

Neil C. Sargent
LL.B., LL.M., D.E.I.
Department of Law, Carleton University

First in a proposed series of titles in Legal Studies published in association with members of the Department of Law, Carleton University, Ottawa, Canada.

LexisNexis®

Private Law, Social Life: An Introduction, 2nd Edition

August 2007

Members of the LexisNexis Group worldwide

Canada	LexisNexis Canada Inc, 123 Commerce Valley Dr. E., MARKHAM, Ontario
Argentina	Abeledo Perrot, Jurisprudencia Argentina and Depalma, BUENOS AIRES
Australia	Butterworths, a Division of Reed International Books Australia Pty Ltd, CHATSWOOD, New South Wales
Austria	ARD Betriebsdienst and Verlag Orac, VIENNA
Chile	Publitecsa and Conosur Ltda, SANTIAGO DE CHILE
Czech Republic	Orac sro, PRAGUE
France	Éditions du Juris-Classeur SA, PARIS
Hong Kong	Butterworths Asia (Hong Kong), HONG KONG
Hungary	Hvg Orac, BUDAPEST
India	Butterworths India, NEW DELHI
Ireland	Butterworths (Ireland) Ltd, DUBLIN
Italy	Giuffré, MILAN
Malaysia	Malayan Law Journal Sdn Bhd, KUALA LUMPUR
New Zealand	Butterworths of New Zealand, WELLINGTON
Poland	Wydawnictwa Prawnicze PWN, WARSAW
Singapore	Butterworths Asia, SINGAPORE
South Africa	Butterworth Publishers (Pty) Ltd, DURBAN
Switzerland	Stämpfli Verlag AG, BERNE
United Kingdom	Butterworths Tolley, a Division of Reed Elsevier (UK), LONDON, WC2A
USA	LexisNexis, DAYTON, Ohio

National Library of Canada Cataloguing in Publication

Atkinson, Logan, 1954-
Private law, social life : an introduction / Logan Atkinson, Neil C. Sargent. — 2nd ed.

Includes index.
ISBN 978-0-433-45201-0

1. Civil law—Canada. 2. Sociological jurisprudence.
I. Sargent, N. (Neil) II. Title.

KE495.A84 2007 346.71 C2007-903790-9
KF385.ZA2A853 2007

Printed and bound in Canada.

General Editor's Introduction

The publication of the second edition of *Private Law, Social Life: An Introduction* represents the launch of a proposed new series of texts from LexisNexis. It is planned that titles in this new series will represent an innovative group of accessible texts, intended for an audience coming to the study of law in context for the first time. While readers will in most cases be undergraduate university students embarking on the social study of law, we anticipate that these books will appeal as well to other non-lawyers looking to widen their understanding of law, legal process and the reciprocally constitutive roles of law and other cultural phenomena.

At advanced levels, the issues canvassed in the present volume and to be addressed in titles in the planning stages for this Series are complex and layered, requiring at least a moderately sophisticated understanding of legal doctrine together with a familiarity with debates in social, cultural and political studies. Finding accessible literature, then, is a challenge, especially for those just beginning their studies or those otherwise looking for suitable introductions to Legal Studies as a discipline. The proposed Series in Legal Studies is intended to address this challenge. Our ambition is that each title in the series will provide a suitable introduction to relevant doctrine (working from conventionally recognized categories) and issues of context, giving readers guides from which they might work as their reading and thinking progresses.

Private Law, Social Life: An Introduction (2nd Edition) is a concise introduction to private law doctrine, and also a guide to some of the interesting critical issues emerging from Legal Studies literature and, perhaps surprisingly, from many of our leading private law cases. Analysis of the often competing philosophical frameworks out of which these issues emerge forms a foundation in the text, and it is hoped that readers will be able to build on this analysis and start to develop their own critical perspectives as they work their way through the book.

As the first title in the proposed Series, *Private Law, Social Life: An Introduction (2nd Edition)* is the initial step in the realization of an idea that originated through many lengthy discussions among colleagues in the Department of Law at Carleton University.

The planned new Series in Legal Studies is the product of a commitment among colleagues to a successful, rich experience for people new to and curious about the discipline, and a genuine spirit of collaboration. Special thanks are due to Neil Sargent, my co-author for the present volume and a principal supporter in the development of the Series.

Logan Atkinson, LL.D.
General Editor

Department of Law
Carleton University

May 2007

Preface

This second edition of *Private Law, Social Life: An Introduction* expands on some of the central concerns of the first edition. Readers will find a stronger emphasis on some of the fundamental assumptions that appear to underlie private law doctrine in the common law tradition. But readers will also find in this edition an assessment of alternative assumptions that have the potential to disrupt convention and, perhaps, lead to a critical reassessment of the structure and function of private law. Is it fair to say that the western turn to individualism that was accomplished with such force in the nineteenth century is not simply the starting point and the defining event in the development of contemporary private law doctrine, but also the continuing and dominant motif in private law decision-making? Or does there remain room for reflection on the significance of healthy relationships *per se* as the source of individual creativity, self-esteem and general well-being, in turn the inspiration for many of our most significant judicial decisions in private law disputes? It is the tension between these two positions (introduced in Chapter 1) that lies just beneath the surface of much of the material that follows, and that we hope will lead to healthy scepticism about the efficacy of private law rules.

While the substantive concerns of this book are investigated with a view to assisting the reader to a more critical perspective, our over-arching pedagogical concerns remain as they were when the first edition was produced in 2003. This book is intended as a brief introduction to the rudiments of private law, combined with a first glance at the role private law plays in our ordinary social experience while remembering the philosophical assumptions lying just beneath the surface of the discussion. We have attempted to provide an accessible short text for those coming to the social study of private law for the first time. In our experience, it is far too challenging for many students to engage adequately with the huge and growing body of literature that takes a critical perspective to the vast world of private law doctrine, without first understanding something of the way in which lawyers look at private law. After all, most of this critical literature on law is written by experts for experts, and as a consequence it assumes a great deal of fundamental knowledge in the reader that, for the most part, is missing in the layperson. This can be a special problem in the study of law outside the professional law school, where there is neither the time nor, perhaps, the inclination to immerse the student in private law rules to the same extent as occurs in the first year law school curriculum.

It is our hope that this book will give those studying private law in its social context a ready source of basic information on the nature of private law categories, and at the same time an introductory overview of some of the issues that emerge from the critical literature. The idea is that this will make the transition to a more complete engagement with that literature less jarring, and therefore more enjoyable. As such, however, the reader is cautioned that this book is not to be taken as either definitive or comprehensive in relating some of the principles of private law. If the reader is intent on a complete and settled statement of private law rules, then one or more of the conventional textbooks ought to be consulted.

Our private law students in Carleton University's undergraduate programmes in Legal Studies have been the inspiration for the second edition of *Private Law, Social Life: An Introduction*. It has been a great pleasure to participate in their engagement with the first edition, but their persistent questions and determination to learn more have been the impetus for a re-focused second edition that, it is hoped, will serve them in better stead. For many students, their first encounter with the intricacies of private law is perhaps little more than a surprisingly interesting diversion from other studies, but it is also true that a great many of those students stay on that diverted path much longer and much more thoroughly than they might have expected. This book is a small step in our attempt to meet their enthusiasm with materials to help sustain their curiosity and encourage further study.

Logan Atkinson
Neil Sargent

May 2007

About the Authors

Logan Atkinson, B.A., LL.B., M. Phil., M.A., LL.D. is an Associate Professor at the Department of Law, Carleton University. Dr. Atkinson practised law for many years in St. John's Newfoundland, and is a member of the Law Society of Newfoundland. His research focuses on interdisciplinary intersections in law and the humanities.

Neil Sargent, LL.B., LL.M., D.E.I. has been a member of the Department of Law at Carleton University since 1974. His research interests include corporate criminal liability, private law relations, legal individualism and alternative dispute resolution.

Table of Contents

Chapter 1

Relationships, Classification and Philosophical Assumptions

I. INTRODUCTION

Imagine that you are a celestial being, inhabiting the heavens and gazing down at the Earth, with a particular interest in observing human life. Now the first thing that you may notice about human life from this lofty perspective is that human beings are extremely busy beings. Humans are constantly on the move, working, studying, traveling, playing, being active in an infinite variety of endeavours and encountering each other in an infinite number of ways. You may notice, too, that human beings participate in this multitude of activities in groups, in communities, and that it is very unusual to observe a human being separate from other human beings for anything but a very short span of time. Virtually everything humans do in their activity is social, meaning that, at some level at least, it involves someone else. There is very little done in the run of a human's day that is absolutely solitary, that has absolutely no connection with anyone else.

When we use the term "connection" in the context of human social activity, we mean connections of the kind that, at first glance, may seem fairly tenuous and obscure. For example, from your special vantage point, you may observe a human taking a shower in the morning, and this may, at first glance at least, seem like a solitary activity. But that human being could not have taken that shower unless the technician at the water purification plant did his or her job properly, unless the plumber who installed the plumbing connected the pipes in the appropriate way, unless the person responsible for the smooth operation of the sewers ensured the orderly disposal of waste water. So even what appear to be the most isolated, solitary acts are actually connected in some way at some level with the acts of others. By thinking of connections in this way, you will ultimately conclude that human activity is almost always social, almost always connected to other activity.

You may also notice that human beings are insistent and consistent classifiers. They catalogue everything, and likely do this as a way to give order and meaning to their world. The community in which humans live is a very chaotic place, and without their various systems of classifying everything they encounter, the world would likely be incomprehensible. Classifying things and ideas gives form out of chaos. The word "taxonomy" means something like "the science of classification", or "the practice of classification", and humans employ taxonomy so as to impose some structure and order on their lives. For example, the ordinary dictionary is a product of the science of classification of words. The authors of dictionaries are practicing taxonomy, but classifying words according to certain pre-determined criteria. What are those criteria? The first and most obvious is that words are classified according to how they are spelled, and this ends up being an alphabetical classification. In grammar, however, humans classify words quite differently, based not on the way in which the words are spelled, but rather on the way in which they are used. So in language we find nouns, verbs, adjectives, prepositions and the rest, and classifying words in this way helps us to make better sense out of the way our language is structured and used in our ordinary day-to-day speech. Further still, humans have something called etymology, the science of word origins, and this science functions as a classification of words according to their ancient roots in founding languages. So humans sort current words according to their origins in Greek or Latin or Sanskrit or some other ancient language, and again this helps them organize and make sense out of what at times appears to be incomprehensible.

One of the principal functions of law is the classification of human social activity, that infinitely various endeavour of humans that you observe from your advantageous perspective. Law classifies human social activity using a particular set of classification criteria, in the same way that the dictionary classifies words based on the alphabet, or grammar classifies words based on function. Legal taxonomy classifies human activity so as to make some order and sense out of this extremely complex set of circumstances that, as celestial beings standing up over the human community and looking down, we might observe first and foremost.

The way in which legal taxonomy responds to the vast array of human social activity is central to our attempt in this book to come to some understanding of the nature of a particular group of relationships that emerges from that activity. The law begins the task of classification by suggesting that human social activity is comprised of relationships.

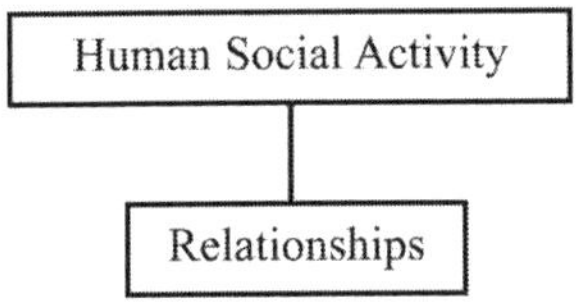

Now ordinarily, when we think of relationships we think of more or less intimate relationships, the ones we have with our parents, our children, our siblings, our extended family, our close friends, perhaps a few others. But from the perspective of legal taxonomy, we have relationships with hundreds, maybe thousands, of other people every day of our lives. The idea of "relationship" in the law is as broad as one might imagine, such that a human has a relationship with the plumber when taking a shower in the morning, and with the sewer maintenance person and the water purification person. If you took the bus to work or school this morning, then you had a relationship with the bus driver, with every other person on the bus, and with every person in every car that drove by the bus as it made its way to its destination. You also had a relationship with the company that made the bus and the one that made its tires, with the municipal government that maintains the roads, with each and every one of your classmates in the classroom or workmates in the workplace, with the executive of the university if you are a university student, and with the university itself. When you buy your lunch in the cafeteria, you have a relationship with the company that operates the cafeteria, with the producer of the food, with the staff that cooks it behind the counter. When you checked your e-mail this morning, you had a relationship with the internet provider. When you brushed your teeth, you had a relationship with the manufacturer of the toothbrush and the maker of the toothpaste. We, each and every one of us, are parties to hundreds and thousands of relationships, in the way that the law defines relationships at least, each and every day of our lives. Legal taxonomy is the means by which we classify that endless number of relationships, the means by which we try to make some sense out of this extremely complex and chaotic web of social activity to which we are all party each and every day.

How does legal classification work? Legal taxonomy starts by sorting out the various possible types of relationship based on the characteristics those relationships share. If apparently diverse relationships share certain types of traits, then they will be lumped together in the classification system, the same way that we think of nouns one way and verbs another in grammar, or the way that the dictionary classifies all the "b" words together and all the "r" words together. The first distinction the law uses in this respect is the difference between what we will call private and public relationships.

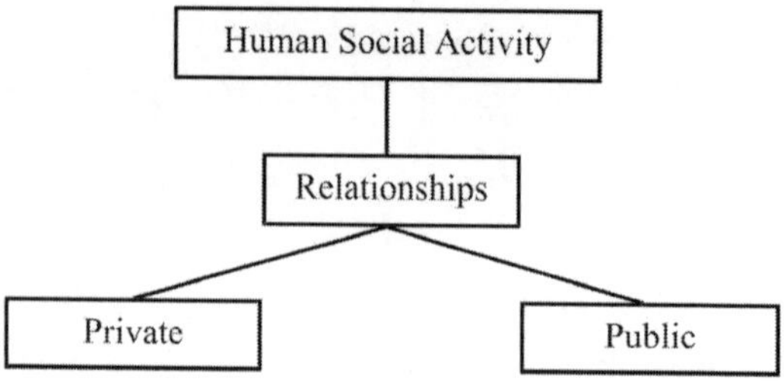

How do we know if a particular relationship is public or private, for the purposes of this first division in our classification system? First, it must be pointed out that the terms "private" and "public" themselves are not free of problems and disputes inside the law, and later in this chapter we will spend some time trying to sort out this very distinction in legal classification. But for the moment, it is enough for us to consider that the way words are used inside the legal classification system is often quite different from the way those same words are used in ordinary speech. From the law's perspective, a "public" relationship is not one that is merely out in the open, in the public eye. In the law, a "public relationship" is one that involves the state in its political or sovereign capacity. Now by the "state" here, we mean government and all its various forms, including agencies of government, the police, public and quasi-public institutions such as our prisons and hospitals, various administrative boards and tribunals such as the "immigration appeal board," and a large number of other agencies and institutions that carry on something of the function of government. For a relationship to be categorized as a "public" relationship, we must have the state (through government or an aspect of government) involved in its political or sovereign capacity, and not as a mere individual. For the moment, that is all that is necessary, but we will explore this idea in a bit more depth later in this chapter.

On the side of our classification system devoted to private relationships, it is important to recognize that we are not necessarily talking about relationships away from public scrutiny, those we have "in private". As already noted, if you took the bus this morning, then you had a relationship with the bus driver, and there is nothing secret about that. Rather, what we mean when we talk about a "private law relationship" is a relationship between or among individuals. Now "individuals" here has a peculiar meaning. By individuals we mean "legal persons", and legal persons are not necessarily the same as ordinary persons. We will consider the question of legal personality in some depth in Chapter 2. For present purposes, it is enough to acknowledge the complexity of the idea of legal personality. For example, adults are almost always legal persons, but not for all purposes if they're mentally unable to look after their own affairs. Children enjoy the benefits of legal personhood, but with restricted legal capacity. Corporations, however, are legal persons, even though they are not human, and the same is true of trade unions. Governments too can act as legal persons for the purposes of private law relationships. In other words, if a government is acting in its political or sovereign capacity, the relationships it generates are aspects of public law, but if it is acting as a legal individual, the relationships are classified as private law. Further, there is a great deal of controversy about whether things (trees, horses, desks and pens) can sometimes become legal persons, and therefore command the attention of private law. But for a relationship to be classified by the law as a private law relationship, the participants in that relationship must be individuals, they must be legal persons to some extent at least, and this very first criterion of classification is an enormously complex idea in itself.

On both the public and the private law sides of our diagram, legal taxonomy, as you may guess, is the ever more specific classification and sub-classification and further sub-classification of the relationships that emerge from human social activity, so as to make some sense out of the enormous complexity of human social existence. This means that there is a limitless number of categories to contend with, if one is to come to terms in any complete sense with the nature of legal rules. So as to give us some context in which to consider the varieties of private law relationships recognized by legal taxonomy, it is necessary first to distinguish the major categories of public law relationships. We will then be able to remove these sorts of relationships from our consideration. While recognizing the complications involved in an attempt to come to terms with the complete number of possibilities in legal classification, we can nevertheless identify three broad categories of relationships on the public law side of our diagram. We will not go into these in any depth; it is enough to introduce them only so as to separate them from relationships on the private law side of our diagram, those classified as "private law relationships".

The three principal categories of relationship on the public law side of our diagram generate criminal law, administrative law and constitutional law.

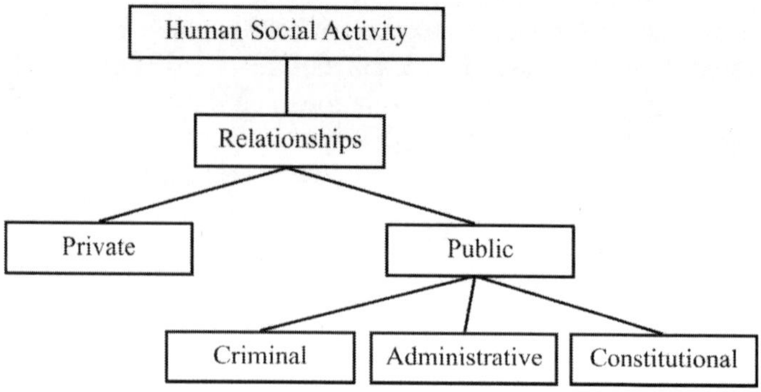

"Criminal law" emerges from the relationship between the person who does a prohibited act on the one hand, and the state in its political or sovereign capacity on the other. It is not the product of the relationship between the perpetrator and the victim; that is a relationship between individuals, and one which therefore would be classified on the private law side. This is why in the criminal law we have state prosecutions of offenders, and state funded penitentiaries — the commission of a crime is a violation of the relationship between the state and the person who does something over which the state has exercised its jurisdiction. It is also the simplest explanation for the difficulty victims of crime often experience in having their interests accommodated in the criminal justice system. Strictly speaking, the proceeding in a criminal court is one between the state and the accused, meaning the victim is not party to the principal relationship under review.

"Administrative law", considered in its most usual sense, is that bundle of rules that governs the way in which state programmes and services are delivered to the population. For example, if the government is to make available employment insurance, then a relationship exists between those of us entitled to collect that insurance, and the government agency (representing the state in its political or sovereign capacity) itself. This is a matter of public law, classified as administrative law. If the state is to provide a mechanism for the review of applications by non-Canadians for citizenship status or landed immigrant status, then the procedures by which that review takes place will be a matter of administrative law, found on the public law side of our legal taxonomy. These are but two examples from a complex network of relationships on the public law side of our diagram known as "administrative law".

In the Canadian context, "constitutional law" sets out the general rules in a number of important legal categories. Perhaps most obvious is the law of rights as between the state (in its political or sovereign capacity) and persons within its jurisdiction, and much of the law in this respect is captured in the *Charter of Rights and Freedoms*.[1] Constitutional law also provides a bundle of rules for governing the relationship between different governments inside the state, including in particular the relationship between Canada's federal government and the various provincial or territorial governments. Further, it is inside this category in the legal taxonomy that we find the law governing the way in which the various levels of government are actually organized, including such matters as the composition of the House of Commons, the Senate and the various provincial legislatures, and including such things as the frequency at which elections must be held. These matters, and a host of other similar questions, are addressed as items of constitutional law and are included on the public law side of our taxonomy.

As we go forward in this book, it is important to keep in mind that the law that emerges from the relationships catalogued on the public law side of our classification system is in most respects quite different from that which emerges on the private law side. The principles current in criminal law and in judicial decisions pursuant to the *Charter* often have only tangential connection to the thinking that underlies private law relationships. In this book we will be spending our time trying to come to terms with the legal taxonomy on the private law side of the diagram, although that will necessarily involve some discussion of public law issues and debates where overlap occurs and where the division between public law and private law is vague.

On the private law side, we have four basic types of relationship, each of which will get extended treatment as the book proceeds. We must be cautious, however, and remember that the way in which we configure the classification system on the private law side is largely a matter of our own convenience. We are developing a classification system primarily as a conceptual tool for the management of an enormously complicated body of thought. Different students of the law may classify legal relationships differently, but in each attempt we are trying to come to terms with the staggering complexity of human social activity and with the limitless number of possibilities inherent in human relationships. For our purposes, we shall call the four categories of relationship between or among individuals on the private law side of our diagram "exchange relationships", "duty relationships", "fiduciary relationships", and "relationships involving property".

---

[1] Part I of the *Constitution Act, 1982*, being Schedule B to the *Canada Act 1982* (U.K.), 1982, c. 11.

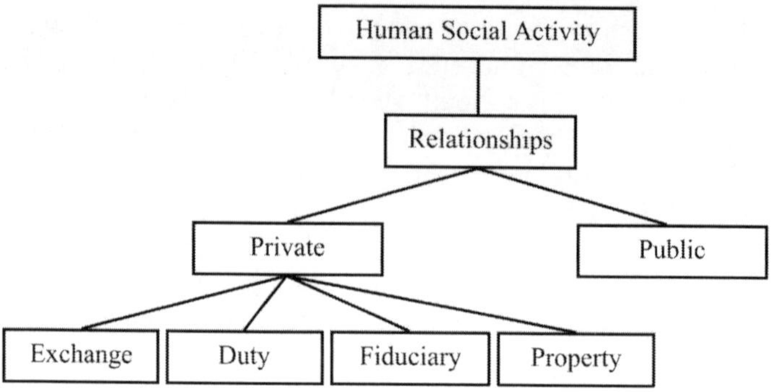

"Exchange relationships" will be explored in some depth in Chapter 3 below. For now, the key thing to recognize is that exchange relationships are those that involve some agreement between the parties, some exchange of promises or bargain, some voluntary submission to an arrangement intended to be binding between the parties. From the perspective of the law, exchange relationships yield contracts as their product. Many of the ordinary relationships in our day-to-day activities are catalogued by the law as exchange relationships, including, for example, the purchase of a bus ticket by a passenger in exchange for the agreement of the bus company to carry the passenger to a specific destination. During the course of our busy lives, we are party to hundreds of exchange relationships, many of them fairly trivial (including the purchase of a bus ticket), and many of them very significant indeed (perhaps the purchase of an automobile or house). In each case, however, the key is that the parties to the relationship *choose* to participate. For a relationship to be recognized by the law as an exchange relationship, it must manifest certain pre-determined characteristics or formal elements, and until such time as those formal elements emerge in the parties' discussions, each of the parties remains free to discontinue the discussions and avoid entering into the relationship. Those formal elements will constitute a major part of our discussions below in Chapter 3.

"Duty relationships" include a limitless number of relationships *imposed* on individuals by law, and we will investigate these relationships in some detail in Chapter 4. The imposition of the relationship on the participants, as opposed to the voluntary choice of the individuals to participate, distinguishes duty relationships from exchange relationships most clearly. In many cases, we participate in duty relationships without ever thinking that there is someone else involved. This is the situation, for example, with the operator of the car that drove by the bus you took to work or school this morning. In our ordinary understanding of the word it would be nonsense to suggest that the car driver and the passenger on the bus had a "relationship", but this is exactly the result in the terms employed in legal taxonomy. The law of duty is extremely complex, but stated simply, a duty relationship is imposed on individuals by virtue of their proximity to each other. Proximity in this context means something such as "causal proximity" — if one individual behaves in such a way as to generate an effect on another individual, then it is likely that the law will impose a duty on the first individual to behave so as to minimize the anticipated impact on the second individual, or so as to avoid impact altogether. On this reasoning, the person who drove by the bus in a car had a legally imposed duty to operate the car so as to avoid injuring the people in the bus. The car driver did not choose this relationship; it was imposed on her by the law. If an individual breaches a duty relationship, failing to exercise the appropriate care so as to avoid injuring the other party to the relationship, and if the other party suffers some injury as a result of that breach, then a special sort of legal wrong results. That legal wrong is called a tort.

The "property" category is different from exchange relationships and duty relationships, primarily because it necessarily involves the introduction of some thing other than the participants in the relationship itself. That thing is called property. The idea of property in private law is fairly obscure, and we will try to come to some understanding of its implications in Chapter 5. For the moment, we can think of property in two separate senses. First, the ordinary use of the term "property" continues to have some meaning in private law. If you were to say "This pen is my property", then most of us would understand that you own the pen. We would recognize the pen as "property". Secondly, however, the law considers the bundle of rights you have with respect to the pen as property too. You are entitled to make decisions about the use and enjoyment of that pen irrespective of what others may think or do. In other words, implicit in the idea of ownership is the understanding that the owner of a thing can use it, possess it, perhaps destroy it or sell it, all without the need to consult someone else.

It is important to recognize that the relationship that ensues by virtue of the introduction of property (in either of its two meanings) is not a relationship between the owner and the thing itself. Remember that private law is about relationships between or among individuals, and it is very rare indeed that something such as a pen could be recognized as an individual for purposes of the law. Rather, the relationship under consideration is the one between the owner and some other individual, mediated by the property. In other words, the introduction of property into a relationship between individuals adjusts that relationship, but it does not change the participants. For example, because you live in a house beside your friend's house, the law may impose a duty on you to behave in such a way that you do not cause injury to your neighbour. However, if your neighbour parks his car (his property) in the driveway, then the law will impose more specific duties on you to refrain from using the car without your neighbour's permission, for example. In essence, the character of your relationship with your neighbour has changed, even though the participants in the relationship are the same. Generally speaking, the types of relationships that emerge from human social activity by virtue of the introduction of property involve a violation of a least part of the owner's rights of use, possession or alienation. For the moment, it is enough to know that the terms "use" and "possession" are generally employed in the law consistent with ordinary understandings, although there are some fairly obscure variations on those meanings in the history of private law. The right of "alienation" in property law means the power to dispose of the thing as the owner sees fit. Each of these senses of the term 'property' will be explored in some depth in Chapter 5.

"Fiduciary relationships" can be either imposed on the participants or chosen by the participants. Sometimes they involve property, and sometimes they do not. The category of fiduciary relationship involving property is known as a "trust relationship", and it will receive extended discussion in Chapter 6. In general terms, a fiduciary relationship results when there is a radical imbalance in the power the parties bring to the relationship, and where there is an expectation on the part of the weaker party that the stronger party will exercise that power for the benefit of the weaker. As you can see, the concept of "dependency" or "vulnerability" is central to the fiduciary relationship. For example, the relationship between a lawyer and the lawyer's client is a fiduciary one, and so is the doctor/patient relationship. The lawyer or the doctor has virtually complete power in this situation, having access to special knowledge that, for one reason or another, is particularly important for the client or patient, making the client or patient especially vulnerable. In addition, it is expected that the lawyer or doctor will behave in such a way that will benefit the client or patient, and that the lawyer or doctor will not take advantage of their powerful position.

In many cases, such as the lawyer/client and the doctor/patient situations, fiduciary relationships are chosen by the participants, but the law also imposes a fiduciary relationship without the consent of the participants, so long as it is clear that such an imposition would be the just result. For example, in almost every case the relationship that exists between you and your banker is an exchange relationship. You choose to put your money in a savings account, in exchange for your banker's agreement to safeguard your money and pay you an agreed rate of interest. However, in certain circumstances the law will impose a fiduciary relationship on parties to a banking arrangement, perhaps where the customer of the bank is particularly vulnerable and new to the world of finance, and where it is evident that the customer had a reasonable expectation that the bank would act only in the best interests of the customer. You can see that the way that legal taxonomy classifies a particular relationship depends on the characteristics that the relationship displays, and for that reason it is impossible to list all potential categories of fiduciary relationships. The possibilities are endless, and we will explore some of these possibilities in Chapter 6.

Legal taxonomy, therefore, is the practice of classifying, making some sense out of, the impossibly intricate web of human relationships that emerges from human social activity. But the question then becomes: "Why is this something that is worthy of our attention? Why should we care if the law catalogues our day-to-day lives by reference to a complicated set of classification criteria that only lawyers and judges can possibly understand?" The important point to note at this early stage of our exploration of private law relationships is that the classification of a particular relationship as "duty" or "exchange" or "fiduciary" has *consequences* for the participants in the relationship. This is an essential idea for you to keep in mind as this book progresses, and in each of the chapters to follow we will explore the range of possible legal consequences in addition to the core principles at work in the classification system itself. If the relationship is classified by the law as a duty relationship, then the consequences that flow from a breach of that relationship may be quite different from those that flow from a relationship classified as exchange. If it is considered that a particular relationship involves the violation of some property right, then the legal consequences will be quite different than a similar situation that does not involve property. If there is a fiduciary relationship under consideration, then the obligations flowing from the stronger party to the weaker will be very onerous, and the consequences attendant on a breach of those obligations may be very serious indeed.

As soon as we recognize that the way in which our relationships are classified may have an impact on the consequences that flow from a breach of those relationships, then we can start to shape our activities, and therefore our relationships, so as to generate certain types of consequences and not others. In our ordinary social activity, we start to make adjustments in how we behave, based on the way in which the legal classification system would respond to what we are doing. For us, this is an important observation, because it raises the idea that the law, represented through this taxonomic system of classification and prescription, is an active participant in our ordinary lives. This leads inevitably to the idea that the law is not necessarily just cataloguing our activities in some sort of disinterested and objective way and prescribing results in the event of problems, but actually may be directing in some fashion the way in which we behave. In other words, the practice of classification and the system of classification that results may actually start to generate activity of certain kinds and discourage activity of other kinds.

Our task in this book is to investigate the extent of this possible connection between private law and social life, and to try to come to terms with the implications of the idea that private law and the rest of our social experience are very closely connected, likely inseparable. This means that the political question about control of the legal taxonomy, control of the way in which private law responds to our ordinary inter-personal activity, and control of the extent to which the law participates in generating certain types of behaviour and discouraging certain others, will be central to the discussions that emerge from the balance of this book. If it is true that the celestial being, gazing down at human life, would notice immediately that humans are inherently social, then the function of private law in cataloguing our relationships, prescribing consequences in the event of a breach of those relationships, and perhaps even actively participating in our decisions about the types of relationships to which we are party, is actually integral to human existence. This possibility is deserving of considerable reflection, and the balance of this book is intended as a beginning of that process.

II. SOME MODERN PHILOSOPHICAL ASSUMPTIONS

The legal classification system is enormously intricate, not simply because the categories of relationship to consider are virtually limitless in number, but because there is no absolutely certain way to distinguish each of the categories from the others. We assign the categories names, and then we try to isolate the central characteristics of each of the categories, but this process is fraught with uncertainty. It is important to re-emphasize that our development in this book of a classification system for private law relationships is done merely for our convenience, to serve as a conceptual tool to assist in coming to terms with some of the significant implications of private law for social life. Our classification system is certainly not the only way that one might think about the law, but it is one way, designed to help us through some difficult ideas.

The diagram we have been using to represent the legal taxonomy is deceptive in certain respects, and this is one of the flaws in trying to represent the extraordinarily complex in a simple two-dimensional form. In subsequent chapters, we will investigate some of these deceptions more completely, especially in the consideration of the often blurry boundaries among the separate private law categories of relationship. In the balance of this chapter, we want to reflect on some of the basic modern philosophical assumptions underlying our classification system, and the implications these assumptions have for establishing the boundary between what is public and what is private. That boundary is not at all clear, despite the complete separation of these two things in the diagram. You will remember that public law concerns the state in its political or sovereign capacity, but it is not certain what exactly we mean by the state, and we are often not sure what it means in each and every conceivable circumstance to act in political or sovereign capacities. Sometimes governments behave in ways that simply defy categorization, and sometimes governments behave in ways that can appear to be both political/sovereign on the one hand, and purely private (purely individual) on the other. Further still, there is a great deal of confusion over categorization between classifications on the public law side and on the private law side. The circumstances that give rise to criminal law and tort law (the law that emerges around the idea of duty relationships) often look the same, for example, but the consequences of classification in one area or the other differs widely.

Let us begin by saying that there may be a public aspect to everything we do, even those things that we would anticipate to be furthest removed from the involvement of the state, representing the public interest. For example, the community at large has an interest of some sort in seeing that the relationship between parents and their children is a healthy one, despite the fact that, for the most part, the law classifies that relationship on the private law side of our diagram. The public wants to be sure that people honour their contracts, too, even though the matter of contract law is considered on the private law side, under exchange relationships. After all, if we respect our contractual obligations, then the marketplace will function more smoothly, and that is conducive to a healthy economy in which we all have an interest. In other words, even in relationships that appear obviously private (from the perspective of the law), there may be something at stake for the community at large. Because of this, it is never perfectly certain the extent to which the public interest will have an impact on the way in which the law might resolve a dispute that is ostensibly private. There is always that lingering possibility that the public interest will prevail, forcing some adjustment in the purely private law considerations that would otherwise direct the consequences.

But the fact that the lines are blurry between the public and private sides of what we do does not relieve us of the responsibility to try to map out the domains of the public and private sides of our legal worlds. It is not easy to sort this out. In fact, the dual aspect of much of what we do may contribute to a great deal of confusion about the nature of law, and about private as opposed to public rights, duties and responsibilities. To start to map out the domain of private law, the domain where the state, in its political or sovereign capacity, apparently has no involvement, we must identify more precisely the "individual" in western thought. The individual, of course, is the focus of private law, the participant in private law relationships, and when we begin to recognize the ways in which the individual has been conceptualized in philosophical terms we can more confidently move to a detailed discussion of the way in which the law considers the individual in Chapter 2. Private law is interested in a particular vision of the individual, the "legal person," but it is likely that vision, perhaps to a very great extent, is derivative of a more general philosophical concept about human individuality. It is that more general concept that will assist us initially in the attempt to distinguish between the public and the private in our taxonomy. At the same time, however, it is necessary to point out that this broader idea is not without its detractors, meaning that the assumptions out of which our private law idea of personhood is generated may have some very significant weaknesses. We will explore the implications of this challenge later in this chapter.

The idea of the individual as a central element of our law is one of relatively recent origin. We are trying to isolate the particular unit of society around which private law will be developed, and the concept of the individual person in this respect is really only about 250 years old. While this may sound ancient to most of us, in connection with the great march of history this is a very short time indeed. If the law is to respond to and possibly direct relationships in the way in which we have briefly mentioned, then it must first identify the basic unit of society that will function as the focus of its attentions, and then build its classification system on the strength of the activities in which that unit of society customarily engages. Prior to the eighteenth century, for example, the law responded most completely in this respect to the family unit, rather than the individual unit, and consequently much of what we today consider to be private law was focused on the family as its fundamental building block.

But the eighteenth century was remarkable for our purposes. The great philosophers of the Enlightenment in Europe began to focus their thoughts on the individual person as the centre of the moral world, as the aspect of life that commanded respect more than any other. The commitment to the primacy of the individual in moral deliberation, as you can imagine, meant that the connections experienced by the individual (in family and in social life generally) started to be viewed as secondary. Jean-Jacques Rousseau, the great Swiss philosopher of the eighteenth century, said that "Man is born free; and everywhere he is in chains",[2] arguing that the most perfect, most beautiful state of human existence is that state we experience

[2] Jean-Jacques Rousseau, "The Social Contract, or Principles of Political Right," in G.D.H. Cole (trans.) and P.D. Jimack (ed.) *The Social Contract and Discourses* (London: J.M. Dent, 1993), at 181.

only momentarily, that is, the moment of perfect isolation and therefore freedom that we have at birth. From this perspective, that moment is then immediately followed by a network of social and political relationships that end up putting us in chains. Now Rousseau was talking primarily of the oppression of the ordinary person by the aristocracy, but the lament for the atomistic individual, enslaved by social, political and economic imperatives, is one that appears over and again in Enlightenment thought, and it is one that had a profound impact on the way in which the law developed over the next 250 years. In philosophical terms, the attempt was made to salvage some of this splendid individual isolation as something like an ideal state of existence for the individual as a subject of our moral deliberations. And as the eighteenth century turned into the nineteenth, the law began to adjust in the attempt to adequately identify for the individual a domain in which the individual could be more perfectly secure from the intrusion of the state.

Many things about the way western societies were organized began to shift at this time, and one of those things was the focus of the non-criminal, call it "civil", law. It was because of the shift in the perspective of moral philosophy toward the individual that the nineteenth century saw the emergence of a great deal of private law doctrine that accepted as its first premise the idea that much of what the individual human being did in their lives ought to be free from outside interference by the state or the state's representatives. This was relatively new. Prior to the nineteenth century, the law considered the human person as first and foremost a person with a particular role (a member of a family, a member of a trade, a serf, a lord), defined almost exclusively for the purposes of what we now call private law as someone whose life was embedded in, perhaps indistinguishable from, a network of relationships that dictated the individual's status at law. But in the nineteenth century, the law started to see the human being as an individual primarily, one responsible for their own conduct and commitments, and one to whose autonomy and individuality we all owed a great deal of respect and deference. The law shifted as a result, and began to map out with some particularity the realm in which the individual's life remained secure from outside supervision and surveillance.

Now let's consider in more detail the idea of "individualism" that emerged with nineteenth century liberal political thought. This idea still informs a great deal of what we do in the political and legal arenas (although, as mentioned earlier, it also suffers a great deal of criticism). For example, the dominant idea of the individual is arguably at the core of the whole rights discourse we engage in day after day, and it is the foundation of almost all of the private law doctrine that we shall consider in more detail as this book progresses. So, what were the elements of this individualism that ultimately compelled the relatively complete re-orientation of private law doctrine in our tradition? First, and perhaps most central, is the notion of human dignity. From the perspective of eighteenth and nineteenth century political and moral philosophy, every human being is possessed of an inherent dignity or value that ought to be given the utmost respect. Once we recognize the primacy of human individual value in philosophical thought, then we must make adjustments in the law so as to protect that dignity from violation, by the state or by other outside interests. The notion of inherent, sacrosanct human value became the first principle, the one around which all other principles appear subordinate.

Ancillary to this first characteristic of the human individual is what moral philosophers call "autonomy", and with it the correlative assumption that human individuals make decisions based first on their self-interest. On the basis of this idea, every human being is something like a free agent, out there in the world making their own decisions, choosing their own life path, ideally unaffected by outside agents (such as the state, or the church, or the master). The individual is only involved in relationships, the argument goes, because the individual chooses to be so involved. The individual scrutinizes these relationships, assesses the responsibilities expected of participants in those relationships, evaluates the contribution others make to those relationships, and then, exercising her or his autonomy, either commits to or abandons the prospect. When we recognize a human being as autonomous in this way, then we are starting to see a being quite different from the status-based, subordinate, relationship-bound person of the earlier era. No longer need the serf suffer at the hands of the lord; no longer is the penitent bound to humble him- or herself before a mystical god; no longer are the connections that the human being has with the rest of society considered to define that individual for the purposes of moral and political thought, and for the purposes of private law doctrine. Instead, we have the human individual, carrying inherent value and dignity, out there in the world behaving according to the way in which his or her intellect directs, autonomously, free of interference, and self-interested.

Flowing from the recognition of human dignity, autonomy and self-interest is the correlative notion of privacy. This is where the whole intellectual movement toward the individual human subject starts to make sense in the world of private law. When we talk of privacy in this context, what we are trying to do is isolate a realm of existence for the individual that is removed from the prying forces of the state. By defining the private realm, we begin to build a foundation for distinguishing between the public and the private as the first division in our legal taxonomy. We bring forward in our thinking around moral and political philosophy this idea of the individual, with inherent value and dignity, acting autonomously and with a dominant view to self-interest, and then we create for this individual so conceived a private realm, a place where the individual can pursue their interests and dreams without undue interference by the state (the "public"). This arena of private activity is more jealously guarded in some societies than in others, perhaps most clearly in the United States, where less government interference is often championed as "more privacy."

The main problem, of course, is drawing the boundaries of this sphere of private endeavour. How do we know the content of this arena? How do we know when state interference is justified, when the life of the individual ought to be encroached upon for the sake of the public good? These are basic questions for us, for it is inside this private world where private law has sway. It is inside this realm of private endeavour that the dignified, autonomous individual is entering into exchange relationships, duty relationships, fiduciary relationships, buying and selling property, building their families, and the like. Some of these activities are the subject of quite careful state scrutiny, and some are relatively free from public concern. This is the shifting boundary between the public and the private dimensions of our lives, and the law must shift right along with our changing conceptions of what is public and what is private. The law must continually be diligent in identifying the social context in which the idea of privacy is understood, since the extent to which we might justify public interference in otherwise private endeavour is largely historically contingent. In other words, our understanding of the boundary between private life on the one hand and areas of concern for the state, acting on behalf of the public interest, on the other, changes as social circumstances change. That said, it is arguable that our law developed over the course of the nineteenth and twentieth centuries so as to give maximum scope for the enjoyment of individual privacy, expressed as the pursuit of economic self-interest. Of course, there were very pragmatic reasons for this, connected with the nineteenth century urge to rapid commercial and industrial expansion. In theory, the privileging of the dignified, autonomous, self-interested individual in nineteenth century reforms of private law allowed the individual to capitalize on the freedom experienced in the world of private endeavour, and the concurrent result was the building of a vibrant nineteenth century economy.

Arguably, however, at the same time as private law adjusted so as to facilitate a greater enjoyment of individual freedom in economic terms, the public interest started to be exerted in other aspects of life so as to shrink the area in which individual autonomy might be more perfectly enjoyed. This was especially true in family life as the nineteenth century turned into the twentieth. Throughout this book, we shall continue to refer to the family as the locus of much dispute in private law. For now it is enough to observe that, prior to the middle of the nineteenth century, the state paid little attention to the arrangements that existed among individuals inside the family. The obligations of support that flow from one family member to another were considered only rarely in the law during the years prior to about 1850, and control over the lives of children was left almost exclusively to the parents. But as the nineteenth century progressed, there was heightened public awareness of abuse and oppression inside the family, especially respecting the subordinate status of married women, the inequitable law of married women's property, and the neglect of the interests of children. As a consequence, the public interest in healthy family life was translated into an enhanced role for the state in supervising the relationships among family members. In turn, at the end of the nineteenth century and into the twentieth we see an array of new law respecting married women's property, divorce and the obligations imposed on spouses during and after the breakdown of the marriage, and concerning the responsibility of the state in seeing to a healthy home life for children. In other words, as the world of private endeavour opened for the pursuit of economic self-interest during the nineteenth century, we find privacy shrinking in the area of family life as the wider community interest in a more fair and safe family was expressed by the state through law.

There are many judicial decisions in both Canada and elsewhere in the common law world that help us understand the extent to which the eighteenth and nineteenth century idea of the autonomous individual has had an impact on the way in which our law has developed, and on the continuing need to define the area of private endeavour that remains immune from state interference. Many of these cases emerge from the public law side of our diagram, especially in the criminal law, but nevertheless these cases are critical in our attempt to isolate the individual as the focus of moral, political and ultimately legal philosophical reflection. When we direct our attention to the often vague boundary between the public and private realms in law, then it is to the idea of the individual that we must turn, and frequently that idea is expressed most clearly in cases that, ostensibly at least, have very little to say about private law relationships. For example, in the famous Canadian case of *R. v. Morgentaler*,[3] the Supreme Court of Canada was asked to consider the constitutionality of a provision of Canada's *Criminal Code* that criminalized a number of stated activities, including allowing oneself to undergo procedures intended to procure a miscarriage.[4] The argument was made that the provision effectively destroyed the dignity of women who, in exercising their choice to have an abortion or not, were expressing their autonomy as free individuals deserving of respect. The Supreme Court of Canada agreed,

---

3 *R. v. Morgentaler*, [1988] S.C.J. No. 1, 44 D.L.R. (4th) 385 (S.C.C.).

4 The provision under consideration was at that time *Criminal Code*, R.S.C. 1970, c. C-34, s. 251.

suggesting that decisions about one's physical integrity are central to individual autonomy and a significant component of that sphere of privacy into which the state ought not to intrude. In this case, the model of individuality inherited from the philosophers of the eighteenth century underlay the Court's decision to overturn the state's intervention in women's decision-making, raising the concept of human dignity to the level of first principle.

The extent of the influence of this philosophical model is not to be underestimated. It is arguable that, even in decisions fairly clearly concerned with adjudicating disputes between private persons, the courts will retreat to the conceptualization of the individual in terms of dignity, autonomy, and respect as an analytical tool to direct the placement of the boundaries of the private sphere. Such was the situation in *Malette v. Shulman*,[5] a 1990 decision of the Ontario Court of Appeal. Here we have a medical doctor faced with a dilemma. Should the doctor respect the patient's wish that she not be given a blood transfusion under any circumstances, even circumstances considered to be life-threatening? Or should the doctor violate that autonomous decision and transfuse the woman so as to save her life? Honouring the woman's decision would respect the model of human individuality on which much of our law is based, but transfusing the woman in violation of that decision would pay obeisance to another honoured principle, the sanctity of human life. The doctor administered the transfusion, and the woman, upon recovering, sued the doctor for a breach of a duty relationship on the private law side of our diagram. The woman succeeded in her suit, even though the judge found that there was no intention to do harm, and that quite the contrary, the doctor acted throughout in what he thought were the best interests of his patient. Oddly enough, the decision appears to be that there are aspects of life which are more important than life itself. If we interfere with a person's autonomy, their freedom to make choices about their life's direction, even when that interference is intended to save their life, then we have violated something perhaps more important than that life, and that is the person's very selfhood. This tells us a great deal about the strength of the model of individuality that we inherited from the philosophers of the eighteenth century, and that continues to inhabit our legal decision-making.

Decisions such as *R. v. Morgantaler* and *Malette v. Shulman* suggest to us that the courts will jealously guard the freedom from interference that the philosophical model of individuality necessarily yields. This is so, whether we are considering state or private interference. Apparently, there is a realm of privacy in which outside interests, state or otherwise, can have no influence. The courts will do their best to ensure that this

---

[5] *Malette v. Shulman*, [1990] O.J. No. 450, 72 O.R. (2d) 417 (Ont. C.A.).

realm endures. Yet, perhaps paradoxically, in many cases the court will override an autonomous individual decision so as to give effect to something such as the public interest, and it is fair to say that the conditions under which such an override will be exercised are rather unpredictable. It depends exclusively on the circumstances of the case, and prevailing notions of right and wrong. For example, we have *Noble and Wolf v. Alley*,[6] a case about the fundamental private right of an individual to enter into exchange relationships of their own design, where the contract that results is prejudicial against identifiable groups. A seller of property made it a stipulation in the contract of sale that the property could never be sold to Jewish people, black people and a long list of other identifiable groups. The purchaser ultimately decided to re-sell the property, and the person interested in buying it wanted to take it free of the original stipulation. The Supreme Court of Canada was asked to rule on the enforceability of the restriction on re-sale. The dispute resolved itself into a contest between the respect we owe to an autonomously struck bargain between two individuals, each supposedly dignified and deserving of respect, and the commitment we owe to the idea that the public interest demands that we act in ways that limit the effects of prejudice against identifiable groups. The Supreme Court of Canada decided in favour of the public interest, and ruled that the restriction on re-sale was unenforceable. This is so, despite the very strong argument in favour of enforcing the restriction on the ground that it was the simple manifestation of the parties' autonomously struck bargain, and therefore an expression of that individuality that ostensibly underlies so much of our private law.

In the world of private law, *Noble and Wolf v. Alley* may appear anomalous, especially considering the slightly earlier Supreme Court of Canada decision in *Christie v. York Corp.*[7] In this case, a tavern owner insisted on a business policy that forbade his waiters from serving black people. A black man sued the tavern owner, alleging that the refusal of service constituted a breach of the conditions under which the tavern was licensed. The Supreme Court of Canada made it perfectly clear in this case that the law was such as to encourage complete freedom of commerce, meaning that the proprietor of the tavern was entitled to deal or not to deal with any member of the public, so long as the result was not against good morals or public order. In this case, it was held that the refusal of service to the black customer was neither, and the suit was lost. In other

---

6 *Noble and Wolf v. Alley*, [1950] S.C.J. No. 34, [1951] 1 D.L.R. 321 (S.C.C.).

7 *Christie v. York Corp.*, [1939] S.C.J. No. 37, [1940] S.C.R. 139. Both *Noble and Wolf v. Alley*, *ibid.*, and *Christie v. York Corp.* were decided prior to the enactment of federal and provincial human rights legislation in Canada, meaning that the decisions would likely be decided on different grounds today.

words, the tavern owner's decision to refuse service to identifiable groups was upheld as an expression of his inherent dignity and autonomy, despite the affront to the customer's dignity, and despite the general public interest in preventing discriminatory behaviour.

As we can see, there is a great deal of tension around the idea of the individual as the building block of the private sphere and as the fundamental social unit that functions as the focus of private law. The place at which we might draw the line between the world of autonomous and private endeavour on the one hand, and the world in which the state or other interests are allowed to have influence despite our apparent commitment to the eighteenth and nineteenth century philosophical model of the individual, is certainly not clear. It is arguable that that line is drawn anew each and every time a court is asked to adjudicate a dispute between competing private interests and public interests, since perhaps everything the human does in the course of his or her activities raises at least a modicum of public concern. The same is likely true when the dispute is between competing private interests, disputes in which the court may be asked to privilege the autonomous choice of one individual over the dignity of another. And further, each of these decisions is grounded in its own circumstances, by which is meant both the general social and historical circumstances prevailing at the time of the decision, and also the more specific circumstances of the case under review.

As was suggested earlier, the dominant philosophical assumptions about the human individual (defined in terms of human dignity, autonomy and privacy) which appear to lie beneath much of our private law doctrine are not without their serious challenges. If these challenges were ultimately successful, then of course our system of private law rules would look quite dramatically different, and the difficulties inherent in our attempt to separate the public and the private spheres of our activities would be transformed into difficulties of another order altogether. Central to the criticism of the dominant set of assumptions is the idea that the human individual is not an isolated, autonomous, self-interested individual at all, but rather an individual necessarily involved in a network of relationships that are inherent in the human condition. From this perspective, the isolated individual does not exist. It is but a construct of political and moral philosophy, an ideal representative of the longing for freedom from oppression which functioned as much of the motivation for the grand theories of Enlightenment thinkers. The autonomous individual is a fiction, so the criticism goes, and therefore the assumptions on which our private law is founded are likewise fictitious.

This criticism of the dominant assumptions at work in private law has considerable strength. Try to imagine yourself making a decision, any decision really, in which the significant people in your life (your parents, your partner, your children, your intimates generally) are unaffected. Try to imagine yourself making such a decision without considering the impact the decision will have on others. It is likely that such an isolated position for a human individual simply does not exist in real terms. We are inextricably connected to others, and the decisions we make as we go about our day-to-day lives are necessarily influenced by those connections, whether we recognize that influence or not. If we allow for this sort of inherent connection as integral to the notion of human individuality, of human selfhood, then our approach to ethical (or "just") behaviour may change quite dramatically. Suddenly, we judge our actions, not on the strength of their support for the idea of human autonomy, but rather for the extent to which they honour and respect healthy relationships. We consider our relationships with others before considering our self-interest.

Some critics suggest that this idea of the inter-connected individual extends beyond our intimate relationships, leading to a conceptualization of the human individual in the context of community-wide relationships and obligations. Not only are the assumptions about autonomy and self-interest in error, but more than that, the assumption that we have important connections and obligations merely with and to a few intimates is incomplete as well. Each of us is a member of a network of wider communities, at work, at school, in our neighbourhoods, across the world of political realities and possibilities, and our participation in those communities is founded on a set of ethical conditions that each of us has a responsibility to meet. Failing this responsibility, then the institutions of our society (our democratic institutions, for example), the ones on which much of our individual freedom ultimately depends, are placed in jeopardy. Viewed in this light, the assumption about individual autonomy, for example, starts to look narrow and ill-conceived, even dangerous and subversive.

As we explore the various private law categories in the remainder of this book, we will see the tension in private law between the commitment to the autonomous individual on the one hand and the commitment to an inter-connected, responsible individual on the other played out in case after case. We will see that, while the former tends to dominate in the underlying structure of our private law doctrine, it is never really clear when the latter will emerge in a judicial decision to contradict the otherwise predictable result. We will see the deference to an autonomous, dignified, self-interested individual sometimes overthrown by a need for the preservation of community values, but in other situations we will see the self-interested individual emerge in a judge's reasons, unscathed by and irrespective of the argument from community commitment. We will see the inter-connected individual described in terms consistent with traditional language about the "public interest", but we will also see the commitment to the autonomous individual described so as to make it central to our very sense of community. This is a complex, difficult philosophical dilemma. The best we can hope to do in this short volume is to recognize the significance of the debate for the structure of private law, and just as importantly, for the individuals involved in the countless cases that come before judges each and every day.

The practice of legal taxonomy is replete with challenges of the sort summarized above, and it is important to keep in mind as we move forward that every decision made when individuals fall into disputes is influenced by moral, political and other broad concerns that are brought to the problem by the participants. The very idea of the individual in our law is one such concern, and it is an idea that functions as the focus of much debate in the very first division in our legal taxonomy, the division between the public and the private. So as to consider the implications of the idea more completely, it is necessary that we explore in some depth the characteristics of the individual considered specifically from the perspective of private law, and that is the subject to which we now turn.

Chapter 2

"Personhood" and the Establishment of Legal Relations

I. LEGAL PERSONS AS ARTIFICIAL CREATIONS OF LAW

In his classic nineteenth century study of legal anthropology, Sir Henry Maine identified what he saw as the most crucial element of a modern legal system. Maine's views on legal anthropology were heavily influenced by Darwin's theory of evolution. Like many followers of Darwin, Maine believed that the evolution of social systems was bound by the same laws of natural selection that Darwin discovered to be at work in nature. Either social systems evolved and adapted in response to stimuli from their external environment, in which case they became stronger and more dynamic; or else they failed to adapt and became static and rigid, doomed eventually to be eclipsed by their more dynamic and successful rivals.[1]

For Maine, it was the movement away from legal relationships based upon the family or kinship networks, towards legal relationships based on the individual, which represented the defining moment in the evolution of a developed legal system. Within a legal system based on family or kinship networks, most legal relationships tend to be defined by one's status within the group. Within a legal system based on individualism, however, it is the individual who has freedom to choose the nature and extent of the legal relationships he or she wishes to enter into. As we will see in subsequent chapters, the nature of the legal relationships that an individual may choose to enter into can vary significantly in different contexts. The marriage contract creates significantly different kinds of legal obligations, and is arguably understood in very different ways, than entering into a contract of employment, or contracting to rent a car at a car rental agency. Similarly, the fiduciary obligations owed by a physician to a patient, or by a parent towards a child, are of a qualitatively different order than the duty to take reasonable care to avoid foreseeable risks towards others that is the basis of the law of negligence. Notwithstanding

[1] Sir Henry Sumner Maine, *Ancient Law* (London: Oxford University Press, 1931).

the variety of ways in which we may classify different kinds of private law obligations, however, it is important to understand that underlying all of these forms of private law obligations is a particular concept of the legal person as the primary unit of analysis around which these other categories of private law relationships are built.

We could put this slightly differently by observing that within the field of private law the concept of legal personality functions in much the same manner as the numeral one in mathematics, or the concept of the atom within atomic physics.[2] Just as individual atoms combine to form more complex molecules in the physical world, so do individual legal persons (the basic particles out of which the legal system is built) combine to create more complex forms of legal relationships based on contract, or family, or property, or fiduciary obligations. Even the most basic economic transaction, such as purchasing a loaf of bread from the grocery store, involves the creation of a legal relationship between two distinct legal persons, the "person" who offers to purchase the bread at the price stated on the one hand, and the "person" who accepts this offer to buy from the purchaser, on the other. The whole idea of contract as a voluntary economic "exchange" is based on the premise that each of the "persons" involved in the exchange is an autonomous legal actor with full capacity to create enforceable rights and obligations by entering into voluntary legal relationships with other persons.

It should be evident that when we are using the term "legal persons" in this context we are not using the term literally or descriptively to denote particular individuals. For example, there is just as much of a contractual relationship formed between two legal persons when a purchaser puts a dollar into a vending machine to buy a chocolate bar or a can of cola. The contract is not made with the vending machine, of course, but with the person who owns and operates the vending machine. In the same way, the "person" with whom the contract is made when a customer purchases goods at a grocery store is not the individual working at the cash till who rings in the transaction and receives the customer's money, but the legal person who owns and operates the store. Moreover, the legal person who owns and operates the store may well turn out to be a corporation, rather than an individual owner. If so, the contract is made between a natural legal person (the customer) and what lawyers call an artificial legal person (the corporation). If we were to alter the transaction to a purchase and sale of computer components, or automobile parts, or unrefined oil, then both of the "legal persons" engaged in the exchange are likely to be corporations or artificial persons. Indeed, it has sometimes been remarked that in a modern capitalist economy, the most significant legal persons

---

[2] See G.W. Paton, *A Textbook of Jurisprudence, 4th ed.* (Oxford: Clarendon Press, 1972), at 394.

are not individuals at all, but large multinational corporations, which may employ tens of thousands of people and have annual revenues exceeding those of many nation states.[3]

When we use the term "legal persons", then, we are not just referring to human beings, or natural persons, but also to artificial legal persons such as corporations. This is a very important point to understand. For most legal purposes, the legal system regards corporations as if they have the same legal capacity to enter into contracts, to sue and be sued in tort, to own property, and to pay taxes as any other natural person, despite the fact that a corporation is in many ways just a legal fiction, an artificial creation of law. Unlike you and me, a corporation has no corporeal body. It cannot speak, think or enter into legal relationships for itself, except through the agency of individuals who are authorized to act on its behalf. Yet for practical legal purposes it is the corporation that is regarded as legally responsible when one of its employees negligently causes injury to a third party, or when the corporation avoids paying corporate income tax on its profits for the year, or when the corporation is in breach of any of its obligations under an employment contract, for example.

The practical consequences of this legal fiction of corporate legal personality are therefore very significant. Perhaps an example would illustrate this point. Let us say that I start a tax consulting business, in addition to my day job as a university lecturer. In legal terms my tax consulting business remains unincorporated. Technically it is referred to as a "sole proprietorship", since I am the individual owner of the business. As an unincorporated business, any income earned by the consulting business is treated as part of my personal income for income tax purposes, and must be declared by me on my annual tax return. Likewise, any legal obligations or liabilities of the business are attributed to me as the sole owner of the business. If I decide to hire a number of researchers to work for me in the consulting business, and to rent office space downtown, I will be personally liable to pay the salaries of the researchers, and the rent for the office, even if the consulting business does not generate sufficient income to cover these expenses.

If, however, I decide to incorporate a company to operate the consulting business, then the legal structure and organization of the business would change dramatically. First, I would have to take the preliminary step of incorporating a company under either the Ontario *Business Corporations Act*[4] or the *Canada Business Corporations Act*.[5] This would be a relatively straightforward procedure involving the registration of a corporate name

---

3 Roger Cotterrell, *The Sociology of Law, 2nd ed.* (London: Butterworths, 1992), at 130.

4 *Business Corporations Act*, R.S.O. 1990, c. B.16.

5 *Canada Business Corporations Act*, R.S.C. 1985, c. C-44.

(hereafter the "XYZ Corporation"), determining the number and classes of shares to be issued by the corporation, and specifying the constitution and articles of incorporation of the corporation. All this can be accomplished quite cheaply and easily by paying the requisite filing and registration fees and completing the requisite forms with the assistance of a lawyer. The result of this process is that a new legal person — the XYZ Corporation — will have come into existence. The legal system will have given birth!

Having created a corporation to operate the consulting business, we now need to know how the corporation will be managed. Under most corporate constitutions, the management powers of the corporation are divided between the corporation's board of directors and the general meeting of shareholders. The board of directors is responsible for the day-to-day management and strategic direction of the corporation, whereas the general meeting of shareholders appoints the members of the board of directors and has the power to approve certain major corporate decisions, such as changing the corporate name or head office, changes in the classes of shares issued, and any alterations to the bylaws of the corporation. In a large corporation, the board of directors may delegate much of its managerial authority to specially appointed corporate officers, such as the chief executive officer and the president, who will often also be members of the board. The board then retains a general supervisory responsibility over management, leaving the operating decisions to the corporation's executive officers. In a small family corporation, such as the XYZ Corporation, on the other hand, the same person or persons may often wear all of these hats at the same time.

Ultimately, it is the general meeting of shareholders, through its power to appoint and remove the members of the board of directors, which retains final control over the strategic direction of the corporation. Most decisions of the shareholders in general meeting require only a simple majority of the votes cast. In some cases, however, a special majority of the shareholders in general meeting is required to approve certain fundamental corporate changes, such as an amalgamation with another corporation, or a change in the corporate name or share structure. In practical terms, this means that those who control a majority of the voting shares of the corporation are in effective control of the corporation.

As the controlling shareholder of the XYZ Corporation, therefore, I will have almost unfettered power over the management of the corporation, since I will be able to appoint the corporation's directors and officers. I can even make the decision on behalf of the board to hire myself as president and chief executive officer. In legal terms, however, it is now the corporation, rather than myself as an individual, which owns and operates the tax consulting business.[6] If the consultancy business is successful and earns money, then it is the corporation that has to declare the profits on its corporate income tax statement each year. If the corporation hires researchers and rents office space in the downtown area of the city, then it is the corporation that is now responsible for the salaries of the researchers and for the rental cost of the office space. The decision to enter into these legal relationships is made by me in my capacity as the chief executive officer and president of the corporation. But the decisions are legally those of the corporation. So it is the corporation, rather than myself personally, which is legally responsible for any obligations or liabilities arising out of these legal relationships.

The implications of this legal fiction regarding the separate legal personality of a corporation from that of its shareholders were clarified by the English House of Lords in the famous case of *Salomon v. Salomon and Co. Ltd.*[7] In a situation very similar to that outlined above, in which one individual was in effective control over a manufacturing corporation, the business eventually became insolvent and the company was put into bankruptcy by its creditors. In this situation the corporation did not have sufficient assets to satisfy the claims of all of its creditors. So the creditors sued the controlling shareholder of the corporation, claiming that he should also be held personally liable for the debts of the corporation, since it was he who had been effectively controlling the business of the corporation. The House of Lords ruled against the creditors' claim, however, holding that as the corporation was in law a separate legal person from the shareholder, and as the creditors were aware of this when doing business with the corporation, they could not be heard to complain if the corporation is subsequently unable to pay its debts. The fact that the founder of the business that was sold to the corporation was also its controlling shareholder did not alter the fact that the corporation was in law a separate legal person from its shareholder, and thus responsible for its own debts and liabilities. Effectively, therefore, the assets and liabilities of the corporation are regarded in law as distinct from the assets and liabilities of its shareholders. Consequently, the personal liability of the shareholders for the debts and liabilities of the corporation is limited to the value of their investment in the share capital of the corporation. This is what is meant by the expression "limited liability corporation".

---

6 In effect, I sell the business to the corporation, in payment of which the corporation issues me a controlling block of its shares. In this way I achieve two of my objectives. I legally transfer ownership of the business to the corporation, while at the same time ensuring that I remain in legal control as its controlling shareholder.

7 *Salomon v. Salomon and Co. Ltd.*, [1897] A.C. 22, [1895-9] All E.R. 33 (H.L.).

The flexibility provided by this method of organizing a business is one of its chief advantages. If the company is successful, and earns a profit after taxes, the board of directors can decide whether to retain the profit within the company to pay for further expansion, or to pay all or part of the annual profit to the shareholders by declaring a dividend. In the case of the XYZ Corporation, since I am in effective control of the board of directors, I can decide whether to leave the profits in the corporation or to pay them out to myself as dividends, depending on which is the most tax favourable strategy to choose. In addition, I may decide to issue more shares in the corporation to enable the corporation to take over or purchase another business, which may then become part of the assets of my existing corporation, or which could be operated as a separate subsidiary or affiliated corporation in which the XYZ Corporation owns part or all of its shares. Once again, the advantage of structuring the second business as a separate corporation is that the assets and liabilities of both corporations remain distinct. So if one of the corporations were to fail and become insolvent, this would not necessarily affect the economic viability of the other corporation in the group, even though both corporations are effectively owned and controlled by the same person.

The economic rationale behind the creation of the limited liability corporation is to promote investment in new business enterprises by limiting the potential liability of shareholders for the debts and liabilities of the corporation. Otherwise it might be too risky to invest in a business with a chance of failure, notwithstanding the potential rewards at stake if the company is successful. In order to benefit from the privilege of limited liability, however, the shareholders must operate the corporation as if it is indeed a separate legal person with its own board of directors, and its own rights and duties. It is not permissible for me, for example, to transfer corporate assets out of an insolvent corporation into a more financially solvent corporation in order to reduce the amount of assets that may be available to the insolvent corporation's creditors. If so, I will be guilty of using my position as controlling shareholder to deliberately deplete the corporation's assets. Since the creditors of an insolvent corporation can normally only sue the corporation, and not the shareholders personally, such an action on my part would be treated as being akin to fraud. In these circumstances, the courts will allow the creditors to "pierce the corporate veil" and sue the shareholders or directors of the insolvent corporation personally, since they will have been guilty of placing their own financial interests over the interests of the corporation and its creditors. But for most other purposes the courts are likely to respect the integrity of the corporation as a distinct legal person with its own rights and interests that remain separate from those of its shareholders. This is one of the major reasons why the limited liability corporation has proven so popular as a means of organizing a business.

In recognizing corporations as a distinct category of artificial legal persons, the question remains, how far should the legal system go in stretching this analogy and treating corporations as if they were the same as natural persons? Should there be any limits placed on the concept of corporate legal personality? After all, corporations cannot vote, or run for public office, or be conscripted into military service in time of war. Should they be entitled to the same constitutional rights as natural persons who are capable of exercising these rights and obligations of citizenship? The courts have responded to this latter question by recognizing that corporations as legal persons are entitled to the protection of the *Charter of Rights and Freedoms*[8] in much the same way as other legal persons. In the case of *R.J.R.-MacDonald Inc. v. Canada*,[9] for example, which involved a constitutional challenge to the validity of provincial anti-tobacco advertising laws, the Supreme Court of Canada unanimously accepted that corporations have constitutional rights to freedom of expression under paragraph 2(*b*) of the *Charter of Rights and Freedoms*, and thus had standing to initiate a legal challenge to the legislation.

Another area in which the courts have been required to examine the scope and limits of corporate legal personality has to do with the question of who should be held legally accountable when a corporation breaks the law — for example by illegally dumping effluents into a river, or violating mandatory health and safety standards in the workplace, thus endangering the lives and health of workers? In these circumstances can the corporation itself be held criminally liable as a party to the offence, together with the managers and directors of the corporation who knew of the illegal activity? Or is it only individuals, or natural persons, who can be convicted of a criminal offence under the *Criminal Code*?

Some commentators have argued that it is irrational to hold a corporation criminally liable for the acts of individuals within the organization. To these commentators a corporation is only an artificial creation of the law, a legal fiction which has no mind of its own and therefore no capacity to form the criminal intent that is necessary in order to be convicted of a serious criminal offence. From this perspective, it is one thing to hold a corporation liable in civil law for breach of contract, or negligence, or for non-payment of property taxes. But it is quite another thing to convict a corporation of a serious criminal offence such as murder or manslaughter. To prosecute a corporation for the crime of murder or manslaughter is

---

8 Part I of the *Constitution Act, 1982*, being Schedule B to the *Canada Act 1982* (U.K.), 1982, c. 11.

9 *R.J.R.-MacDonald Inc. v. Canada (Attorney General)*, [1995] S.C.J. No. 68, [1995] 3 S.C.R. 199 (S.C.C.).

like prosecuting the car driven by a drunk driver that runs down an innocent victim, or like prosecuting a gun for the crime of shooting someone! The car, or the gun, is only the tool or weapon used by those individuals who were truly responsible for the commission of the crime. It is these individuals who should be held criminally responsible for the harm done by the car or the gun, not the other way round.[10]

The courts have responded to this dilemma by developing a theory of corporate criminal liability whereby a corporation can be held criminally liable for the illegal actions of those of its employees, senior managers and directors who are regarded as part of the "directing mind and will" of the corporation.[11] Part of the reasoning behind the courts' willingness to hold a corporation criminally liable for the acts of its senior managers is that this is more likely to deter future illegal corporate behaviour than just punishing the individual managers and officers. One of the problems of viewing individual human agents as the real "authors" of a corporation's criminal behaviour is that this ignores the problem of who really benefits from the unlawful activity. When the managers of a company knowingly dump dangerous effluents into a municipal water supply, or fail to install necessary ventilation equipment into a mine shaft, it is the corporation that saves the money that is not spent on the installation of emissions control technology or a new ventilation system. It is not the managers who pocket the savings. Moreover, by holding the corporation criminally liable for the unlawful acts of its managers and officers, there is a greater likelihood that preventive actions will be taken by the company to avoid this type of risk occurring again. If a corporation is effectively permitted to retain the benefits of illegal activities carried out in its name, there is too great an incentive for the corporation to continue breaking the law, rather than complying with it.

It is evident from this brief discussion that the consequences of regarding a corporation as a legal person do not just follow as a matter of course from the nature of corporate legal personality itself. Instead, courts and legislators are required to work out the practical legal implications of the theory of corporate personality on a case by case basis. Far from being a straightforward legal idea which simply reflects our common sense views of social relations, the concept of legal personality turns out on closer inspection to be a very open-ended legal category, the precise limits of which may vary considerably at different times, and in response to

---

10 Nicolette Parisi, "Theories of Corporate Criminal Liability (or Corporations Don't Commit Crimes, People Commit Crimes)", in Ellen Hochstedler, ed., *Corporations as Criminals* (Beverley Hills: Sage Publications, 1984), 41-68.

11 *R. v. St. Lawrence Corp.*, [1969] O.J. No. 1326, [1969] 2 O.R. 305, 5 D.L.R. (3d) 263 (Ont. C.A.); *R. v. Canadian Dredge & Dock Co.*, [1985] S.C.J. No. 28, [1985] 1 S.C.R. 662 (S.C.C.). See also Celia Wells, *Corporations and Criminal Responsibility, 2nd ed.* (Oxford: Oxford University Press, 2001).

different sets of social conditions. Is there any natural limit, for example, on the capacity of the legal system to recognize new categories of artificial legal persons? This question has given rise to much debate among animal rights activists and environmentalists in recent years.

In an influential article Christopher Stone asked why it is that the environment is not accorded the same legal rights of personhood that are accorded to corporations? Corporations, after all, are artificial legal persons. Unlike the natural environment, they have no independent existence outside of the legal arena. So it is the legal system which, in a sense, gives them birth and recognizes their rights and obligations as legal persons. Why, then, could we not extend the categories of artificial legal persons to include the natural environment, he asks?[12]

According to Stone, the lack of legal rights for the environment tends to encourage behaviour that promotes exploitation rather than conservation of natural resources, thus leading to problems of environmental degradation and waste. Our contemporary legal approach to protecting the environment is fundamentally flawed, he asserts, since it is influenced by a Judeo-Christian ethic which still views nature as a wealth of untapped resources which humankind has a natural right to exploit and claim dominion over. According to this Judeo-Christian ethic, natural resources such as land, water, air, soil, trees, minerals, even genetic material derived from human or animal sources, are regarded as *things* or resources which can be the objects of property rights held by human beings or by corporations, but which are not recognised as having inherent or legal rights in themselves. In much the same way, he argues, the legal system formerly viewed women and slaves as the property of their husbands and masters, rather than as autonomous legal persons in their own right.

One of the benefits of extending the categories of legal personhood to include the environment is that this would encourage us to think of the environment in a more holistic way, as a natural organism with its own interests and needs. At present, many forms of environmental injury tend to remain invisible in the eyes of the law. Only where environmental degradation results in injury to health or property of other human beings is there any legal right to bring an action at common law for environmental injuries. Where this cannot be shown — for example, where a polluter emits acid rain into the atmosphere in such a way that it is impossible to identify or quantify the precise consequences for health or property damage — there is no possibility for a lawsuit by private or public interest groups. The only legal mechanism for preventing or policing such environmental damage is through government enforcement of existing

[12] Christopher Stone, "Should Trees Have Standing? — Toward Legal Rights for Natural Objects" (1972), 45 *Southern California Law Review* at 450-501.

regulatory standards, which may often be more sympathetic to the interests of industry than to the issues of loss of environmental quality of life.

One way to address this risk of "regulatory capture" would be to permit third parties to bring legal proceedings against private and public polluters in the name of the environment itself. This could be achieved by recognizing the environment as having a distinct legal status, akin to that of a child, or legally incompetent person, who needs to have a legal guardian or "next friend" to represent them in any legal proceeding. In much the same way, public interest groups concerned with preservation of the environment could apply to the court to be appointed as a legal guardian or next friend of environmentally endangered species or locations. This would then enable lawsuits to be brought on behalf of the environment to claim compensation for environmental damage, for example, by farmers, loggers, developers, or mine owners, without having to show proof of additional personal injury or property damage on the part of individual claimants.

Stone's argument for natural rights for the environment has been raised in a number of lawsuits. In one high profile case, *Sierra Club v. Morton*,[13] the United States Supreme Court rejected a claim by the Sierra Club for legal standing to intervene in a lawsuit as the next friend or legal representative of a wilderness area that was due to be commercially developed as a ski resort. The majority of the Court refused to grant the Sierra Club legal standing as an intervenor on the grounds that existing federal and state environmental laws were sufficient to ensure that environmental interests were taken into account in the decision-making process governing the ski development. A minority of the Court, however, in a dissenting opinion strongly reminiscent of Stone's natural rights argument, would have been prepared to grant the Sierra Club legal standing to represent the interests of the wilderness area. Taking a very different approach from the majority of the Supreme Court Justices, Justice Douglas found that there is a separate environmental interest that needs legal representation, over and above existing governmental regulatory processes, because of the risk of conflicts of interest on the part of governments and regulators, who may tend to promote economic development and increased tax revenues over legitimate environmental concerns.

Had Stone's natural rights argument been accepted by the United States Supreme Court, the effect would have been to open up environmental decisions to increased judicial review in the courts, with the possibility of lawsuits brought on behalf of the environment in cases where environmental damage or injury has been caused by industrial or urban development, for example. According to Stone, any damages awarded by the courts for

---

[13] *Sierra Club v. Morton*, 405 U.S. 727 (1972).

environmental injuries in a lawsuit of this nature could be held in a special trust fund that could be used to pay for environmental clean-up or improvement costs. However, if the environment were to have sufficient legal status to sue or be named as a party in such proceedings, the question arises whether the environment also has sufficient legal status to be sued in cases of injury or damage caused by the environment, for example by ice storms, floods, hurricanes, tornadoes, or forest fires? In this context, it is much less obvious whether the policy arguments in favour of extending legal rights to the environment are so compelling. If the effect of a damage award against the environment might be to bankrupt an environmental group seeking legal guardianship status, or to force a sale of environmentally sensitive wetlands or forest areas to pay the costs of personal or property damage caused by flooding or by forest fires, then the benefits of recognizing the environment as a distinct legal person with its own natural rights could easily be exceeded by the potential legal costs. Insofar as there is a need for greater legal protection for the environment, therefore, it may be that this is best achieved through legislative reforms to existing environmental protection laws, without the uncertainties and risks involved in extending a special status of personhood to the natural environment.

Nevertheless, this example does illustrate that the categories of legal persons are not necessarily unchangeable, and can be contested and challenged. Indeed, much of the past century and a half has witnessed a progressive widening of the categories of legal persons to include many groups and entities which had formerly been precluded from exercising the rights and obligations of personhood. As Stone suggests, every extension of legal rights to new categories of persons involves a breach with the past, a leap into the unknown, a willingness to think the unthinkable. It is often hard to step outside the legal categories or boundaries that we are already familiar with. Yet it is the very capacity to be able to think outside of existing boundaries that makes it possible for the legal system to respond to new challenges and adapt to changing social conditions.

II. LEGAL DEPENDENCY AND THE FAMILY

One of the areas in which changing social values have resulted in very significant shifts in the categories of legal personhood has been in the context of family relationships, particularly with regard to the legal status of women. Historically, married women were regarded at English common law as being under the special legal protection (or "coverture") of their husbands, and as such did not have any separate legal personality or identity from that of their husband. Under the doctrine of unity of legal personality, the English common law viewed a husband and wife as being "one person" in law, with the consequence that a married woman had very limited capacity to enter into legal relationships on her own behalf. Thus, she was very far from being seen as an independent person in her own right.

The practical implications of this doctrine of unity of legal personality in marriage were very significant and affected every aspect of women's lives. A married woman could not enter into a contract in her own name without the agreement of her husband, unless the contract was for household necessaries (in which case the husband's consent to the transaction was presumed). Nor could a husband and wife enter into a binding agreement with each other during the marriage, since in order to make an enforceable contract there must be two parties to the agreement, and under the common law doctrine of unity of legal personality the husband and wife were considered to be one person in law. Even where the wife owned property before entering into the marriage the effect of the doctrine of unity of legal personality was to take away the wife's legal capacity to execute deeds or other transactions in respect of her own property, and thus to transfer effective powers of management and control over the property to her husband. Indeed, in one celebrated case in the nineteenth century, the husband of a widely published author who had written a number of pamphlets arguing for more liberal divorce laws for women, sued her publishers for the royalties she had earned from her books, on the grounds that although they were legally separated, she was in law still his wife, so he should be entitled to her earnings as her husband![14]

In many respects, therefore, the legal status of a married woman at common law was akin to that of a child, or a person of unsound mind who is considered to be legally incapable of managing their own affairs. Unlike a child, however, a married woman's status as a legally incompetent person did not change on reaching the age of majority, but remained throughout the duration of the marriage. The husband's legal authority within the family even extended to the power to forcibly confine or punish a disobedient wife or child. The common law would only intervene where the husband or father exceeded his legal authority by using unreasonable or excessive force (hence the common law "rule of thumb" whereby use of a rod or stick greater than the width of a man's thumb was considered to be unreasonable force). If a married woman were to be injured through the actions of a third party, she could not bring a legal action in her own name, since in law the injury to her was also considered to be done to the husband, so that any legal action must also be brought in the husband's name. Likewise, a married woman could not bring a legal action against her own husband (other than in very limited circumstances), or give

---

[14] Lee Holcombe, *Wives and Property* (Toronto: University of Toronto Press, 1983), at 55-56.

testimony against him in an action brought by a third party, since husband and wife were considered to be one person in law, and a person should not be required to give evidence against himself![15]

Effectively, therefore, the common law viewed marriage not as a relationship based on choice between two equal partners, but as a hierarchical relationship based on status, in which a husband was delegated considerable legal authority over both the person and the property of his wife. Moreover, these common law restrictions on women's legal rights as "persons" within the marriage were not only operative as between husband and wife in the private sphere of the family. The same traditional view of gender roles that denied women rights as persons within the family was also frequently invoked by legislators and by judges to deny women the right to vote or to run for public office. Even where the right to admission to a university, or to practise as a lawyer or doctor, was nominally open to all "qualified persons", the courts still tended to interpret this term restrictively to apply only to qualified *male* persons. Qualified female persons, therefore, need not apply!

Over time the traditional assumptions about the role of women within the family that were used to justify such exclusionary legal rules have undergone a significant transformation.

Legislative reforms beginning with the enactment of statutes respecting married women's property in the second half of the nineteenth century successively removed all of the old common law restrictions on women's legal autonomy within marriage. Marriage is no longer viewed as a semi-private legal realm in which a married woman is legally dependent on her husband. Indeed, the preamble to Ontario's *Family Law Act* explicitly declares that marriage is a partnership in which both partners contribute equally, regardless of their respective roles in the marriage.[16] Thus, even if one partner stays out of the work force to bring up the children, while the other partner works, both partners are deemed to have contributed equally to the marriage. Consequently, both parties should be entitled to an equal share of the family assets if the marriage ends in divorce. In short, marriage is now viewed as a relationship based on contract rather than status, in which both husband and wife are seen as autonomous legal actors with full capacity to enter into legal relationships and create enforceable rights and obligations with respect to persons outside the marriage, as well as vis-à-vis each other.

This shift in the legal status of women within marriage has been accompanied by legislative and judicial reforms respecting the rights of

---

[15] See Sir William Blackstone, *Commentaries on the Laws of England, vol. 1* (Chicago: University of Chicago Press, 1979), at 442-45.

[16] *Family Law Act*, R.S.O. 1990, c. F.3.

women in the public sphere. In what have come to be known as the "persons cases" in the late nineteenth century and the early part of the twentieth century, the legal incapacities imposed upon women as a result of the old common law rules concerning unity of legal personality within marriage were successfully challenged before the courts and in the legislature. One of the obstacles facing women who sought to challenge these legal disabilities in the courts was that the judges were all men who had been steeped in the very legal traditions that had denied women any separate legal personality at law. The litigants in these persons cases were therefore confronted with the task of changing not only the formal legal categorizations of persons at common law or in specific Acts of Parliament, but more significantly, the weight of centuries of tradition that had invested these categories of persons with the immutable authority of law.

The complexity of this challenge can be seen in the United States Supreme Court decision in *Bradwell v. The State*.[17] In this case, the plaintiff sought to overturn a decision of the Supreme Court of Illinois, upholding a restrictive interpretation of the rules governing admission to legal practise of the State Bar of Illinois. The plaintiff was a married woman who had completed all the technical requirements for admission to the practise of law, but who was refused admission to practise solely on the grounds that she was a woman. The plaintiff appealed this decision to the United States Supreme Court, arguing that the lower court's refusal to grant her admission to the practise of law amounted to an infringement of her rights as a citizen under the 14th Amendment of the Bill of Rights to engage in any lawful occupation of her choice. The Supreme Court rejected her appeal, however, on the basis that nowhere in the United States Constitution was it specifically stated that this right is accorded to women as citizens.

In denying the plaintiff's appeal, the Supreme Court relied not only on the laws of man, such as the common law doctrine of unity of legal personality, but also invoked the divine order of nature, which had ordained that women were best fitted for the domestic sphere of home and hearth, and were temperamentally as well as physically unsuited to the rigours of practising law.

Bradwell v. The State was decided in 1872, before women had won the right to vote in federal or state elections either in Canada or the United States. A different judicial attitude was apparent some sixty years later, in the famous Canadian persons case of *Henrietta Muir Edwards v. Canada (Attorney General)*.[18] In this case, the question before the court was once

---

[17] *Bradwell v. The State*, 16 Wall. 130, 21 L. Ed. 442 (1872).

[18] *Henrietta Muir Edwards v. Canada (Attorney General)*, [1930] A.C. 124 (J.C.P.C.).

again whether women could be considered "legal persons". However, the context this time was whether women were eligible to be appointed to the Canadian Senate in accordance with the provisions of s. 24 of the *British North America Act, 1867*.

At the time of their petition to the Attorney General in 1927, the five appellants were all women who either had been or were currently holding public office in the Province of Alberta. Two of the appellants had been members of the legislative assembly; one was currently a sitting member of the legislative assembly and a member of the provincial Executive Council; one was a police magistrate; another was the Alberta Vice-President of the National Council of Women for Canada. Despite their status as professional women who were well qualified to hold public office, the Supreme Court of Canada unanimously held that the term "qualified persons" under s. 24 of the *British North America Act* did *not* include women. The basis of the court's ruling was that since women were still excluded from most public offices at the time the legislation was enacted, in 1867, Parliament must have been aware of this in drafting the wording of s. 24, and thus must have intended women to be excluded from eligibility for the Senate.

The onus of proof was thus placed on the female petitioners to show conclusively that the legislature had meant to include women within the category of persons eligible for appointment to the Senate at the time of enactment of s. 24. Since the legislation nowhere gave any indication that women were to be included as persons under this section, the Court concluded that it must be presumed that the legislature intended to *exclude* women.

The appellants appealed this decision to the Judicial Committee of the Privy Council, then the senior appellate court for Canada, which overturned the decision of the Canadian Supreme Court. In handing down their historic decision, the judges on the Judicial Committee of the Privy Council took a very different stance towards the interpretation of the *British North America Act* than the judges of the Supreme Court. Rather than looking backwards to discover the intention of Parliament at the time of the enactment of the legislation, the Court ruled that the wording of s. 24 of the Act should be given its natural meaning in the context in which the question of interpretation arose. That context includes the fact that social mores and political values had changed considerably in Canada between 1867 and the commencement of the litigation in 1927, after women had already won the vote.

Thus the reasons for denying women rights as persons under the ancient common law of England were not necessarily relevant in interpreting the wording of constitutional legislation in Canada at a much later date. Instead of presuming a Parliamentary intention to exclude women, as the

Supreme Court had done, the Judicial Committee of the Privy Council asked whether the wording of s. 24 could be interpreted to include women in the category of "qualified persons"? Certainly it could, since the expression "qualified persons" is gender neutral on its face, and thus capable of application to both men and women. This being so, the Court asked whether there was any clear evidence of Parliament's intention to deliberately *exclude* women in the wording of the legislation? There being no deliberate use of the male pronoun to restrict the interpretation of "qualified persons" under s. 24, as there was in other sections of the legislation, the Judicial Committee held that Parliament did intend women to be included in the category of "qualified persons" eligible to be appointed to the Senate. In so doing, the court not only contributed to the legal emancipation of women as legal persons under Canadian law, but also adopted a new liberal approach to interpreting the constitution, referring to it as a "living tree", which must be allowed to flourish and grow within its natural limits in the constitutional soil in which it has been planted, rather than remaining sterile or hide-bound to tradition.

III. CHILDREN AS LEGAL DEPENDANTS

If Maine's prediction about the movement of progressive societies from relations based on status to relations based on individual autonomy and contract has been borne out with respect to women's legal rights as persons, this cannot be said with the same degree of confidence about the legal status of children. For most purposes, until they reach the age of majority (which varies according to the legal activity in question among the different provinces), children are still regarded as legal dependants within the family, with limited capacity to enter into voluntary legal relationships or to create enforceable legal rights and obligations on their own behalf. In the eyes of the law, minor children are not regarded as competent legal persons who are rationally capable of acting in their own best interests. Consequently, the legal system imposes significant limits on a minor child's freedom of choice, and restricts the number and types of legal relationships which a child has legal capacity to enter into. These restrictions range from minimum age limits on the purchase of cigarettes or alcohol or prescription drugs, to more substantial restrictions on the minimum age at which it is legally permissible for a young person to hold a driver's licence, to vote, to marry, to leave school, to change his or her name, or even to leave home and remove him or herself from parental supervision. Provincial and federal age of majority laws therefore operate as important legal thresholds between the restricted status of childhood dependency, and the legal autonomy of adulthood, in which the young adult is no longer subject to the formal legal authority of others (in the family, or at school, for example).

The status of dependency in law, therefore, implies a corresponding transfer of legal powers to one person to make certain decisions in the "best interests" of the other, dependent person. Within a family context, these legal powers will normally be vested in the child's parents. The parent or guardian is implicitly delegated legal authority by the state to make decisions in the child's best interests. In a way, therefore, we can say that the law places the dependent child under the protective custody of a parent or guardian, who is given a considerable degree of authority over the child. The essentially *custodial* nature of the parent/child relationship is clearly evident in the context of a parental divorce or separation, which is likely to involve a separate custody hearing before a judge in order to determine in whose custody any dependent children of the relationship should be placed. In reaching its decision, the court will exercise its *parens patriae* jurisdiction — that is to reach a decision regarding custody that, in all the circumstances, is in the child's best interests. This could result in either a sole custody order in favour of one parent (with the other parent being accorded access or visitation rights), or a joint legal custody award between the two parents, in which case both retain their legal authority as parents vis-à-vis their children. In some circumstances, a custody hearing could even result in an order of custody being made in favour of a third party, such as a child's grandparents, where the court decides that this would be in the child's best interests.

It is important to realise, however, that the legal authority which a parent can exercise over dependent children within the family is not unlimited, and indeed has undergone considerable modification over time. As we have seen, the common law view of the parent/child relationship regarded the child as being almost the property of the father. Other than the limits placed by the so-called rule of thumb, the common law placed very few restrictions on the legal authority which a father could exercise over his children while they remained subject to his authority and under his roof. As a result, the common law provided very little protection to a dependent child in the event of abuse or neglect within the family. The father's legal obligation towards his dependants was to feed, clothe and shelter them, and otherwise look after their physical and spiritual needs. In return, the legal system imposed an obligation of obedience on his dependants. Any act of disobedience or disrespect towards the father's will by any of his dependants could therefore be subject to severe punishment, qualified only by the father's duty at common law not to use excessive or unreasonable force.

This common law stance of virtually untrammelled parental authority remained largely intact until the emergence of a "child saving movement" in the last decades of the nineteenth century. The philosophy behind the reformers' efforts was to provide more legal protection for children in need of care, specifically those at risk of abuse or neglect or abandonment. As a result of these efforts, legislation such as Ontario's *Children's Protection Act* in 1893 was enacted which provided greater legal powers to the State to remove children from the legal custody and control of their parents, and to place them under the temporary or permanent legal guardianship of the Crown.

The effect of such legislation is to give child protection authorities considerable power to intervene within families in order to protect the welfare of children. Such forms of intervention may be voluntary and take the form of providing therapeutic services to families with children in need of care. Or, they may be coercive and take the form of legally "apprehending" children from the parental home. Because of the infringement on family privacy which apprehending children at risk necessarily involves, the onus lies on child protection workers to provide evidence before a court that such an intervention is necessary. However, where the risk of abuse or neglect is perceived to be high, and the need for speed is great, the legislation often gives the legal power to child protection agencies to apprehend children at risk without obtaining a prior court order in appropriate circumstances.[19]

Where a child is removed from a home, the legal effect of a temporary wardship order is to give temporary custody of the child to the local children's aid society or provincial child protection authorities. Where a child is placed in temporary care, the parent/child relationship may be re-established if the conditions of a care order or ongoing supervision by child protection workers are complied with by the family. While under a temporary wardship order, the parents still retain a legal right of access to their child, even though the child may be placed in a short term foster home or in an institutional environment. If the court determines that the care order should be made permanent, the parents' legal relationship with their child will be terminated. The child then becomes a permanent ward of the State and may be placed for adoption.

The effect of an adoption order is to transfer permanent legal custody over the child from the child's biological parent(s) to the adoptive parent(s), who thereby become invested with the full custodial powers of a parent in law. At the same time, the parental rights and obligations of the biological parent(s) are extinguished by operation of law. In legal

---

[19] Dick Barnhorst and Bernd Walter, "Child Protection Legislation in Canada", in Nicholas Bala, Joseph P. Hornick and Robin Vogl, eds., *Canadian Child Welfare Law: Children, Families, and the State* (Toronto: Thompson Educational Publishing Co., 1991), at 25.

terms, the prior parent-child relationship has ceased to exist. The child is now a member of a new family.

We can see from this discussion that the existence of a parent-child relationship, in legal terms at least, does not necessarily depend on a prior biological relationship between parent and child. Instead, the terms "parent" and "child" more properly refer to the existence of a *custodial* relationship between the parent and the child, the precise nature of which may vary in different contexts, and can be terminated or modified substantially through operation of law, such as in the event of death or divorce, or the intervention of child welfare authorities.

The implications of this essentially custodial view of the parent-child relationship were explored in the United States' Supreme Court case of *Stanley v. Illinois*.[20] The case involved an application for custody brought by the biological father of three minor children, who had been taken into care by the child welfare authorities in Illinois, following the death of the children's mother. Although the children's biological father had lived with the mother at different times over a period of eighteen years, the two had never married. Under Illinois law, at this time, children of unwed mothers were regarded as wards of the state in the event of the death of the mother. In other words, the status of illegitimacy meant that the law did not regard the biological father of the children as having any legal rights or obligations as a parent towards the children. It was as if the children had a mother, but no father. Consequently, when the mother died, the children were regarded legally as orphans, and thus became wards of the state.

The biological father sought legal custody of the children on the basis that he was their biological father, and that the child protection authorities had shown no sufficient legal cause for removing the children from his care and control. In response, the child welfare authorities argued that under Illinois law he had no custodial rights with respect to the children, and thus he had no legal standing to challenge the order making them wards of the state. However, they suggested that he could apply for an adoption order and seek to regain custody of his children from the state in this manner!

On appeal from the decision of the Illinois Supreme Court, which upheld the Illinois law denying custody rights to biological fathers in these circumstances, the United States Supreme Court ruled that the relevant provisions of Illinois law violated the petitioner's constitutional rights to due process of law. In any other circumstances, the onus would be on child welfare authorities to provide evidence that the children were at risk before intervening to remove them from their settled home environment.

---

20 *Stanley v. Illinois* (1972), 405 U.S. 645 (U.S. Supreme Court).

The fact that the children's biological father had not married their mother was not presumptive evidence of his legal unfitness to care for his children. Thus, he should be entitled to the same due process rights to a hearing to determine his suitability to remain in custody and control of his children as any other parent would be in similar circumstances. The status of illegitimacy should no longer be a legal barrier to recognizing the importance of the parental relationship between an unwed father and his children in these circumstances.[21]

A related legal context in which a child's needs may come in conflict with the principle of family autonomy may arise in a situation requiring consents for medical treatments. In Chapter 1 we briefly considered the case of *Malette v. Shulman*,[22] which concerned the legal dilemma posed by a doctor's decision to order a blood transfusion for a patient who had made known her wishes to refuse any blood transfusion on religious grounds. In that case, the court held that the patient's right to autonomy and dignity should override the doctor's decision that the transfusion would be medically in her best interests. As a legal person of full age and capacity, the patient was entitled to make her own decisions regarding her consent or lack of consent to particular medical treatments. The doctor's decision, backed by the hospital, to proceed with the blood transfusion while being fully aware that she did not consent, amounted to a battery on her person, for which they were held liable in damages to the patient. The doctor's view that the transfusion was medically necessary was no defence to an action brought by the patient in tort, since he lacked legal authority to override her lack of consent.

Consider now, the case of a young child in a similar situation in which a physician wishes to give a blood transfusion to the child. This time, the parents state their wishes that the child not be given a blood transfusion on religious grounds, notwithstanding that the hospital or the attending physician may believe that a transfusion might be necessary to save the child's life.

As in the case of *Mallette v. Shulman*, the doctor or hospital cannot override the parent's authority or proceed without their consent. However, in a similar case, *B.(R.) v. Children's Aid Society of Metropolitan Toronto*,[23] when the attending physician felt that the child's life was in serious danger

---

21 In Ontario the status of illegitimacy has been formally removed from the law by sections 1(1) and 1(4) of the *Children's Law Reform Act*, R.S.O. 1990, c. C.12, s. 1(1) provides:

> "Subject to subsection (2), for all purposes of the law of Ontario a person is the child of his or her natural parents and his or her status as their child is independent of whether the child is born within or outside marriage".

22 *Malette v. Shulman*, [1990] O.J. No. 450, 72 O.R. (2d) 417 (Ont. C.A.).

23 *B.(R.) v. Children's Aid Society of Metropolitan Toronto*, [1994] S.C.J. No. 24, [1995] 1 S.C.R. 315 (S.C.C.).

without a blood transfusion, the physicians contacted the Children's Aid Society, which in turn applied to court on very short notice for a temporary wardship order, which would have resulted in the child becoming a temporary ward of court for a period of 72 hours, so that a blood transfusion could be administered to the child. Despite the parent's objections, the court granted the temporary wardship order (subsequently extended for a period of 21 days) while the child was still hospitalized. The senior physician testified that the situation was a medical emergency, and wished to maintain the legal authority to transfuse if the situation, in the eyes of the physicians, warranted it. A transfusion was administered to the child while under the temporary wardship order. When out of danger, the temporary wardship order was rescinded, and the child returned to the custody of the parents.

The parents appealed the ruling of the Provincial Court granting temporary custody of the child to the Children's Aid Society, arguing that this amounted to a violation of their right to choose medical treatment for their child in accordance with their own religious beliefs under ss. 7 and 2(a) of the Canadian *Charter of Rights and Freedoms*.[24] In this context, the Supreme Court of Canada upheld the constitutionality of the Provincial Court's ruling, holding that the provisions of the *Child Welfare Act*[25] granting the court power to make a temporary wardship order did not amount to a violation of the parents' constitutional rights.

Fundamentally, the Supreme Court ruled that parents do not have an unqualified right to make decisions on behalf of their children, or to deny them access to necessary medical treatment where this may conflict with the parents' religious views. Where circumstances warrant and there is evidence that a child is in need of care, the court in the exercise of its *parens patriae* jurisdiction is justified in making a temporary wardship order so that treatment can be given to the child. As Justices Iacobucci and Major observed, "Although an individual may refuse any medical procedures upon her own person, it is quite another matter to speak for another separate individual, especially when that individual cannot speak for herself."[26] In these circumstances, therefore, the Supreme Court found that the child's best interests outweighed the parents' interest in preserving family autonomy and religious freedom.

Having said this, however, it is important to recognize that there may be some situations in which the State's powers of intervention to protect the welfare of children may themselves be qualified by other constitutionally protected legal rights. In the case of *Winnipeg Child and Family Services*

---

[24] *Supra*, note 8.

[25] The statute under consideration was the *Child Welfare Act*, R.S.O. 1980, c. 66.

[26] *Supra*, note 23, at para. 217.

(Northwest Area) v. G.(D.F.),[27] for example, an apparently similar set of legal issues came before the courts. In this case, an application was brought by a Children's Aid Society for an order to take a child temporarily into care so that appropriate medical treatment could be given to the child, and to ensure that consents for necessary medical treatments would not be unreasonably refused. However, this case differed from the previous fact situation in that the application for a temporary wardship order was brought by the Childrens' Aid Society before the birth of the child, while the fetus was still *in utero*.

The expectant mother was pregnant with her fourth child, and had a history of addiction to glue sniffing, which could damage the central nervous system of the fetus. Two of her previous children had been born permanently disabled and were permanent wards of the State. The Children's Aid Society was concerned about the risk of the mother's addiction for the health of the child if the mother was unsupervised during the pregnancy. Effectively, in order to protect the developing fetus, the Children's Aid Society applied for an order to have the mother taken into care in a protective medical treatment facility during the remaining course of the pregnancy.

The temporary care order was granted by a judge of the Superior Court of Manitoba. However, the order was stayed two days later, and appealed to the Manitoba Court of Appeal, which overturned the decision of the Superior Court judge. The Children's Aid society then appealed the case to the Supreme Court of Canada, which held, by a 7-2 majority, that the courts have no jurisdiction to make wardship orders over unborn children.

In the event, the mother voluntarily remained at the treatment centre for a number of days, and gave up sniffing glue, giving birth to an apparently healthy infant some months later. Notwithstanding the relatively happy outcome of the pregnancy for the participants concerned, the Supreme Court ruled that the courts have no authority, either under the law of tort, or under the court's *parens patriae* jurisdiction, to order a mother into custody against her will for the purpose of protecting her unborn child. In contrast to the situation of a child after birth, a temporary wardship order to protect a fetus does not simply involve an interference with the parental rights of a mother to make decisions on behalf of her child. Instead, such an order necessarily involves an interference with the physical liberty of the pregnant woman. Since a fetus has no separate rights as a person until birth, the effect of a temporary wardship order under these circumstances would be to take the pregnant woman into care, and make her effectively a temporary ward of the State, something which neither the Children's

---

27 *Winnipeg Child and Family Services (Northwest Area) v. G.(D.F.)*, [1997] S.C.J. No. 96, [1997] 3 S.C.R. 925 (S.C.C.).

Aid Society, nor the court, even under its *parens patriae* jurisdiction, has authority to do.

In this kind of situation there are a number of competing issues at stake. The Court of Appeal and the Supreme Court of Canada adopted similar reasoning to that followed in previous court decisions such as *Malette v. Shulman* and *R. v. Morgentaler*.[28] The proposed temporary wardship order would have involved an unjustifiable infringement on the expectant mother's rights to autonomy and dignity as an individual. In the absence of her voluntary consent to treatment, the only way to compel a pregnant woman to receive treatment during her pregnancy would be to apply for an order declaring her temporarily legally incompetent under the provisions of the *Mental Health Act*.[29]

This argument was rejected by both the Court of Appeal and the Supreme Court of Canada. Such an approach would not only be coercive, and subject to practical problems in enforcement. It would also involve the courts in regulating and supervising women's behaviour during pregnancy, something which courts are ill-equipped to do. At what point should the legal system intervene to prevent a woman from making choices that could injure her fetus? Should women be allowed to drive while pregnant, to smoke, to drink alcohol? And are there any circumstances in which a woman could choose to terminate her pregnancy? These are all questions which the courts would be faced with if they were to expand their coercive jurisdiction to include protecting the welfare of an unborn child. In many respects, the consequence of this approach, as the Supreme Court appeared to realise, would be to turn back the clock to the old common law attitudes about women's legal incapacity. As with the rights of the patient in *Malette v. Shulman*, the Supreme Court of Canada therefore upheld the rights of the pregnant woman to refuse treatment during the course of her pregnancy, even where medical or social work professionals believed this to be in the best interest of the fetus, on the basis that to coerce her to undergo treatment would violate her inherent rights to dignity and autonomy as an individual.

---

[28] *R. v. Morgentaler*, [1988] S.C.J. No. 1, 44 D.L.R. (4th) 385 (S.C.C.). See also *Tremblay v. Daigle*, [1989] S.C.J. No. 79, [1989] 2 S.C.R. 530 (S.C.C.).

[29] The consolidated version of the relevant legislation in Manitoba is *The Mental Health Act*, C.C.S.M. c. M110.

Chapter 3

Private Law Relations Established by Agreement

I. INTRODUCTION

The relationships in which human beings choose to participate function as perhaps the clearest expression of that autonomy, privacy and self-interest we identified in Chapters 1 and 2 above as central to the model of individuality on which much of our private law doctrine appears to be based. If autonomous choice and decision-making are as significant to private law as we suspect, then we can anticipate a fairly clearly developed and perhaps rigorously enforced body of legal doctrine that will protect those choices and decisions against violation by others. This is especially the case in a situation of exchange, a particular type of private law relationship in which two or more individuals negotiate the content of their relationship, settle on the terms, and then agree to conduct a certain aspect of their lives on the strength of those negotiations and terms. In effect, the result is a body of rules developed and agreed upon by a small number of individuals that will govern their lives in certain defined respects, with no necessary or apparent direct involvement by other members of the community. The appearance is that the participants in these relationships effectively constitute themselves as a separate community for a specific purpose, and impose their own "private government" to regulate their involvement in that purpose.[1]

Ideally, a private government so constructed and negotiated between two independent, equal decision-makers in the marketplace would function perfectly to give expression to the dominant assumptions at work in the structure of private law, the assumptions about individual autonomy, dignity,

[1] Stewart MacAulay used the term "private government" to describe the way in which individuals design their own regulatory framework to govern their day-to-day lives, sometimes irrespective of other normative systems (including the formal law) that may direct behaviour in certain ways. Stewart MacAulay, "Law and the Behavioural Sciences: Is There Any There There?" (1984) 6 *Law & Policy* 149. In negotiating the terms of an exchange relationship, and then agreeing to conduct themselves according to those negotiated terms, individuals construct their own norms of behaviour, albeit with limited application.

privacy, and self-interest introduced in Chapter 1. In fact, we understand the equality of the negotiators in just these terms — they are assumed to be equally rational and self-interested, for example, and this equality of autonomous contractors contributes to the idea that, barring something highly unusual, the bargain struck through negotiation is one that ought to be enforced in private law. However, consistent with the criticism of the dominant assumptions of private law explored at the end of Chapter 1, the wisdom of this result ought to be scrutinized very carefully, both on the grounds of the possible failure of the assumption of equality between negotiators (a criticism grounded in a fresh interpretation of the nature of the inter-personal relationship at stake), and of the idea that the relationship negotiated between the parties is in fact private (a criticism which recognizes the "public", or community-wide, implications of even the most mundane of contracts). As we go forward in this chapter to investigate the formalities of contractual relationships, it will be these two criticisms that we shall keep in mind.

Of course, it would be inconsistent of the law to privilege human autonomy and privacy in the many ways in which private law is developed (at least as we suspect), and then fail to recognize relationships that, on the surface at least, appear to be autonomously negotiated. Despite this, however, the law does impose some controls, some fairly rigid rules that direct the formalities that must be present before the law will recognize a particular relationship as an exchange relationship, that is, the expression of at least two individual wills deserving of the law's support. An exchange relationship that manifests the necessary formalities generates a "contract", and a contract is one of the most carefully defined concepts in all of private law. Perhaps paradoxically, the law insists that a relationship demonstrate certain pre-determined characteristics before it can be recognized as a contractual relationship, even though the terms of that relationship are considered to be the result of negotiation by two autonomous individuals, establishing their private government in the way that their wills direct.

In this chapter, we will begin by investigating the formalities that must be present in a negotiated relationship to establish it as a contractual relationship in private law. It must not be forgotten that, at least occasionally, individuals choose to behave in certain ways so as to attract particular legal consequences and discourage others, and this pattern of behaviour is perhaps most obvious in the law of contract. We will see that, in almost every situation, the law will support the autonomous choice of the participants to take part in a contractual relationship, so long as the necessary formalities are present, and even where the participants themselves have had second thoughts about their involvement. It is important to remember that lying behind this support is the assumption that the parties come to their negotiation as equals, that is, equally rational and self-interested, such that neither might take undue advantage of the other. To honour such negotiation through private law support is to respect the dignity of the participants; to intervene is an affront to their autonomy. At the same time, however, we will see that on certain grounds the law will nevertheless intervene in an apparently autonomously negotiated arrangement and refuse to recognize it as a contractual relationship, despite the appearance of the formalities on which contract law is based in the first place. In other words, the mere presence of the necessary formalities is not enough to ensure the law's support in enforcing the relationship if those formalities were achieved in a way that denies the dignity of the participants themselves. We will conclude by considering aspects of the role of contracts in family life.

II. FORMAL ELEMENTS OF CONTRACT

It is helpful to recall that the law performs its function of classifying human social activity by recognizing certain characteristics that relationships share, and then by grouping those relationships together in the legal classification system. If a relationship manifests pre-determined formal aspects, then it will be classified according to legal taxonomy in the same way that other relationships manifesting similar aspects are classified. To the extent that the law also performs a prescriptive function, that is, prescribing the consequences attendant on breach of a relationship once it is catalogued in a certain way, then we can anticipate those consequences in advance of a breach when we are astute enough to recognize the formal aspects of relationships in the same way as the law. If we can learn to respond to relationships on the same basis as the law responds, then we can predict with some certainty the way in which the law will prescribe consequences. Our investigation of the formal characteristics of exchange relationships is the first step in that process.

It is also helpful to recall that sometimes words used in legal terminology have meanings quite different from meanings ascribed to the same words in ordinary discourse. This we saw in the case of the words "public", "private", and "individual", for example. The term "contract" has a particular meaning in legal terminology, too, distinguished from other words common in ordinary usage by virtue of the formal elements necessary to establish a contract at law. Ordinarily, we use terms such as "agreement", "undertaking", "promise" and others virtually interchangeably with each other, and sometimes we use the word "contract" in the same way. Each of these words shares something in the way we understand them, yet the term "contract" in law is distinct in certain respects. Now in ordinary understanding, we acknowledge that two individuals have an agreement by first recognizing that one of those individuals has made an offer, that is, an offer to do something, to refrain from doing something, to pay some money, to perform some service. This is the first step in the creation of an agreement in ordinary terms, and also the first step in the creation of a contract in the sense of our legal classification system. To this extent at least, ordinary understandings and legal classification are similar.

But even in ordinary language, an offer made in isolation does not constitute an agreement, and the same is true in the law of contract. Even in day-to-day interpretation, an offer must be accepted before an agreement results, such that an acceptance is the second stage in the formation of an agreement. If an individual makes an offer to do some thing, perhaps wash your car once weekly for the balance of the summer, then it is nonsense to suggest that there is an agreement to perform that service unless you have accepted the offer. An agreement results from both offer and acceptance, and the same is true in the law of contract. Without an offer to do something, to refrain from doing something, to perform some service or pay some money, followed by an acceptance of the offer so made, then neither an agreement in ordinary terms nor a contract in formal legal terms can result.

In ordinary usage, however, there really is nothing more to an agreement than the offer and acceptance. If I offer to wash your car once weekly for the balance of the summer, and you accept my offer, then in ordinary language it is clear that we have an agreement, but in the law it is equally clear that there is no contract. In order for a legal contract to result, something more must be evident, something more than the simple offer and acceptance. It is not every agreement that we would recognize in ordinary discussion that yields a contract at law. The reason is that there are additional formal elements of the relationship between the individual making the offer (sometimes called the "offeror") and the individual accepting it (often referred to as the "offeree") that must be present before the legal classification system responds by categorizing the relationship as a contractual relationship. The first of the missing formal elements is the idea of "exchange". It is the concept of "exchange" that first distinguishes a contract recognized as such in the legal classification system from other sorts of relationships that manifest the characteristics of an agreement.

By "exchange" we mean something such as "both parties to the relationship must give something up in order for a contract to result from the offer and acceptance". So, when I offer to wash your car once weekly for the balance of the summer, and you accept that offer, no legal contract can result because you have not given anything up in exchange for my efforts in performing my obligation. If I fail to honour our agreement by neglecting to wash your car, then there is no doubt that I have broken our agreement. This may be a moral wrong, and there may be consequences for that. Perhaps you will not trust me in the future, or perhaps our friendship will be damaged as a result of my unreliability. But the law will not come to your assistance in this circumstance because there is no contract at law. One of the formalities of a contractual relationship, the idea of an exchange, has not been met, and so the law does not recognize the relationship in the legal classification system. Therefore, the prescriptive function of law is not engaged.

Now suppose that, in exchange for my offer to wash your car once weekly over the balance of the summer, you accept by agreeing to pay me $200 for my efforts. In this situation, you have agreed to give something up in exchange for the fulfilment of my obligation, such that this additional formal element of a contractual relationship has been met. As a result, the prescriptive function of law is available to you if you pay me the stipulated amount and I fail to wash your car as agreed. You can seek the assistance of the law by claiming that a formal contract was negotiated, that there was an offer and an acceptance, and that both parties to the arrangement gave something up in exchange for the other's obligation. In legal terms, the thing given up by one party in exchange for the other's performance of their obligation is called "consideration", such that when a judge says that there is no contract "for want or failure of consideration", the judge means that the law does not recognize the relationship as a contract in formal terms because one of the parties did not agree to give something up in exchange for the other party's agreement to perform their obligation.

Simply put, the coincidence of offer, acceptance and consideration is ordinarily enough to generate a relationship that the law will catalogue as a contractual relationship, and if that is the case, then certain results ensue. The law prescribes fairly precise remedies in the event that one party to a contract (established by demonstrating that the required formalities have been met) fails to perform their obligation as agreed. In Chapter 7 below, we will consider some of the remedies available for breach of contract. But there is an additional element of the relationship between the parties that must be considered before we can be certain that a legal contract is the result of the parties' discussions, and this final element is perhaps the most difficult to establish with precision. This fourth element we shall call the "mental element", and it consists of two related components.

The first component of the formal mental element in contract law is known as "the intention to create legal relations". The law has developed in such a way that a contract will not be recognized by the law if one or both parties to the discussion did not intend that a contract result. Suppose that you need your car washed before leaving home to attend a wedding. However, you have a number of other important things to do in a very short time, and likely will be unable to finish everything. You are standing in your driveway, talking to your neighbour, and in your exasperation you say "I'd give a million dollars if only someone would wash my car!" Your neighbour immediately says "I'll do it", and she proceeds to wash your car. In this situation, you made an offer, your neighbour accepted it, and the element of consideration is present, such that the first three formal elements of a contract can easily be demonstrated. But it is unlikely that a court would force you to pay your neighbour the million dollars offered in the first place, as it seems clear from the facts that you did not intend to be bound by your offer. As can be imagined, it is often very difficult to demonstrate whether or not individuals intended to be bound by their apparent offers and acceptances. After all, how do we prove what was in someone's mind? Generally, the matter will be resolved by looking at objective tests of intention, that is, evidence that does not necessarily depend on the testimony of one or the other party to the arrangement. And so the court will infer intention through considering all the surrounding circumstances, and in the situation described it appears clear from the facts that the intention to create legal relations was absent, that the offer to pay was made without the required intention to be bound.

The second aspect of the mental element in the formation of a contract is called *consensus ad idem*, literally translated as a "meeting of the minds". Ordinarily, this requirement means that not only must the parties demonstrate agreement through offer, acceptance and consideration, but that in addition the parties must be agreeing to the same thing. Their minds must meet on the essential terms of the agreement in order for a contract to result. For the most part, essential terms include such things as price, the quantity of goods in a transaction of sale, the quality of goods, the time of delivery, and other terms of key significance to the performance of the parties' obligations. However, in each case in which the court is asked to consider issues of *consensus ad idem*, the court will review questions of essential terms on the basis of the particular negotiations that took place between the parties. In other words, while price is almost always an essential term, colour will likely not be an essential term unless the negotiations of the parties suggest otherwise. Every case is different, of course, such that the essential terms on which the parties must agree cannot be defined with complete precision without knowing the exact circumstances of the negotiation. And, if there is disagreement between the parties on a term of the arrangement that is not considered an essential term, then the court will imply something reasonable, and enforce the parties' obligations on the strength of the implied term.

It ought to be noted that the two aspects of the mental element in the formation of a contract, being the intention to create legal relations and *consensus ad idem*, are often considered together, that is, as one formal requirement rather than two. In other words, if there is no manifest intention to create legal relations in the making of an offer, then it is obvious that there can be no agreement on essential terms. However, conceptually and for analytical purposes, it is sometimes helpful to think of the intention to create legal relations as prerequisite to a discussion of a meeting of the minds on essential terms. After all, both parties may demonstrate an intention to be bound, but to different terms as to price, delivery and so on. For our purposes, the important thing to remember is that, for the law to respond to a particular set of circumstances by classifying a relationship as a contractual relationship, the required mental element must be formally established, and that mental element includes both an intention on the part of all parties to be bound by the arrangement, and agreement (a "meeting of the minds") on essential terms.

Each of the four formal elements of a contract at law have been considered in innumerable cases over the years, such that there are extensive discussions in the literature about the peculiarities that occur in ordinary life and that may have an impact on the way in which each of these four elements are identified and understood. Some of these peculiarities have a direct effect on whether or not an apparent offer will qualify as such for the purposes of legal classification, whether an acceptance according to ordinary understanding will be a valid acceptance in the law, and so on. Remember that, if the law is to respond to a particular relationship by classifying it as a contractual relationship, then the required formalities must be present. These requirements are strictly defined and understood, such that, to qualify as an offer or an acceptance or consideration in the law of contract, the activity must meet the strict tests of an offer or an acceptance or consideration as they are defined at law.

It is not possible in this short book to investigate the wide range of particular rules that have emerged from thousands of judicial decisions in the law of contract. We will have to be content with a few examples of such rules, and leave detailed investigation to longer studies. Perhaps the most notorious example we might consider is the set of circumstances known as the "invitation to treat". Suppose you go to a grocery store and see a box of cereal displayed on the shelf with a price tag saying $3.99. You take the box of cereal to the cashier, and present him with the necessary funds to purchase the cereal. The cashier refuses to sell you the cereal. Now, superficially it appears as though the grocery store (through its representative, the cashier) has broken its contract to sell the cereal to you. It appeared to offer the cereal at $3.99, and you purported to accept that offer by tendering the necessary funds. There is an apparent intention to create legal relations, and agreement on essential terms. Now our ordinary understanding of these events suggests that a contract has been made and then broken by the cashier's refusal, but the law responds to this situation differently. The law construes the store's display of the cereal as an "invitation to treat", rather than an offer to sell. From a legal perspective, the display of the cereal is merely an expression of the store's intention to enter into negotiations with prospective purchasers, and an indication of a desire to sell if a suitable arrangement can be made. According to the law, the necessary formal offer is made, not when the box of cereal is displayed with a price tag attached, but rather when you tender an amount of money to the cashier, and there can be no contract until the cashier accepts the offer so made. In other words, the cashier has done nothing in breach of contract by rejecting your tender of money. There is no contract until the offer is accepted. This situation often arises in commercial contexts where one party will be looking for expressions of interest from a number of parties to perform specified work, and the court is forced to struggle to pinpoint the exact moment at which a contract is created.[2]

The law has developed additional peculiarities respecting offers, too. For example, it is clear that the person claiming to have accepted an offer must have been aware of the offer at the time of acceptance in order for a contract to result. This situation arises most often in the case of offers of reward money in exchange for information. Sometimes the information will be supplied by someone who is unaware of the offer of reward. Strictly speaking, there is no contract in this situation, and therefore no obligation to pay the reward money. As well, offers are sometimes limited in time, meaning that if an offer is not accepted within the time limited for acceptance, then no acceptance is possible and no contract can result. Even this apparently simple rule is sometimes complicated by circumstances. Suppose that the time within which an offer must be accepted has expired, but that a person interested in accepting the offer approaches the offeror, asking for a clarification of terms. If the offeror provides such a clarification, after which the person purports to accept the offer, then the court may conclude that the offeror impliedly demonstrated an intention to extend the time for acceptance through discussing terms after the original time of expiration. You should also note that an offer, once made, can be revoked by the offeror at any time prior to its acceptance. This is true, even where the offer states on its face that it will remain open for a stipulated period of time. The principal qualification to this rule is that the revocation of the offer must be communicated to the person to whom

---

[2] In Canada, the common law respecting retail sales has been adjusted in many important respects through the federal *Competition Act*, R.S.C. 1985, c. C-34, and at the provincial level through the various consumer protection statutes.

the offer was addressed, without which the revocation is not effective and the offer remains open for acceptance. The requirement of communication is introduced by the law to prevent fraudulent claims of revocation in an attempt to avoid the creation of legal relations after an acceptance has been made.

These are just a few examples of the complexity of the law of contract as it relates to offers. There are many, many cases on each of these examples, and of course many, many further oddities that the law of contract must be flexible enough to address. It must be remembered that every single situation that arises in ordinary negotiation between or among individuals is different, meaning that it is virtually impossible to state with complete certainty the range of possible circumstances that must be addressed by the law. To perform its functions of classification and prescription, then, the law must establish a set of formal rules that, while certain and predictable enough to allow ordinary persons to measure their activity relative to the law's predicted response, nevertheless maintains a sufficient level of flexibility to allow for the infinite variety of ordinary human social relations.

The same is true of acceptance, the second formal requirement in the law of contract. For an apparent acceptance to qualify as an acceptance so as to contribute to the establishment of legal relations, it must be an acceptance of the actual offer, with all of the essential terms agreed. If I offer to wash your car once weekly for the balance of the summer if you pay me $200, and you accept my offer, so long as the fee required is only $150, then there is no contract. The law will construe your acceptance as a counter-offer, and if I agree with its terms, then my response will be the acceptance.

You should note as well that an acceptance does not qualify as such until it is communicated to the person making the offer. This rule has caused great confusion in the common law of contract. What actually constitutes communication of the acceptance? Ordinarily, of course, our basic understanding of communication applies here, such that actual communication of the acceptance is required. But there are situations in which there is a lapse of time between attempted communication and actual communication, and sometimes during that period circumstances change. Suppose I send you a note in the mail, offering to wash your car once weekly over the balance of the summer if you pay me $200. You prepare a letter of acceptance, address it to me, and put it in the mail. Now the mail takes two days to reach me, and during that two day period I call you on the telephone and revoke my offer. Have the formalities of a contract been met, or not? The ordinary response would be that there is no contract, since the revocation of the offer was communicated prior to communication of the acceptance. But the law developed an odd rule known as the "postal rule", which says that the acceptance will be deemed to be communicated as soon as it is deposited in the mailbox. It will be at that point that contractual relations are crystallized. This rule appears fairly anachronistic today, given our advancing communications technologies, but the question remains about the moment of communication of an acceptance. Considering progressively more sophisticated and quicker modes of communication, does it occur when a telegram is sent, or a telex, or a fax? Does it occur when a voice mail message is left, when the offeree hits the "send" button in their e-mail programme, or when a text message is sent? Suppose an acceptance is sent to the offeror by e-mail, but the offeror checks her e-mail only once weekly. Is the acceptance valid so as to create legal relations, even though it has not actually been communicated to the person making the offer?

A further difficulty arises in a few unusual cases where the courts have decided that actual communication of the acceptance, or even attempted communication, is unnecessary to constitute a formal contract at law. In the English case *Carlill v. Carbolic Smoke Ball Co.*,[3] the defendant advertised widely that it would pay a sum of money to anyone who used their pharmaceutical product but caught influenza in any case. The plaintiff used the product, caught the disease, and sued for breach of contract when the defendant refused to pay. In finding in favour of the plaintiff, the Court stated that the offer was not one in which communication of the acceptance was either necessary or desirable, and that the plaintiff had signified acceptance by his actions. In relation to the vast number of cases in which the law of acceptance is scrutinized so carefully, this case (and those that have followed it[4]) appears to be anomalous.

It is not necessary for present purposes to resolve these various difficulties in the law of contract. It is enough for us to acknowledge that the law must be flexible enough to recognize the vagaries of ordinary human social interaction, addressing oddities such as those just described, and contemplating the virtually limitless number of situations that emerge in day-to-day life. The postal rule is just one of many special rules that have developed in the law of contract over the course of generations and generations of judicial decisions, and the law has been compelled to adapt to changing conditions as technologies develop and social situations evolve. The same holds true in the law of consideration, the third of our formal elements in the classification of contractual relationships. Ordinarily, consideration will take the form of money in exchange for goods or services, but that is not always the case, and the law must be flexible enough to recognize the sufficiency of all sorts of different exchanges as fulfilling the requirement of consideration.

---

[3] *Carlill v. Carbolic Smoke Ball Co.*, [1893] 1 Q.B. 256 (C.A.).

[4] See, for example, *Dunham v. St. Croix Soap Mfg. Co.* (1897), 34 N.B.R. 243 (C.A.).

Perhaps the most interesting aspect of the law of consideration involves the question of adequacy. It is in this area that the law's commitment to the image of the autonomous, self-interested individual, behaving rationally and deserving of respect, holds clearest sway. The general rule respecting the law of consideration is that the law will not inquire into the adequacy of the exchange. In other words, the law will not relieve against a bad bargain, objectively considered. Suppose that I have a diamond ring that, if purchased at retail, would command several thousand dollars. You offer to wash my car in exchange for the diamond ring, and I agree. Now objectively considered, the ring is worth far more than the effort you put forward in washing my car, such that the consideration flowing from you to me is radically insufficient to compensate me for the transfer of the ring to you. However, if I change my mind after negotiating this contract with you, and attempt to renege on my obligation to give you the ring in exchange for your effort because of this remarkable difference in consideration objectively considered, the law will not assist me in terminating the contract. I will continue to be bound by the contract I have negotiated, notwithstanding the fact that the relative value of the things given up is widely different.

This reluctance of the law to inquire into the relative value of consideration and to make adjustments in the parties' obligations based on objectively determined value is the necessary consequence of elevating the autonomous, self-interested individual negotiator to privileged status. The law assumes that each of us bargains in ways that are unique to our particular situations, such that the contracts we strike with each other are considered to be expressions of our autonomy and self-interest, and therefore deserving of the greatest respect. It would be disrespectful to substitute an objectively determined assessment of value for one arrived at by an autonomous, rational, self-interested individual, despite the fact that many observers would consider the consequence ridiculous. But, from the perspective of contract law, it is not for us to judge the wisdom of what superficially appears to be a bad bargain. As individuals taking part in a market economy, however, the price we pay for this deference to our autonomy and for commanding such respect for our decisions is that we will be held to our bargain, notwithstanding that, after the contract is negotiated, we have second thoughts about its advisability. Consequently, I can be pleased that I am free to negotiate a transfer of a diamond ring to you in exchange for your washing my car, and can be secure in knowing that the contract so negotiated will be held in the greatest esteem by the law. At the same time, however, I cannot seek the law's assistance when, having reflected upon the terms of my contract, I change my mind. Later in this chapter we will consider some of the significant situations in which the assumptions about the equal rationality and self-interest of the contracting parties are not maintained, that is, where the underlying framework of private law appears to be disturbed by a thorough review of the interpersonal relationship at stake and an inquiry into the very nature of the participants. These situations generate excuses for non-performance of obligations that, otherwise and perhaps superficially, appear to meet the contractual formalities we have just summarized.

There are grounds for the intervention of law in apparent contractual relations that relate to wider community implications as well. One of the significant exceptions to the rules respecting consideration involves the interposition of public policy in questions relating to validity. Ordinarily, as we have discussed, the world of private law is a world where the autonomous, rational individual has fairly complete scope for the pursuit of his or her self-interest, and, in many situations at least, the law is loathe to interfere in those pursuits on behalf of something such as public policy. This is the domain of privacy, the space in our lives where we can enjoy our own decisions relatively free of outside interference. The insistence of the law that we be held to our contracts, despite their sometimes ridiculous results, is an expression of this respect for the private realm. However, there is a limit to our autonomy in this respect, a point beyond which the interest of the community at large will be held to overcome the obeisance paid to autonomously negotiated bargains. In the law of consideration, there are certain sorts of exchanges that are held to be against public policy, and therefore not capable of functioning as the necessary formal elements in the establishment of contractual relations. For example, a promise to do an illegal act is not valid consideration in the law of contract. If I promise to wash your car in exchange for your promise to steal a diamond ring for me, then the law will not assist me in seeing to the completion of your obligation. The consideration you have offered is illegal, and public policy will not allow the enforcement of an obligation that is itself against the law. This is so, even though the overarching concern with the enforcement of autonomously negotiated bargains would seem to direct otherwise.

Earlier in this chapter, when the formal requirement of consideration was introduced, it was remarked that both parties to the arrangement must agree to "give something up" in order for a contract to result. While this is true, it is important to point out that it is not necessary for each party to receive the direct benefit of the other's consideration. In other words, it is perfectly legitimate for one party to the negotiation to agree to confer a benefit on someone who is not a party to the contract. The person receiving the benefit in such a circumstance is known as a "third party beneficiary". Suppose you and I negotiate a contract whereby I agree to wash your car once weekly throughout July and August next summer, in exchange for which you agree to mow my mother's lawn whenever the need arises during the same period. It is clear that both you and I have agreed to give something up here, my time and energy in washing your car, your time and energy in mowing my mother's lawn. Therefore, the formal requirement of consideration is met, and the contract can be enforced by me, even though I have received no direct benefit through this contract. The interesting aspect of this situation is that the third party beneficiary, my mother, cannot sue to enforce the contract in the event that I wash your car as agreed and you fail to mow her lawn. As a third party beneficiary, my mother is not directly a party to the contract, is not a participant in the "private government" you and I have negotiated to govern certain aspects of our relationship, and therefore she has no remedy in the event obligations are breached. The law says that she is not "privy" to the contract, and as a result cannot sue.

Despite the various quirks that emerge from even a quick review of the formalities of contract law, the image remains of the self-interested individual taking part in the marketplace, freely negotiating their contracts, establishing sets of rules designed for particular situations in their lives, agreeing to be bound by those rules for specific purposes, and then coming to the law for assistance when the expectations established through these contracts are not met. It is fair to say that this image depends for its appeal on an assumption that individuals come to a negotiation on relatively equal terms, and from the perspective of the law at least, this assumption is valid. The law considers each of us to be equally free, autonomous and rational, and equally deserving of the respect that human individuality ought to command both in philosophical terms and in ordinary life. This assumption of equality in formal terms, however, ignores a great deal about the substantive inequality that we experience every day of our lives, inequalities based on imbalances in economic power, for example, or on advantages open to members of one ethnic group as opposed to another, or perhaps even on simple variations in levels of intelligence. Is it reasonable to assume that everyone equally enjoys the autonomy and can pursue the self-interest on which much of the modern law of contract is based, while at the same time being driven by radical imbalances in economic strength? Are particular situations of real life need nullified by the assumption of an equality of bargaining power in the law of contract? Is it not evident that much of what appear to be formally acceptable contracts are actually the product of the exploitation of one party's weaknesses by a stronger party? Is this an acceptable consequence of a body of law that purports to hold individual dignity and respect as its first principles?

III. EXCUSES FOR NON-PERFORMANCE

The law of contract becomes more complicated as we attempt to resolve some of the anomalies that appear between autonomously negotiated, formally recognized and legally enforceable obligations on the one hand, and the dignity and respect that ostensibly lie at the base of the formal law of contract on the other. Not every case presents an anomaly, of course, but it remains true that many discussions between individuals in ordinary, day-to-day existence apparently yield all of the formalities necessary for the recognition of the resulting relationship in legal terms, yet for one reason or another offend against the ideal of individuality that the law of contract, in many ways at least, is intended (we think) to capture. To accommodate these situations, the law has developed a series of justifications for interference in what appear to be valid contractual relationships. That is, if the circumstances are appropriate, the law will make adjustments in the way it responds to negotiated relationships so as to relieve one party or the other from the legal consequences.

The most obvious situation in which the law will relieve against performance involves the negotiation of a contract by someone who does not possess the necessary legal capacity to contract. As we saw in Chapter 2, one of the incidents of full legal personhood is the capacity to contract, such that, unless the person apparently bound by a contractual commitment is a legal person in the complete sense of the term, the law will not assist in the enforcement of the contract. A contract with a child is unenforceable on these grounds, for example, and this is the result, even where the other party to the contract has completely performed her side of the bargain. Although there are some exceptions, each party to a negotiation, therefore, is vested with the responsibility to ensure that the person with whom they are negotiating has the legal capacity to enter into the contract, and therefore the legal capacity to be bound to performance.

Beyond this fairly obvious consequence of the doctrine of legal personality, the grounds on which the law will relieve against performance are somewhat murky. For our purposes, there are four categories of such grounds, and in the balance of this section of this chapter we will consider some of the situations that give rise to these categories. We shall refer to the categories as "mistake", "misrepresentation", "unconscionability", and "inequality of bargaining power". It must be remembered that we are trying to isolate the circumstances in which the law ignores the apparent formalities of a voluntarily negotiated relationship, and by which the law overcomes the assumption of equality that lies at the basis of much of the law of contract in the first place. Superficially at least, this is a significant realignment in the theoretical framework of contract law. But in fact, the grounds on which the law will intervene to prevent the strict enforcement of apparent obligations in contract are often construed so as to negate one of the formalities that function as conditions precedent to the very creation of contractual obligations. In other words, the situations we are about to consider function so as to allow the law to conclude that, for want of a valid offer, acceptance or consideration, or perhaps for failure of the requisite mental element, there is no contract at all. In a sense, then, we are preserving, even enhancing, the model of human individuality on which to a large extent the law of contract is founded by saying that the formalities of contract cannot result unless the assumption of equality between the parties is undisturbed. The grounds on which the law will relieve against performance are raised by one of the parties to the relationship to demonstrate that one or the other of the formal contractual requirements has not been met. In effect, the party argues that the apparent relationship was not the result of the party's autonomous, self-interested choice after all. The summaries of excuses for non-performance that follow, therefore, ought to be read as illustrations of circumstances in which the fundamental assumptions at work in the law of contract are sufficiently upset to render the appearance of contractual formalities at least doubtful. This is then enough to make the enforcement of the interpersonal obligation impossible in legal terms.

There are a number of different sorts of mistake that will relieve a party from performance of an apparent contractual obligation. Generally speaking, if the offeree knows that the offer contains a mistake, the court will not allow the offeree to accept the offer and then insist on strict performance by the offeror. Suppose I offer to sell you my two carat diamond ring for $5000. Now you know that my diamond ring is actually three carats, but you accept the offer anyway. Upon discovery of my mistake, I try to renegotiate the terms of our contract, but you refuse and sue me for completion of the transaction. In this situation, it is likely that the court would not hold me to my offer, since the mistake as to an essential term of the contract was enough to negate my intention to contract, one of the necessary formalities we have considered already. This is the situation, so long as the mistake can be considered to go to the essential character of the contract, and of course that is a question of fact to be considered separately in each and every case.

The cases in which mistake is considered as a ground for relief from performance can be divided into two general groups, bilateral mistake and unilateral mistake. A bilateral mistake can arise where both parties are in error, although on different aspects of the contract. Suppose I agree to sell you a ring. The ring is two carats, and I believe you want a two carat ring. At the same time, however, you believe that the ring is three carats, and it is a three carat ring that you want. This situation of bilateral mistake, known as "mutual mistake", will likely not be enforced by the courts. It is clear from the separate mistakes made by the parties that one of the required formalities, *consensus ad idem* on essential terms, is missing. Bilateral mistake can also arise where both parties make the same mistake. Suppose you express a desire to buy a three carat ring from me. I believe that the ring I am selling is a three carat ring, and you share that belief. Ultimately, we discover that the ring is only two carats. This situation of bilateral mistake is known as "common mistake", and will likely not be enforced by the courts. While there is agreement on essential terms, there was a shared mistake on the identification of the subject matter of the contract, enough to render the contract a nullity.

It must be remembered that the courts will often look to objective criteria in the attempt to determine *consensus ad idem* and the intention of the parties to the negotiations. From our perspective, the key is that a contract is considered to be the expression of the parties' individual wills, such that mistakes as to the essential character of the relationship are often enough to deny that the negotiated terms and the autonomous choices made by the parties are coincident. The same is true in the case of unilateral mistakes, although, because of the opportunity for fraud, the court must be much more cautious in deciding whether to allow the mistaken party to escape their contractual obligations. Generally speaking, when one party has made a mistake about an essential term of a contract, the court will tend to relieve that party from performing their obligations when the other party to the negotiation knew of the mistake before the terms of the contract were finalized. If the non-mistaken party was not aware of the error, then it is unlikely that a court will relieve the mistaken party against performance. In effect, the law is placing the responsibility on the parties to the negotiations to make certain that the key terms of the contract are as they suppose, underscoring the assumption that parties act out of self-interest and ought to be held to their bargains as a result. This is so, unless the non-mistaken party knowingly takes advantage of the mistaken party's error.

A court will always have great difficulty in allowing a dishonest party to enforce a contractual obligation against an innocent party, and such is the situation in the case of misrepresentation, the second of our grounds on which a court will relieve a party from performing an apparent contractual commitment. Actually, the situation in the event of a fraudulent misrepresentation is quite clear. Where one party to a negotiation misrepresents some fact that is material to the making of a contract, with knowledge that the represented fact is untrue and with the intent to deceive the innocent party to the negotiations, then a fraudulent misrepresentation has taken place and the court will not enforce the innocent party's obligations. This is true, so long as the innocent party actually relied on the misrepresentation when deciding whether to enter into the contract or not. This situation functions to negative the innocent party's consent to the terms of the contract, and so denies the assumption of equality that generally supports much of contract law doctrine.

However, there are misrepresentations that are not fraudulent, and this is where the law becomes more complicated. Ordinarily, at common law only fraud entitles an innocent party to deny that they have given the required consent to contractual terms. An innocent misrepresentation, that is, one made in the situation where the party making the representation was not aware of its untruth, is generally not enough to allow the innocent party to escape contractual obligation, although there are limited exceptions in the cases. Sometimes, too, innocent misrepresentations are made negligently, and this circumstance can lead to more complex discussions. Suppose that I represent to you that the ring I am selling is a three carat ring. Now I believe this representation to be true, such that I am not committing a fraudulent misrepresentation. However, had I used my ordinary manner of checking the quality of the diamond before offering it for sale, I would have discovered that it was a two carat stone. As a result of my negligence in failing to verify the quality of the ring, I have misrepresented the character of the ring to you. You act on my representation, and buy the ring, paying much more than you ought to, given the nature of the diamond. In the law of contract, this situation is simply unclear. The common law is still developing in this respect, and it opens up one of the more obvious areas of overlap between the law of contract and the law of duty relationships, to be introduced in Chapter 4.

Our third category of situations in which a court may relieve a party from performing their apparent contractual obligations is "unconscionability", actually a group of related grounds which we shall call "duress", "undue influence" and "unconscionability". Remember that we are investigating the circumstances in which a court will feel justified in interfering in what appears to be an autonomously negotiated bargain struck by two self-interested individuals. To take this step, the court must feel fairly comfortable in concluding that what appears to be so is really something else, that the autonomy and self-interest apparently expressed by the parties to the contract is not what it appears to be. This conclusion allows the court to protect the image of the independent negotiator to which we have referred before by denying that a valid contract was ever concluded. It is in this category of related grounds, grouped together under the term "unconscionability", that the court's task in this respect may be easiest, for the very definitions of the terms at work here speak directly to the state of mind of the innocent party to the arrangement, denying that party's independence and freedom of thought.

There are two sorts of duress to which we might refer, being duress to the person and something we can call "economic duress". A contract entered into as a result of actual or threatened physical violence or unlawful imprisonment of the innocent party or a member of the innocent party's family can be avoided on the grounds of physical duress. Note that there must be actual threats of physical action for this defence to succeed, although the threat may be made against someone other than the innocent party. The idea of duress as a defence to the strict enforcement of contractual obligations has been extended in recent years to include threats to economic well-being, perhaps a threat to destroy one's property or to jeopardize one's employment. It should be obvious that courts will be reluctant to uphold a contractual obligation entered into by someone whose independent will was manipulated through threats to their well-being, whether those threats are physical or economic. The underlying intent to create legal relations is impossible to establish if one party to the arrangement is unable to form the required intent due to duress. From the law's perspective, coerced consent is not consent at all.

Undue influence as a ground for avoiding contractual obligations is akin to duress, but it involves something we might call "moral coercion", that is, non-physical pressure against the mind and ultimately the consent of the party influenced. The use by one contracting party of any form of oppression, coercion, compulsion or abuse of authority or power for the purpose of obtaining the consent of the other party may result in a successful defence of undue influence. In such situations, the courts assume a paternalistic responsibility to protect individuals against victimization by others. Often, undue influence will be fairly obvious. Suppose you are heavily involved in a charitable organization that needs my continued contribution of funds in order to sustain operations. I use the threat of a withdrawal of my support from the charity to exact favourable contractual terms from you on an unrelated transaction. It is fairly certain here that a court would consider your consent to the contract to have been unduly influenced by the threat of withdrawal of support from the charity, and so would likely refuse to enforce your obligation.

Sometimes, however, undue influence is presumed by the court to arise from the mere fact of the relationship between the two parties to the contract. In situations where one party to the arrangement is in a position where that party is in possession of confidential information about the other party, then the court will presume that any contracts entered into by the parties will have been struck on the strength of an undue exploitation of power. This arises in solicitor/client, doctor/patient, parent/child and other like relationships where there is an imbalance of power in negotiation based on possession of confidential information. In these cases, it will be the responsibility of the stronger party to demonstrate to the court that the weaker party entered into the contract free from the undue influence that is presumed to lie at the heart of the contract.

In considering the further sub-category that we can refer to generally as "unconscionability", the central point to remember is that there are some bargains that are so manifestly unfair and one-sided that a court cannot help but relieve against strict enforcement. Given our earlier discussion of the law of consideration, in which we concluded that a court is reluctant to disturb a contract on the ground that there is a radical imbalance in the consideration flowing between the parties, it is difficult, at first glance at least, to conceive of situations where a court would nevertheless feel justified in excusing performance of a contract on the ground of manifest unfairness. Remember that the sanctity of the formalities of contract introduces some stability and predictability in the marketplace, allowing parties to know that, once the formalities are established, their obligations are fairly certain and secure. Besides, strict adherence to the formalities of contract gives support to the idea of the autonomous individual, striking bargains in the marketplace in pursuit of their self-interest.

On the other hand, it is arguable that, at some level at least, we have a general obligation to protect the more vulnerable members of society. This obligation emerges from our moral orientation, if not directly from our law. Such moral proclivities find their way into judicial decision-making in the same way that they find their way into ordinary decision-making, and as a consequence, the formalities of the law are sometimes justifiably overcome by reference to the more basic demands of justice. In terms of our general critical perspective on the assumptions that we think lie at the foundation of private law rules, we can see here the recognition that, at some level and when circumstances are right, there is something at stake in the law of contract that is greater than the autonomy and self-interest of the immediate parties to the arrangement. That something is a widely shared community understanding of the nature of justice itself, that is, justice as a moral claim perhaps transcendent of mere private law rules. Unconscionability, as a ground for the avoidance of contractual obligation, is conveniently considered as an expression of this ordinary commitment to justice as a moral imperative, rather than as yet another exception to the strict enforcement of legal rules. It arises in situations where one party takes advantage of another simply by exploiting that other party's obviously weakened position, giving the entire arrangement an odious character. Despite the appearance of contractual formalities, the law tends to respond to this situation by recognizing the violation of our recognized commitment to justice in ordinary moral terms.

In order for the test of unconscionability to be met, the evidence must suggest a fairly pronounced or dramatic inequality of bargaining power between the parties, and an improvident transaction. Suppose that you must take your child to the hospital immediately because of an asthma attack. Ordinarily a taxi ride of similar length will cost $10. However, the taxi driver, knowing the urgency of the situation, stipulates that this particular ride will cost $1000. Having no alternative, you agree. In this situation, there is no physical or economic duress exerted by the taxi driver, and no moral coercion so as to justify a plea of undue influence. But it is unlikely that a court would hold you to this bargain. It offends our moral sensibilities, our over-arching commitment to justice, such that the appearance of all the necessary contractual formalities is rendered of secondary significance. The taxi driver took advantage of your radically weakened position in the marketplace, and exacted an improvident transaction as a result.

The final main ground on which courts occasionally interfere with what appear to be formally constituted contracts is known as "inequality of bargaining power". This ground emerged from the English case, *Lloyd's Bank Ltd. v. Bundy*, decided by the Court of Appeal in 1974.[5] It is unclear from Lord Denning's judgment in this case whether inequality of bargaining power is a separate ground on which weak parties might escape contractual commitments, or whether it is simply a particular type of unconscionability. Mr. Bundy was a farmer who mortgaged his family farm to Lloyd's Bank to secure a guarantee of his son's debts. The Bank called the guarantee, and attempted to realize on the farm. Despite the fact that, in the ordinary law of contract, the law will not interfere in a bargain no matter how ill-advised it might have been, Lord Denning found the grounds in this case to relieve Mr. Bundy of the obligation to give up his farm. He said that relief in this case was a matter of "common fairness", relying on the idea of general moral demands in place of a strict construction of legal rules. After a review of the principles at work in duress, undue influence, unconscionability and other like excuses for non-performance, Lord Denning said the following in the most often quoted section of his judgment:

> ... I would suggest that through all these instances there runs a single thread. They rest on "inequality of bargaining power". By virtue of it, the English law gives relief to one who, without independent advice, enters into a contract upon terms which are very unfair or transfers property for a consideration which is grossly inadequate, when his bargaining power is grievously impaired by reason of his own needs or desires, or by his own ignorance or infirmity, coupled with undue influences or pressures brought to bear on him by or for the benefit of the other.[6]

Now it remains unclear whether by these words Lord Denning was intending to create an additional category of defence to the strict

---

5 *Lloyd's Bank Ltd. v. Bundy*, [1974] 3 All E.R. 757 (C.A.).

6 *Ibid.*, at 765.

enforcement of contractual obligations, or whether he was simply making the attempt to reserve some flexibility to judges who are confronted with situations of gross unfairness that do not comfortably fit into one of the more well-established categories. It may be that the idea of "inequality of bargaining power" is simply an extension of the idea of "unconscionability", for example. In any event, however, we ought to be cognizant of the possibility that the categories of situations in which the court will relieve against performance of contractual obligations are likely not completely contemplated through mistake, misrepresentation, duress, undue influence and unconscionability.

The consistent theme in the categories we have considered in this section of this chapter is that the law will strive to find some ground on which to relieve a weak and defenceless party against a manifestly unfair bargain. This is especially the case in relationships of dependency, situations that arise simply by virtue of the pre-existing relationship between the parties, or by virtue of particularly stressful circumstances that allow the exploitation of one party by another. Courts are loathe to allow one person to take advantage of another when a relationship of dependency exists. Judges will almost always feel free to intervene for the purpose of protecting against the exploitation of the weak by the strong, and this is accomplished either through the application of legal rules, or through drawing on the ordinary moral demands of justice and equity. In this way, the law preserves the model of individual dignity, autonomy and respect that underlies much of contract law doctrine, not through a slavish commitment to the formal rules of contract, but rather through a sensitive protection of individual dignity when the circumstances demand it.

IV. CONTRACTS AND FAMILY LIFE

Relationships of dependency are perhaps most obvious inside family life, and it may be for that reason that family law and contract law have had a fairly uneasy relationship over the course of the last two hundred years. Adults in intimate relationships are particularly vulnerable to exploitation by each other, and children are always at great risk of manipulation by their parents and guardians. Family law has developed a sophisticated network of principles and instruments to justify intervention by the state in intimate relationships where the situation demands it, and so over the course of the nineteenth and twentieth centuries we saw the emergence of legislative regimes for divorce, matrimonial property, maintenance and alimony, and child protection. The common law of contract, meanwhile, remained relatively uninvolved, only rarely developing exceptional rules (including the presumption of undue influence, referred to above) that had particular application inside the family.

In fact, it is arguable that the very intimacy that accompanies family life is inconsistent with the model of individual autonomy and self-interest that underlies much of the modern law of contract. If privacy as an ideal survives at all in the modern manifestation of private law rules, then one would expect that it would survive most thoroughly inside the family, for many of us our most intimate space. This is especially the case when we consider traditional views of the conventional family, in which the man and woman were considered to join together as one person, united spiritually in a common endeavour. In this view of spousal relations, it would be nonsense to think of a wife and husband negotiating a contract on how household duties might be divided, for example, or bartering as separate, individual wills when deciding how best to spend the household income. Such was the case in *Balfour v. Balfour*,[7] a famous example of the reluctance of the common law of contract to become involved in matters of marital disagreement. In this case, the English Court of Appeal considered a negotiation between husband and wife as they prepared for a *de facto* separation. Upon his return to Ceylon, the husband agreed to pay his wife in England £30 monthly, in exchange for which she agreed not to pledge his credit for her various purchases. Ultimately, the wife sued the husband for enforcement of the contract.

The court decided that there was no enforceable contract in this situation, despite Lord Atkin's finding that the formalities of a typical contract, including offer, acceptance and consideration, were present. Lord Duke said that, as between married couples, all sorts of obligations arise because of the very relationship of husband and wife, and these should be fulfilled because of that relationship first, not because of any apparent contractual obligation. Besides, he argued, if every exchange of promises inside a marriage led to possible suits for breach of contract, then we would be promoting quarrelling and dissension inside marriage, and as a matter of public policy that is to be avoided. And in a famous statement on the flexibility of judges when faced with common law difficulties emerging from the conventional family, Lord Atkin said that "each house is a domain into which the King's writ does not seek to run, and to which his officers do not seek to be admitted."[8]

Despite the fairly obvious relationship of dependency that subsisted inside the Balfours' marriage, the judges were reluctant to impose a legal regime designed, for the most part at least, for the commercial marketplace. It is easy to see the commitment to a public policy position that only

---

7 *Balfour v. Balfour*, [1919] 2 K.B. 571 (Eng. C.A.).

8 *Ibid.*, at 579.

rarely will interfere in the intimate relations that prevail inside the family, especially where such interference could be construed to be disruptive to harmonious family relations. But the idea of dependency, discussed above in the context of the grounds on which the law will interfere in apparent contractual relations, is actually misleading when we consider *Balfour v. Balfour*. Dependency gives us a framework for understanding ways in which a court might relieve a party from performing contractual obligations, and really has little to do with the idea of imposing contractual obligations where none exist. To some extent, this was what the court was asked and refused to do in this case.

As the twentieth century progressed, the reluctance of courts to enforce ordinary contractual relations inside marriage was remedied to some extent through legislation. In each of the provinces of Canada, we now have legislative sanction for a number of different domestic contracts, including contracts negotiated in contemplation of marriage, contracts negotiated during the currency of a marriage, co-habitation agreements between adults who are not spouses, separation agreements, and a number of others. So long as the parties negotiate a contract that meets the formalities set forth in the legislation, and so long as there is no evidence of duress, undue influence or other excuse for non-performance, it is likely that a court will enforce a domestic contract. Such contracts often contemplate the way in which property will be shared, the ownership of assets acquired before the marriage, and like matters.

Therefore, we can see that there has been a shift in public policy toward a more active role for law inside family life. This shift has taken place, to a large extent, in an attempt to prevent the abuses that, it is fair to say, have always existed to some degree inside intimate relationships. While the common law of contract has been slow to respond, the legislatures have taken up the task of expressing a shift in public expectations in this respect, intervening so as to allow adults in intimate relationships to contract in ways that can lead to a more equitable sharing of assets and to more economic security for weaker partners. In some ways, these legislative developments highlight a shrinking private sphere, a greater public intervention in the space in which private decision-making was thought to reign independent of community supervision. In other ways, however, a legislative framework for domestic contracts has done what the common law could not or would not do. It has widened the territory in which the idea of contract has influence, adjusting the concept of intimacy through the introduction of negotiation by autonomous, self-interested individuals.

While it is fairly easy to see an expanded role for the idea of contract in public policy changes relative to intimate adult relationships, such is not the case when we consider the law respecting children. Since the second half of the nineteenth century, the state has assumed a fairly rigorous supervisory responsibility for the welfare of children, with mixed success of course. Courts have clung to the notion of "the best interests of the child" as the dominant guiding principle in cases where children are involved, and this paternalism became more entrenched as the twentieth century progressed. This is not surprising, of course, because the law's urge to protect the vulnerable and dependent lies at the heart of many principles, as we have seen. This has meant that, in relation to the law of contract, the formalities demonstrating the establishment of legal relations can be overcome by appeal to the higher standards of protection for children that, in almost every situation, override mere common law rules.

Such was the situation in the famous American case, *In re Baby M.*[9] A man contracted with a woman to have her act as a surrogate mother. She was impregnated with his sperm, and carried the baby to term. The arrangement was that the mother would release the baby to the father in exchange for a fee of $10,000, and that the mother would relinquish all parental rights to the child, thereby lifting any impediment to the adoption of the baby by the father's wife. When the baby was born, the mother refused to honour her contract, and fled with the baby. The father sued to enforce the arrangement. Now it is clear that all of the formalities of a contract, including offer, acceptance and consideration, and specifically including the intention to create legal relations and *consensus ad idem*, were present in this case. In fact, the court pointed out without equivocation that the mother knew exactly what she had bargained for, that she had done similar things before, and that she was under no duress or undue influence. In other words, the conventional grounds on which a party might argue to be released from contractual obligation were not available to the mother.

Yet the court refused to enforce the surrogacy contract at the suit of the father. There were many reasons for this result, discussed at length by the judges on appeal. For present purposes, however, we need consider only that the formalities of the contract, which superficially were enough to support the father's claim, were not enough to compel the termination of the relationship between a mother and her child. The underlying principle at work here is that there are some aspects of our lives that are not open to negotiation, that cannot be bargained away, even by two autonomous, self-interested individuals approaching each other independently in the marketplace. The law of contract is particularly well-suited, we might argue, to economic transactions, but the relationship between parent and child cannot be commodified in the way contemplated by that law. The best interests of the child are not served by the abandonment of parental rights for a fee, and so the mother's relationship

---

9 *In re Baby M*, 537 A.2d 1227 (N.J. Sup. Ct. 1988).

with the child was preserved by the court despite contractual formalities. In an interesting twist, however, the court decided that it was also in the best interests of the child that custody be granted to the father. Although the privilege of adoption was not vested in the father's wife, the result was that the father succeeded in having and keeping the child that he and his wife wanted, without resort to the formal law of contract at all.

In the world of private law, the image of the autonomous, self-interested individual is perhaps captured best in exchange relationships, and this image functions to generate much of the common law doctrine that has emerged in modern jurisprudence. The formalities of contract, the characteristics that are recognized by the law as essential to the establishment of legal exchange relationships, are founded on the assumption of two equal participants in the marketplace, each one negotiating in their self-interest, and each one possessed of a formal equality only occasionally investigated in the course of legal decision-making. As we have seen, however, this image is not as deeply entrenched as we might first predict. While it is true that particular decisions might be criticized for being too formalistic, it is also true that the law of contract often comes to the aid of the defenceless, despite the presence of the formalities. Especially in cases of demonstrable weakness or dependency, the law retains the flexibility to look beyond the formalities, to inquire into the substantive positions of the parties involved in the ultimate attempt to ensure that justice, perhaps in the way that justice is ordinarily understood, is served through the law of contract. This is the situation we discover when we consider conventional excuses for the non-performance of contractual obligations, and it is also the situation when we consider the refusal of courts to rely strictly on contractual formalities in the face of compelling public policy alternatives.

Chapter 4

Tort Law and the Concept of Duty

I. INTRODUCTION

As we move across the private law side of our legal classification system, away from exchange relationships and toward other categories, we encounter a somewhat bewildering array of relationships that the law groups together under the heading "duty". This is the vast area of classification that generates the law of tort, a difficult, complex mixture of rules, sub-rules, exceptions and sub-exceptions that serves to adjudicate relationships *imposed* on the participants by the very classification process itself. It will be remembered that one of the major distinctions between exchange relationships and duty relationships is the role of the participants in *choosing* to take part in the former, while in the latter the relationship is *imposed* by the law irrespective of the participants' willingness. That distinction is key to understanding both the role that legal classification plays in ordinary social life, and the more specific legal framework that underlies the law of tort.

It must not be assumed, however, that the reduced role for the idea of autonomous choice in the classification of duty relationships results in a lessened significance generally for the model of individualism that formed much of the foundation for our inquiries into the rudiments of contract law. Rather, we shall encounter that model yet again, this time serving to generate a set of basic assumptions about the way that individuals ought to relate to each other as they go about their day-to-day lives. It is on the strength of these assumptions that the law identifies the characteristics of the various legal wrongs known as "torts", that is, civil wrongs separate from breaches of contract and fiduciary obligation. Central to a discussion of the fundamentals of tort law is the idea of duty, that is, the overarching obligation we owe to each other to refrain from acting in such a way that injury is caused to someone's person or property. The types of activity prohibited through recognizing the significance of duty in this manner are in fact limitless, and therefore impossible to list comprehensively. As a result of considering duty in this sweeping way, we recognize in the law the attempt to preserve individual separateness by creating wrongs where that separateness is violated in defined ways. Arguably at least, the idea of individual dignity is thus preserved by a shield of protection erected in tort law.

But the law of tort goes still further in maintaining the significance of the individual. In the same way that the law insists that, short of extenuating circumstances, an autonomously struck bargain must be kept, the law maintains that individuals accept responsibility for the reasonably predictable consequences of their actions. The question of what constitutes a predictable consequence is one of the most difficult in all of tort law, phrased in judicial decisions and commentaries as the question of "reasonable foreseeability". If we assume that a hypothetical ordinary reasonable person, standing in the place of an actual person performing an action, had directed their mind to the consequences of that action before carrying it out, then to what extent were the consequences that actually ensued reasonably foreseeable to that hypothetical person? This is a difficult test to consider, as might be expected. Generally speaking (there are exceptions, as always), if the law concludes that the consequences were reasonably foreseeable according to the test, then the actual person taking the action will be held responsible for those consequences. They will be considered to be "at fault". It is reasonably foreseeable that, if a bus driver does not operate her bus in accordance with ordinary standards of good driving, then accidents will occur. If injuries result from those accidents, then the bus driver is at fault, and must accept responsibility for the consequences. The idea of fault is central to our discussion of duty relationships and tort law. It is the mechanism by which the individual actor is held accountable for interfering in the enjoyment of separateness by others.

As may be imagined, the cases in which the extent of the duties we owe to others have been examined and delineated are virtually unlimited in number and variety, and therefore impossible to summarize at all completely except in a lengthy treatise. But there are some things about the law of duty that we can state fairly succinctly and confidently. The law of duty generates a particular family of legal wrongs known as torts, and torts can be defined as civil wrongs, being neither breaches of contract nor breaches of fiduciary duty. Therefore, it is convenient to consider torts as a residual category of legal wrongs, that is, as wrongs not recognized in the other major categories. By using the term "civil wrongs", we are isolating torts from criminal activity. A tort is not a crime, although oftentimes the same activity is capable of classification as both a crime and a tort. But a crime, as will be remembered, is considered in our legal classification system to be a breach of a relationship between the state (acting in its political or sovereign capacity) and a person performing an illegal act, whereas the law of duty arises on the private law side of our system, and involves a relationship between individuals.

Then, so as to separate a tort from other types of wrongs on the private law side of our system, we distinguish it from breaches of contract and fiduciary duty. Again, however, it is often the case that a particular activity will generate one or several of these legal wrongs, manifesting the characteristics necessary for the purposes of legal taxonomy to be classified in several different categories at once.

In the balance of this chapter, we will investigate some of the major sub-categories in the law of tort, describing briefly the characteristics of an array of activities that, over the course of extended litigation, has been adjudged to be tortious. Because of the complexity of this area of the law, it will be necessary to return to the diagrams introduced in Chapter 1, and to develop the major category of duty relationships by reference to sub-categories based on the particular wrongs (torts) that result. As pointed out in Chapter 1, it must be remembered that this process of classification and sub-classification is only one way to consider the nature of law and the relationship law bears to ordinary social life. There are other ways to reflect on the functions of law, and other ways to configure the classification system itself. But for our purposes the classification system (as we develop it) is a convenient starting point for further inquiry.

Following our exploration of some of the sub-categories in the group of duty relationships, we will examine briefly the way in which the law establishes liability for failing to act in accordance with the appropriate standard. It is in this discussion that the law becomes fairly subtle, as we try to reconcile actual behaviour with the presumed behaviour of a reasonable person, and as we attempt to stand in the place of actual persons following actual events and, retrospectively, predict what might have been foreseen. Before becoming involved in that discussion, however, it is necessary to explore (in at least an introductory way) the range of possibilities at work in the law of tort.

II. THE TORTS CLASSIFICATION SYSTEM

As indicated in Chapter 1, the law of tort emerges from duty relationships, one of the major categories on the private law side of our diagram. Sub-categories in tort law are conveniently constructed by reference to a blend of, first, the nature of the wrong committed, and secondly, the nature of the interest violated by that wrong. So it is on this basis that we shall proceed to develop the classification system in tort. Initially, we configured our general classification system in the following way:

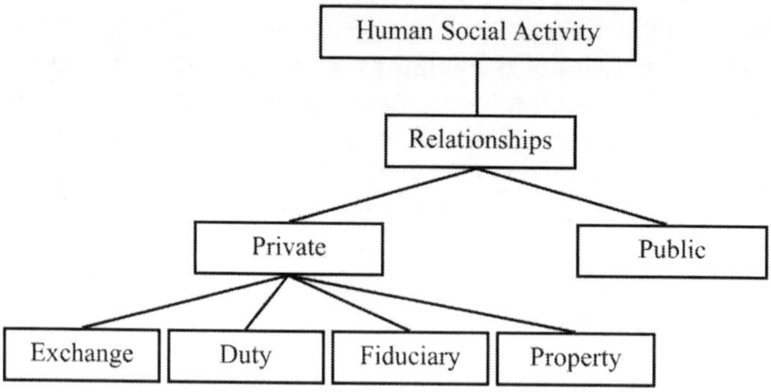

Now the first thing for us to recognize in the development of the "duty relationships" classification is that there can be no tort, no legal wrong in this classification, unless a duty is found to exist according to law. For our purposes, the general way to describe the circumstances in which a duty is deemed to exist is as follows: Individuals have a duty at law to refrain from acting in such a way that causes injury to some other individual's person or property. Injuries can be caused simply by virtue of the actual physical proximity of one individual with another (as in the situation where one person hits another with his or her fist), or by virtue of some causal connection between the activity and the injury, perhaps irrespective of physical proximity. The latter might occur where one individual dumps a dangerous chemical in a river, and the chemical is ultimately deposited on and does damage to another individual's property many kilometres downstream.

After finding that a duty exists in the manner contemplated by tort law, then we must proceed to consider the various types of interest liable to be injured by a breach of duty, and the extent to which those interests are protected by the law. If one individual hits another with his or her fist, then the bodily integrity of the individual receiving the blow has been injured. If one individual pollutes a river, then the interest held by downstream property owners in a safe and clean riverside is liable to be adversely affected. The nature of the wrong that is constructed in tort law by virtue of a breach of duty is based on an assessment of the violation of interests, such that the violation of bodily integrity gives rise to the tort of battery, while the breach of duty that results in downstream contamination may be the tort of negligence. To understand the range of possibilities, it is therefore crucial that we explore the various interests intended to be protected in the law of tort, out of which emerge the more specific sub-classifications of particular torts. In fact, for the purposes of this discussion it is helpful to think of the human individual as an amalgam of interests, that is, interests in bodily integrity and physical freedom from restraint, in their reputation, in their property and in certain of their relationships with others. It is the adverse effect on one or more of these and other interests that is an essential aspect of the legal wrong known as a tort.

But as a first step, we might develop the large category of duty relationships by reference to the intention of the individual alleged to have breached the general duty not to act so as to injure others or their property. The law considers intentional breaches of duty in one way, and unintentional breaches of duty in another. This serves as our first subdivision of the category.

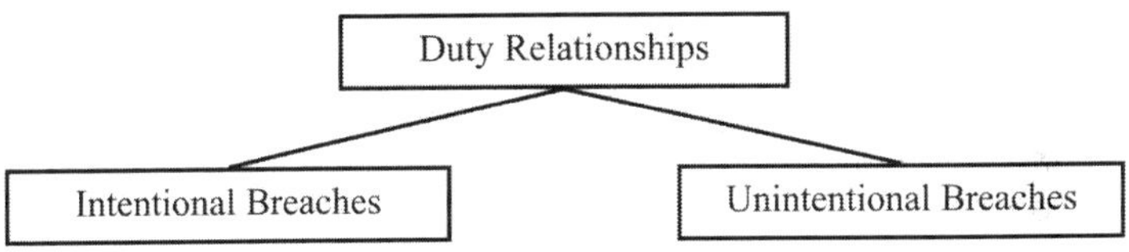

As a result of this first subdivision, we create a category of legal wrongs known as "intentional torts", and another group known as "unintentional torts". Curiously enough, the variety of intentional torts is much more extensive than that of unintentional torts, but despite this, virtually all litigation in tort law occurs as a result of alleged unintentional breaches of duty. Because of the relative frequency of torts of the unintentional variety, the last section of this chapter will consider the question of liability exclusively as it might be established under the heading of unintentional torts. But before proceeding to that discussion, we must investigate the range of possibilities a bit more carefully.

A. Intentional Torts

To consider the extensive array of torts that might result from an intentional course of conduct, it is convenient for us to reflect on the type of interest intended to be protected by tort law. What is it that the law is trying to preserve or protect through the process of imposing duties and adjudicating alleged breaches of those duties? As mentioned above, we must not lose sight of the model of individuality that has occupied much of our attention in the earlier chapters of this book. If we assume the separateness of each individual in the way that this model suggests, then we can identify characteristics of that separateness that might be deemed worthy of protection by the law. As a first step in this process, we can consider the individual's interest in personal well-being, and the individual's continuing interest in the things the individual accumulates, that is, their property. So we anticipate torts resulting from injuries to personal interests and from injuries to interests in property.

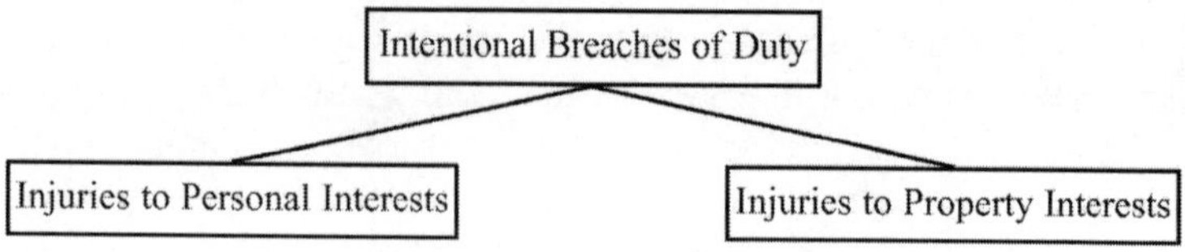

These sub-categories can be further divided, based on a more particular consideration of the sort of individual interests that might be adversely affected. Injuries to personal interests might be either injuries to the person's body, or injuries to their reputation. Injuries to property interests might be either injuries to interests in land, or injuries to interests in movable property (called "chattels" in the law). Our diagram, therefore, can be expanded as follows:

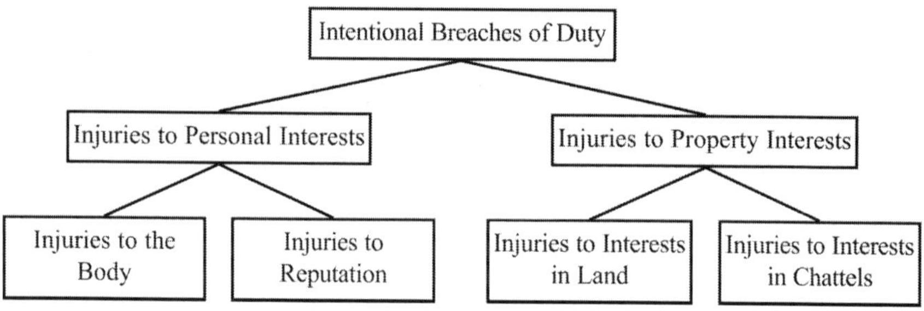

Each of these four sub-categories, developed by reference to the type of interest intended to be protected by tort law in the case of an intentional breach of duty, containing a number of specific legal wrongs. These separate wrongs or torts are complex in themselves, discussed at length in many judicial decisions and containing an extensive number of rules, sub-rules and exceptions. It is not within the ambit of this short book to consider the possibilities in this respect in any great depth. All we can do is give a quick introduction to the legal requirements that give rise to particular torts. To begin, under the heading "Injuries to the Body" there are three major categories of wrong.

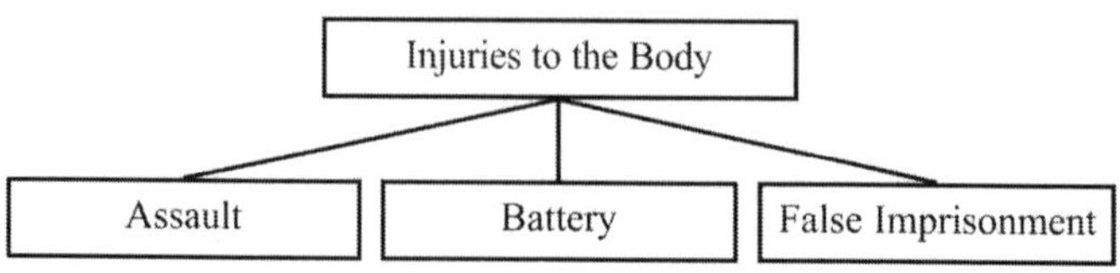

The tort of assault is the intentional creation in another person of a reasonable apprehension of imminent offensive or harmful contact. There are some particular issues to be noted in this definition. It is not necessary that the activity actually generated fear in the person complaining, nor is it necessary that the threatening person actually had the means to carry the threat into effect. All that is required is that a reasonable apprehension of imminent harmful or offensive contact is created. Therefore, if one person threatens another with physical injury at some time in the future, the tort of assault has not been committed. While this may be classified as some other sort of legal wrong, there is no reasonable apprehension of imminent contact, and therefore no tort of assault. Likewise, if an individual is threatened through an e-mail communication, then the tort of assault has not been committed, although, again, the activity may constitute some other legal wrong. However, if one individual raises his or her fist in a threatening way to another individual standing in the necessary physical proximity, then the tort of assault has been committed. All the requirements of the legal definition have been met.

It is convenient to think of the tort of battery as the logical extension of the tort of assault. If one individual raises his or her fist to another individual standing in the necessary physical proximity, and then follows through on the threat and actually makes contact with the second individual, then the tort of assault has been committed, followed quickly by the tort of battery. Battery is the intentional infliction by one individual of harmful or offensive contact on another. Oddly enough, however, it is not necessary that the tort of assault occur immediately prior to the tort of battery. If one individual hits another in the back with his or her fist, then the tort of battery has been committed. But the tort of assault was not committed because the second individual was not under a reasonable apprehension of harmful or offensive contact. Note that, in the tort of battery, it is not necessary for the complaining party to have suffered some demonstrable bodily injury to succeed. All that is required is that the contact be offensive. A slight touching, therefore, can be an injury to the interest in bodily integrity and therefore a battery, if it is offensive to the recipient and if it was intentionally inflicted.

We can see in both the torts of assault and battery that the law developed so as to protect the individual's separateness relative to their bodily integrity. A similar protection is afforded through the tort of false imprisonment. This tort results from the intentional confinement by one person of another within fixed boundaries and without lawful justification. It occasionally happens, for example, that a suspicious looking customer in a retail store will be held by store security personnel against their will, not because there was a reasonable belief that the customer was engaged in or about to engage in shoplifting, but rather because the customer was suspicious looking.[1] Confinement in such a circumstance could be the tort of false imprisonment, confinement of the customer in the security office without lawful justification. Now there is a variety of particular rules employed by the courts to unravel situations of alleged false imprisonment. For example, if the confined person has a reasonable means of escape, then there is no tort of false imprisonment. Suppose the suspicious looking customer were left alone in the security office, and the door to the office was open or unlocked. If the confinement were unlawful in the first place (and it would have to be if the tort of false imprisonment were to be established), then there is nothing to prevent the customer from walking away. This is one example among many that could be given to illustrate special rules in the tort of false imprisonment.

It should be noted that each of the torts briefly described under the heading "Injuries to Personal Interests — Injuries to the Body" have their counterparts in criminal law. The circumstances that give rise to the tort of assault also give rise to the crime of assault; we have defined a tort of battery, and the crime of assault contemplates similar circumstances; the tort of false imprisonment can yield the crime of assault, or confinement, or even kidnapping. But the interests at stake in these separate classifications of the same activity are quite different. In the criminal law, the state prosecutes an alleged offender for committing an act that the state has determined to be a breach of the individual's relationship with the state. The offence is against the state, and the offender, if convicted, is punished accordingly. It is only rarely in the criminal law that the victim recovers some restitution for the wrong done to them.[2] Ordinarily, the victim's remedy is pursued on the private law side of our classification system, where the judge is asked to adjudicate an alleged breach of a relationship between individuals, without the necessary involvement of the state in its political or sovereign capacity.

There is a small group of torts under the heading "Injuries to Personal Interests — Injuries to Reputation", but these torts often give rise to very high profile litigation. Under this category we can position defamation, made up of the separate torts of libel and slander. We can categorize the tort of malicious prosecution under this larger heading as well.

---

1 Such was the situation in *Chaytor v. London, New York and Paris Assn. of Fashion Ltd. and Price* (1961), 30 D.L.R. (2d) 527 (Nfld. S.C.), where the falsely imprisoned individuals were "spies" from a competing department store.

2 See, for example, ss. 738 *et seq.* of the *Criminal Code*, R.S.C. 1985, c. C-46 as amended, in which the court can sentence an offender to compensate victims of crime for various bodily and property injuries. This is one of very few instances in the criminal law where the victim's loss is adjudicated, and was added to the *Criminal Code* in respect of bodily injury only in 1996. Note too that the order for restitution is made by the judge on application of the prosecution or on the judge's own initiative, and not on application of the victim.

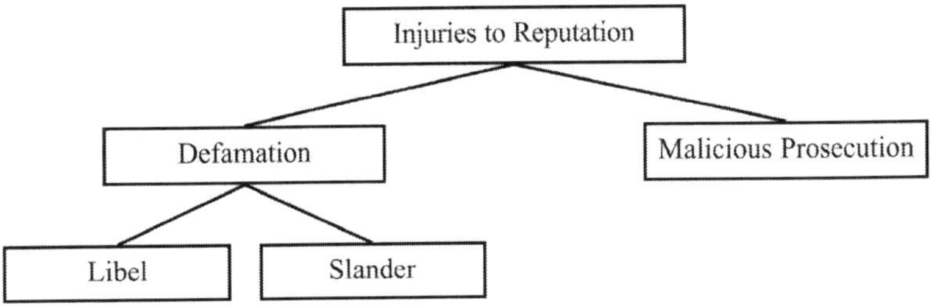

The Supreme Court of Canada has defined defamation as the publication of a statement "which tends to lower a person in the estimation of right-thinking members of society, or to expose a person to hatred, contempt or ridicule."[3] Libel involves defamation given in some sort of permanent form, perhaps published in a book, a newspaper, a movie or on television. Slander involves a defamation through spoken words or gestures. The law of defamation is enormously complicated, primarily because if the statement alleged to be defamatory is actually true, then the tort has not been established. This defence leads to very difficult evidentiary contests over interpretations of the truth. Further, a person defending against an allegation of defamation can argue that the statement made was merely "fair comment", that is, it was not motivated by malice (remember that defamation is an intentional tort), the subject is one of public interest, and it was an opinion that any reasonable person might express on the facts of the situation as they are known. Further still, there are some statements made that are protected by privilege, meaning that they are defamatory but cannot form the basis of a successful lawsuit in tort. Statements made in Canada's parliament, for example, are protected by privilege, even if they are found to be defamatory and untrue. Despite all of this, however, if the person claiming to have been defamed is able to establish that a statement has been made which meets the test set out by the Supreme Court of Canada, and if the utterer of that statement is unable to establish one of the recognized defences to the court's satisfaction, then the suit will succeed. The law of tort will be enlisted to protect the injured person's reputation in the community.

The other major tort in the category "Injuries to Personal Interests — Injuries to Reputation" is malicious prosecution. This tort arises during prosecution for a criminal offence. The Supreme Court of Canada has set out the four fundamental requirements to be established in a suit for malicious prosecution. First, the person accused in the criminal trial must

3 *Botiuk v. Toronto Free Press Publications Ltd.*, [1995] S.C.J. No. 69, 126 D.L.R. (4th) 609 at 622-23 (S.C.C.).

be acquitted. This is the person who will ultimately complain of having suffered injury as a result of tortious conduct. Secondly, the defendant in the civil suit for malicious prosecution must be the person responsible for the criminal proceedings against the person complaining of injury. Thirdly, the injured party must demonstrate that the defendant was motivated by malice in causing the criminal prosecution to take place. And finally, it must be established that the criminal proceedings were commenced without reasonable cause.[4] This tort arises on occasion where it is demonstrated that public officials (the police or the prosecutors) pursued criminal proceedings in situations where the charges are not reasonably founded and the official is motivated by something other than solving a particular crime. Although rare, this does occur.

It must not be forgotten that this short description of intentional torts relative to injuries to personal interests is necessarily incomplete, in two senses. First, the detail given is but a quick look at a body of law that has emerged through hundreds of cases over the years, meaning that there is a great deal of subtlety in the law that cannot be considered except in extended study. Secondly, there are additional torts identified under this broad category that have not been mentioned here, primarily for the sake of brevity. But our main purpose is not to become fully familiar with the vast range of tort law doctrine. Rather, our goal is to gain an appreciation for the relationship between duty as it is defined in tort law, and the interest each of us is assumed to have in maintaining our separateness from others as a manifestation of our dignity and privacy. In its recognition of a catalogue of intentional wrongs that emerges around the security of bodily integrity and reputation, the law of tort confirms that, in the construction of legal rules, the protection of individual dignity and autonomy is apparently an ideal of the first order.[5]

The same could be said of our next major category of intentional torts, the category we will refer to as injuries to property interests. In our short description of this family of torts, we will see that the focus of the law shifts from the bodily integrity of the injured individual, to the integrity of the individual's claim to the control of *things* relative to other individuals. The nature of ownership will be discussed more fully in Chapter 5. For now, it is enough to recall from Chapter 1 that ownership implies some sort of dominion over property (land or chattels) that affords the owner the power to bar others, in whole or in part, from the use, possession or alienation of that property.

---

4 *Nelles v. Ontario*, [1989] S.C.J. No. 86, 60 D.L.R. (4th) 609.

5 The extent to which the law of tort is successful in this endeavour remains a subject of some debate. This question will be introduced later in this chapter, and in Chapter 7.

The ownership interest, in its various forms, is protected in the law of tort through a group of wrongs which we will divide between injuries to interests in land resulting in the tort of trespass to land, and injuries to interests in chattels. For our purposes, we can further subdivide the latter by reference to the torts of detinue, conversion, and trespass to chattels.

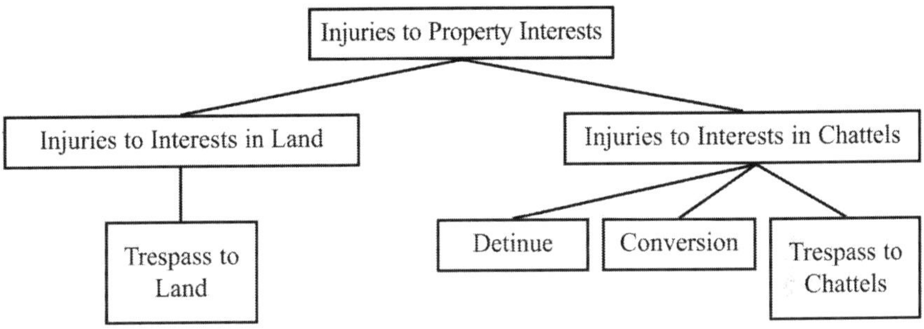

As we briefly describe these various torts, remember that it is the interest in the thing that is presumed to be violated through the breach of duty, rather than the thing itself. In other words, and with some notable exceptions, there is no need for the complaining individual to demonstrate that the thing has somehow been damaged or that its value, objectively determined, has been diminished through the wrongful act. Instead, all that is required in most cases is proof that the owner's rights of use, possession or alienation have been violated, in some measure at least, through the defendant's behaviour.

Trespass to land occurs through interference with the use or possession of the land of another. The individual complaining need not have the full range of ownership interests to sustain an action in trespass. All that is necessary is that the injured party be legally entitled to assert a right to the land in priority to the right of the trespasser. Therefore, this means that a tenant entitled to mere use and possession of land, and not entitled to exercise the right of alienation, is nevertheless capable of maintaining an action in trespass against someone who enters on the land wrongfully and without consent. The key here is that the person asserting that an interest has been violated must be able to demonstrate that that interest is recognized by the law and superior to the interest of the trespasser. In most cases, of course, the situation is straightforward. A person claiming full ownership of the land alleges that another has violated that ownership interest by building on the land, by using it for recreation, or by some other non-consensual use. Even a simple act such as throwing something on another's land without permission can constitute a trespass. Such violations of the ownership interest are actionable *per se*, meaning that it is not necessary for the complaining party to demonstrate that the trespasser's actions have actually diminished the value of the land objectively considered, nor that the trespass has caused some other direct economic loss to the owner. Rather, all that is necessary to succeed in a suit in trespass is to demonstrate that the ownership interest (generally use or possession in the case of trespass to land) has been violated.

Each of the torts grouped under the heading "Injuries to Interests in Chattels" is referable to a violation of some aspect of ownership rights to movable property. The tort of detinue is a wrongful retaining of possession by one individual as against the individual lawfully entitled to possession. Suppose you borrow my car for the weekend with my consent. When Monday comes, I ask for the return of the car, and you refuse. You keep the car over my objections until Wednesday, and then return it. In this situation, you have committed the tort of detinue, and I am entitled to recover an amount of money from you to compensate me for the injury to my right to possession for the period from Monday to Wednesday, the time during which your detention of the car was without my consent.

The tort of conversion occurs where the wrongdoer converts one or more of the rights of ownership to his or her own use without the consent of the individual lawfully entitled to assert that particular right. Suppose I allow you to borrow my car for your own use this weekend. During the weekend, however, you lease the car for one day to your friend. While your possession and use of the car was done with my consent and is therefore lawful, your lease of the car to your friend is an exercise of the right of alienation, and that right was not transferred to you from me. You have converted the right of alienation to your own use, and that is tortious at law. It should be noted here that, while we have catalogued the tort of conversion under the broad heading of "Intentional Breaches of Duty", even an innocent conversion of chattels will, in most cases at least, result in commission of the tort. The relevant intention, for our purposes, is the intention to turn the chattel to use, rather than the intention to violate the injured party's interests.

When we consider the tort of trespass to chattels, it is convenient to recognize that this tort is virtually identical to the tort of trespass to land. Any non-consensual touching of another's chattel will constitute the tort, even in the case where no actual damage (considered objectively) can be demonstrated. It is quite rare, of course, that a lawsuit would be initiated for very minor, technical trespasses, and this is the case both in trespass to land and in trespass to chattels. Even if such a suit were successful, a modern court would award only the smallest monetary compensation for such a slight injury to one or the other of the ownership interests. But for our purposes, we must remember that the very availability of the tort is a demonstration of the extent to which the law privileges certain types of interests that emerge in our ordinary social activity. It is arguable that the interests most directly connected to the assertion of our individuality, either through a claim to bodily integrity or through the exercise of dominion over things, are the interests that attract the most attention from the law of tort. This is perhaps most clearly demonstrated through the continued protection of the slightest injury to our rights in movable property.

There is a third category of intentional torts that continues to expand and develop through the cases. While the torts that result from breaches of duty generating violations of personal and property interests can be summarized fairly quickly, the third category is more vague, and less settled. This third category results from breaches of duty generating injuries to economic interests, and we shall call this group "economic torts". There are a number of possibilities here, but we shall limit our summary to the torts of conspiracy, unlawful interference with contractual relations, and fraud.

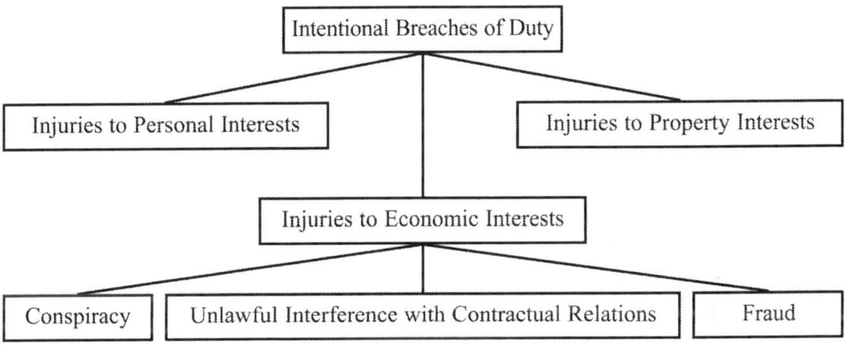

Often, of course, torts resulting from actions causing injuries to personal interests or injuries to property interests will result in injuries to economic interests as well. For example, if I need my car for the purposes of my profession, and you commit the tort of detinue by keeping my car two days longer than allowed, then you have interfered in my performance of my profession, and that could cause some form of economic loss. But the torts known as economic torts generally arise in a commercial setting, and they are direct actions against economic interests, rather than actions that generate economic loss as a mere ancillary consequence of some other wrongful act. Occasionally, one of the torts in this group occurs outside of the commercial world, but for the most part it is business interests that are at stake.

The tort of conspiracy looks much like the crime of conspiracy. In tort law, a conspiracy occurs where two or more individuals plan an action together with no legitimate object or purpose other than injuring the target individual's interests. Again, we are talking of economic interests here, for the most part. The significant differences between a criminal conspiracy and a tortious conspiracy are two (other than the basic difference related to the state's involvement in criminal law). First, the planned act in the tort of conspiracy need not be a criminal act. All that is required is that it is an act directed toward damaging the interests of another, with no other legitimate purpose. In criminal law, the planned act must itself be a crime for the crime of conspiracy to have taken place. Secondly, in criminal law the crime is complete when the planning or discussion takes place. It is not necessary that the conspirators actually act on their conspiracy. In tort law, however, the target individual must demonstrate to the court that their interests have in fact been adversely affected in order to succeed in a suit for conspiracy.

Another name for the tort of unlawful interference with contractual relations is inducing breach of contract. This tort occurs in the situation where one individual takes steps to cause another individual to breach an existing contract with a third individual. The steps taken must have no legitimate purpose other than inducing the breach of contract, and the complaining individual must have suffered some actual damage as a result of the breach. The question of what constitutes a legitimate purpose is not completely clear in the cases, but it is likely true that the self-interest of the defendant is not a sufficient purpose. Such was the situation in the early English case of *Lumley v. Gye*,[6] one of the more famous cases in this area of tort law. There, an opera singer was under contract to perform at a particular theatre. Managers of a competing theatre convinced the singer to breach her contract so as to allow her to sing at their location. This was sufficient to ground a successful suit for unlawful interference with contractual relations, despite the obvious competitive impetus that we assume governs much of what takes place in the ordinary commercial marketplace.

It is in cases of fraud (often called deceit) that we find the most opportunity for the commission of an economic tort outside of the ordinary commercial world. Conduct is fraudulent where the defendant makes some statement, knowing that the statement is false (or at least being reckless as to whether it is true or false), and intending that some other individual take some action in reliance on the truth of the statement. The target individual must in fact act on the strength of the statement, and suffer some loss as a result. This tort occurs frequently in ordinary commercial matters where, for example, one individual deliberately inflates the value of shares in a corporation so as to induce some other individual to invest. But it also occurs in more private settings. The traditional literary image is the vulnerable person convinced by a charming cheat to transfer her

---

6 *Lumley v. Gye* (1853), 2 El. & Bl. 216 (Q.B.).

wealth to the cheat's benefit in return for promises never intended to be kept. This is the tort of fraud.

There are many further examples of economic torts we might describe, but the main thing for us to remember is that this group of torts arises through actions intended to cause damage to economic interests. The network of protection is thus completed by tort law. Personal dignity and security is intended to be assured through the group of torts emerging from intentional acts against personal interests; property interests are protected through another family of torts; business interests are supported through a group of related torts specifically designed, for the most part, for the commercial world. We start to see a picture emerging in tort law of the dignified, autonomous individual as an amalgam of their various interests, meaning that, in some sense at least, we recognize and respect the ideal individual by virtue of their claims to bodily integrity, dominion over property and the pursuit of self-interest in the marketplace. The system of intentional torts can be construed as the mechanism by which that individual so recognized is protected from deliberate violation. However, the picture is not complete. So far, we have not taken sufficient account of the standard of conduct we demand of others. It is easy enough to justify the protection of the individual against deliberate interference, but what of the situation where an injury occurs by accident?

B. Unintentional Torts

To address situations in which injury to one or the other of the personal, proprietary or economic interests of an individual are injured through accidental occurrences, the law of duty relationships has developed a small number of torts which we shall call "unintentional torts". It is in this group of wrongful activities that the concept of fault, introduced at the beginning of this chapter, starts to have real resonance. It is obvious that responsibility for injury ought to lie at the feet of those intending to cause injury, but it is not so obvious that those causing injury by accident ought to be responsible too. Through reflection on this large category of wrongful conduct, yielding a small number of important torts, our focus shifts from the ideal individual as victim of wrongdoing, to the ideal individual responsible for the necessary and foreseeable consequences of their acts, whether those acts or their consequences were actually intended or not. For our purposes, this shift in focus allows us to consider two separate torts, nuisance and negligence. This side of our diagram, therefore, can be represented as follows.

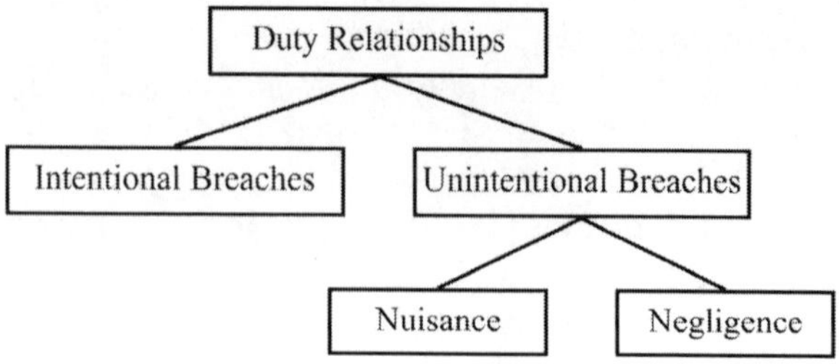

Nuisance in its most common form is a tort that arises through the conduct of neighbouring property owners. It is considered by some scholars to be an intentional tort,[7] but for our purposes we shall consider it as the result of unintentionally causing damage through acts that may or may not be intentional. Simply stated, a nuisance occurs where one property owner or occupier uses their property in such a way as to adversely affect the use or enjoyment of neighbouring property. An unreasonable level of noise, the escape of unpleasant or dangerous fumes, the seepage of water from one property to the next — all of these things and many others have been adjudged to be nuisances when they interfere with a neighbour's use or enjoyment of their property. Such interference must be continuing to constitute the tort of nuisance, meaning a one time or merely occasional disturbance will not be grounds for a successful suit in nuisance. For our purposes, the tort is unintentional because, despite the fact that the actions complained of are almost always carried out intentionally, it is not necessary that the defendant intended to cause a disturbance to the neighbour.

One interesting and difficult aspect to the law of nuisance is the way in which it compels a judge to reconcile competing, similar interests. We know already that, relative to our property, we command a set of private law rights, including possession, use and the power of alienation. Ordinarily, the law does not prevent our exercise and enjoyment of these rights in whatever way we feel is appropriate. In other words, there is nothing at law to prevent me from destroying my desk, so long as no one else can claim some of the rights of possession, use or alienation relative to that desk. I am at liberty to use or abuse my things in the way I choose,[8] free of the interference of others. This is the right asserted by an individual

---

7 See, for example, Margaret Kerr, JoAnn Kurtz and Laurence M. Olivo, *Canadian Tort Law in a Nutshell* (Toronto: Carswell Thomson Professional Publishing, 1997), at 21.

8 This is simplistically stated, of course, because there is a vast regulatory framework that has an impact on the way in which we exercise our rights relative to certain types of property. The state protects items of cultural or historical significance, for example, despite their private ownership, and it is contrary to law to abandon property of certain types and in certain situations (*e.g.*, littering). But apart from such controls, ordinarily imposed to advance a perceived public interest, we are free to deal with our property as we see fit.

complaining of a nuisance. But, in response, the target of the complaint asserts the same right, the right to use their property in whatever way they see fit, so long as that use does not adversely affect the interests of others in the same property. In deciding that a claim in nuisance is successful, a judge is ultimately adjudicating competing claims to the use and enjoyment of property, restricting the exercise of property rights by one neighbour so as to preserve the enjoyment of the rights of the other.

The tort of negligence generates virtually all litigation in tort law, and it contemplates every possible activity in which we engage every day. It is designed to protect each of the victim's interests we considered in our summary of intentional torts above, but in doing so it focuses on the standard of care employed by the alleged wrongdoer so as to ensure that his or her actions are not harmful to others. In other words, even short of an intentional infliction of harm, individuals are held legally responsible for the harm they generate where the standard of care they employ to prevent harm is considered insufficient to meet the common law duty in tort law. In thinking about negligence, therefore, our principal focus shifts from the protection of the victim's interests to the conduct of the alleged wrongdoer.

The law of negligence imposes on each of us the obligation to refrain from acting in ways that cause reasonably foreseeable injury to another's personal or property interests. Each of us is responsible to act in accordance with a reasonable standard of care so as to avoid such injuries. The question of reasonableness, an essentially objective determination, is therefore fundamental to the law of negligence. In effect, the law imposes on us a set of assumptions about right conduct based on the way in which we expect reasonable persons to behave in like situations, and then requires us to live up to that standard of reasonableness. These assumptions, driven by the circumstances out of which the litigation arose, are developed by reference to guidance afforded by earlier case law, but it is likely unavoidable that they also depend to a large extent on the decision-maker's own perspective on right and wrong. Consequently, while we cling to the idea of objective standards of proper behaviour, doing our best to turn the fictional reasonable person into a real and meaningful guide to our thinking, in truth the determination of appropriate standards of care towards others during our ordinary activities has a large subjective component. This reality has a substantial impact on the predictability of the law, and also on the extent to which the law is evenly applied in the assessment of the conduct of different defendants.

In the last section of this chapter, we shall look a bit more carefully at the way in which the law imposes liability on defendants in negligence cases. This will require a return to the fundamental formula in tort law, that is, the coincidence in one set of facts of duty, breach of duty, and resulting damage to an interest protected by the law. Before doing that, however, it must be pointed out that not every interest of an individual complaining of wrongful conduct is recognized and protected in the law of negligence. While the interests in bodily integrity, property and economic endeavours are protected through the network of intentional torts, and, to some extent, through the torts of nuisance and negligence, the law of negligence has always been hesitant to compensate for psychiatric injuries and for economic injuries that are not consequent on injuries to the person or injuries to property. In other words, there are some interests we might identify as consistent with our image of the dignified, autonomous individual, but which are nevertheless not compensable in the case of negligently caused injuries. Although there has been some movement in recent years toward allowing for these imperfectly protected interests,[9] our understanding of tort law as a web of protection for the defining interests of the dignified individual must be adjusted somewhat when we introduce the law of negligence.

III. LIABILITY IN NEGLIGENCE

The law of negligence emerged with full force in the English case of *Donoghue v. Stevenson*, a decision of the House of Lords in 1932.[10] In one of the most famous decisions in the entire common law, the Court outlined the grounds on which one might be held liable for injuries caused outside of intentional infliction of harm in tort, and outside of the relationship recognized in the law of contract. While prior to this decision, the law of negligence did have significant influence on the way in which the unintentional infliction of harm was adjudicated, after 1932 the law of negligence developed so expansively that it threatened to overwhelm the entire tort law arena. The impact of *Donoghue v. Stevenson* is not to be underestimated.

The facts of the case were quite simple. A bottler of ginger beer sold its product to a distributor, who in turn sold it to members of the public. A particular bottle was purchased from the distributor, and then given to the purchaser's friend to be consumed. The bottle contained a decomposing snail, not discovered by the friend until after a portion of the ginger beer had been consumed. The friend suffered shock and an attack of gastroenteritis. She sued the bottler of the ginger beer. Now the law to be

---

[9] See Allen M. Linden, *Canadian Tort Law, 6th ed.* (Toronto: Butterworths Canada Ltd., 1997), at 385-422.

[10] *Donoghue v. Stevenson*, [1932] All E.R. 1 (H.L.).

applied in this situation was quite complex. First, if ordinary prudence exercised by anyone who handled the bottle would have led to the discovery of the snail, then the bottler ought not to be responsible. If there were a reasonable opportunity for inspection of the product prior to its consumption, then responsibility for the injury would shift to the person who failed to act on that opportunity. The Court did not hesitate in finding that there was no reasonable opportunity to inspect the product prior to its consumption.

Secondly, there were three separate transactions between the act of bottling the ginger beer and the act of consuming the ginger beer. The bottle was sold to the distributor, then sold to the purchaser, then given to the consumer. In the law of contract, this separation of act and event would be fatal to the claim. The consumer would fail in her suit based on the argument that she had no direct contractual relationship with the bottler. For the consumer to succeed, therefore, she had to successfully argue that the bottler was liable to her in tort law. The bottler argued, of course, that there was no liability. After all, how could it be argued that the bottler owed a duty to the consumer when there were three separate intervening transactions between manufacture and consumption? If the bottle had been passed from friend to friend a dozen times before it was consumed, was the bottler to remain liable? In such circumstances, how would it ever be possible for the bottler to know the range of persons to whom it owed a duty to take care in the manufacture of its products? Is it conceivable that the bottler owed a duty to a limitless number of persons, impossible to identify at the time the ginger beer was bottled? Is this a rational result?

In one of the most famous statements in the common law, Lord Atkin decided that the law of negligence was designed to accommodate this very situation. In his opinion, each of us has a duty in law not to act in such a way as to cause injury to the person or property of others who might reasonably be foreseen to be affected by our actions. This is the famous "neighbour principle", summarized by Lord Atkin in the following terms:

> The rule that you are to love your neighbour becomes in law, you must not injure your neighbour....You must take reasonable care to avoid acts or omissions which you can reasonably foresee would be likely to injure your neighbour. Who, then, in law, is my neighbour? The answer seems to be — persons who are so closely and directly affected by my act that I ought reasonably to have them in contemplation as being so affected when I am directing my mind to the acts or omissions which are called in question.[11]

---

[11] *Ibid.*, at 11.

It can be seen that Lord Atkin was particularly careful to establish that the test for negligence is an objective test. He qualified his language in three separate places by inserting the term "reasonably". This means that the conduct complained of must be assessed based on ordinary expectations of right conduct, and it is that standard against which our acts will be measured. As indicated earlier in this chapter, the objective standard of reasonable conduct is very elusive, with the result that the decision-maker must of necessity rely on their subjective understanding of proper behaviour, although guided at all times, of course, by precedent. But the standard of care expected of ordinary persons in ordinary activities is one of the most difficult concepts in the entire common law, and is generally re-assessed on a case by case basis.

Lord Atkin's neighbour principle also emphasizes the problem of causation, introduced briefly in Chapter 1 above. Whereas in the area of intentional torts there is a fairly direct connection between the tortious conduct and the injury, in the law of negligence the connection is sometimes quite obscure. Often, a particular act will set in motion a complicated chain of events that ultimately causes injury. Suppose the operator of an automobile negligently injures a pedestrian. The pedestrian is a grandparent, the voluntary caregiver for his two small grandchildren while his daughter works outside the home to support the family. Because the accident renders the grandfather unable to assist in raising the children, the mother of the children is forced to hire a replacement. This means that she cannot save funds for her children's university education. The children's prospect for a lucrative career and comfortable lifestyle is therefore jeopardized. Is it reasonable to argue that the adverse impact on the prospects of the injured person's grandchildren was caused by the negligence of the automobile operator? It seems clear that it was so caused, but should the automobile operator be compelled at law to compensate the children for this injury? Is it fair to suggest that the grandchildren ought reasonably to have been in the contemplation of the automobile operator as she drove down the street?

Questions and complications such as these render negligence law one of the most difficult areas in all of private law. It has an impact on everything we do. It provides the standard against which our conduct is measured for the requisite level of care, and, through the test of reasonable foreseeability, allows successful claims for some injured parties and denies recovery for others. For the most part, we owe the idea of *duty* in negligence law to *Donoghue v. Stevenson*. But the tort is not complete simply by finding that a duty exists. In the law of negligence, there will be no successful suit unless there is also a *breach* of duty, and then *damages* (some sort of injury to personal or property interests) consequent on that breach. Duty, breach and damage must co-exist, and must be referable to each other, without which there can be no recovery by the injured party. This raises an array of very difficult questions in negligence law, some of which are based on the objective standards of assessment of conduct introduced by Lord Atkin.

For example, it is clear that the operator of an automobile owes a duty not to act in such a way as to cause injury to other users of the highway, or to anyone who might reasonably be foreseen to be affected by the operation of the car. However, what if the driver breaches her duty to other users of the highway, but causes damage to them in unforeseen ways? Suppose the driver accidentally allows her car to swerve across a sidewalk. No one is struck, but a nearby pedestrian is alarmed, jumps into the air and strikes a passerby with his arm. Is the driver of the automobile liable for the injury suffered by the passerby? According to Lord Atkin's concepts of duty and neighbourliness, is this injury compensable? It was caused by the negligence of the driver, but in a way that was not likely in the reasonable contemplation of the driver when she directed her mind to the operation of the vehicle. Does this matter when the courts consider the extent of liability in negligence?[12]

For our purposes, it is enough to recognize that the combination of duty, breach of duty and resulting damages is ordinarily enough to establish liability in negligence. The law has developed an extensive system of rules to govern duty relationships under this category, both in ordinary circumstances such as the traffic mishaps used in our examples, and in special circumstances. For example, in dealing with people relying on their expertise, professionals are held to a standard of care somewhat higher than the ordinary person. Further, there is a special set of rules about the way in which property must be maintained by the occupiers of that property so as to ensure that people visiting (or sometimes even trespassing on) that property are not injured. This is known as the law of "occupiers' liability". As well, there are special categories of negligence for governments ("Crown liability") and manufacturers ("products liability"). Strictly speaking, *Donoghue v. Stevenson* was an example of products liability. And there is a host of other sub-categories of negligence that make mastery of this area of the law a challenging prospect.

It is likely that the law of negligence is intended to provide a relatively comprehensive legal framework to afford compensation to injured individuals where their injuries are caused by the unintentional acts of others. This is a just and attractive result, so far as it goes. But it is arguable that the law of negligence is deficient in at least two significant

---

[12] The general rule in such cases is that the injury is compensable, so long as the injured party is someone contemplated by the neighbour principle, and so long as questions of causation can be answered satisfactorily. Ordinarily, the manner by which the act leads to the injury is not significant.

respects. First, it is not every injury that is compensable in the law of negligence. As we saw earlier in this chapter, certain types of interests are not protected in tort law, including some psychiatric injuries and particular types of economic losses. The rationale for preventing recovery for these difficulties, where they are demonstrated to be the result of a breach of a duty established through Lord Atkin's neighbour principle, is not entirely clear. Is there any meaningful difference between a damaged limb and a damaged mind? Is there any justification for allowing recovery to economic interests when they are the target of intentional tortious acts, but denying recovery for the same loss where it is a consequence of negligence? After all, an injury to bodily integrity is compensable, whether caused deliberately or negligently. Are economic interests different in some qualitative way? Although these questions continue to perplex torts scholars and judges, there is some movement in the cases toward more comprehensive coverage of injured interests, and it is likely that the law of negligence will continue to develop in this respect.

Secondly, the law of negligence focuses primarily on the conduct of the person alleged to have caused the injury. This focus raises the question of fault, alluded to earlier in this chapter as a central concern of the law of tort. If fault cannot be established, then there is nothing that can be done for the injured party inside the tort law framework. It is the first element in the establishment of liability in each and every case. In the law of negligence, fault is demonstrated through showing that the required standard of care was not met, and that the failure to meet the standard of care was the proximate cause of the injury. It is felt that imposing liability on those who are found to be at fault is the just result where individuals are injured through no fault of their own, and the accomplishment of just results is a social good that motivates much of the way in which our legal system is structured and operated. But this leaves open the question of compensation for injuries suffered in situations where no one is at fault, according to the appropriate legal standards. Can it be argued that it is also a social good to leave parties suffering such injuries without compensation? If not, then is there some community-wide obligation, derived from morality if not from law, to ensure that every member of the community is protected against injuries they suffer through no fault of their own? The "no fault" automobile insurance programme in place in some jurisdictions is an attempt to recognize such an obligation, and to provide a level of protection for every member of the community, whether injury is caused through negligence (as defined in law) or some other accident. Is there any reason why the concept of fault ought to continue to have such significance in other types of accidentally caused injuries? Is there any reason why "no fault" compensation ought not to be the entitlement of every injured person, where the injury is suffered through no fault of their own, and irrespective of the fault of others?

Over the course of many, many generations and thousands of cases, tort law has developed a variety of ways in which these questions are answered, at least in part. For example, the doctrine of vicarious liability provides a mechanism whereby employers are held liable in tort law for the wrongful acts of their employees, even in the situation where there is no fault (as it is ordinarily understood) in the actions of the employer. If, during the course of employment, an employee commits a wrongful act causing injury, then the employer can be held liable in damages for those injuries, even where the employer has done no demonstrably wrongful act itself. This rule is engaged in situations where the wrongful act committed by the employee is either an act authorized by the employer, or an act which, while not itself directly authorized by the employer, is a manner of completing an authorized act. For example, a truck driver employed to deliver goods is authorized by the employer to drive a truck, make stops, and unload, but is not authorized to drive the truck negligently. However, the negligent operation of the truck is a manner of doing the authorized task of driving and delivering, and as such is sufficient to invoke the doctrine of vicarious liability and impose responsibility on the employer for injuries resulting to others.

It can be seen, therefore, that vicarious liability appears to violate the idea that responsibility ought to lie where fault resides, that is, at the feet of the wrongdoer. In our example, it is clear that the wrongdoer is the truck driver, not the employer, such that our previously developed model of liability should protect the employer and render the employee responsible. But yet the law of tort reaches more deeply into the various relationships at work in this situation, and finds the employer liable irrespective of fault conventionally understood. The policy reasons behind this apparently aberrant situation have been considered by many courts and academics over the years, the general conclusion seeming to be that, because employers have economic or other interests to promote in having their employees engaged in various activities, then they ought to be responsible for the acts of those employees. The risk of loss ought to lie with the risk of reward, in the ordinary commercial sense. The policy consequences are twofold. First, injured parties have an additional target from which to recover the damages to which they are justly entitled, a consequence driven by the overarching concern in tort law to see just compensation flow to deserving parties. Secondly, the employer may have some additional incentive to more thoroughly supervise the activities of its employees, even in the situation where its ordinary course of supervision is not so deficient as to make the employer directly liable in negligence to the injured party. This result satisfies in part the goal of deterrence that, arguably at least, is built into our tort law system.[13]

There are other doctrines developed in the law of tort to address in part the situation where a person is injured through no fault of their own, and with no apparent fault lying with others. Most prominent here is the doctrine of strict liability, by which responsibility may be found in a party who has nevertheless done all reasonably expected acts to prevent injury to others. A nineteenth century English case, *Rylands v. Fletcher*,[14] is the starting point in any discussion of strict liability. In that case, the defendant stored a large volume of water in a reservoir on his land. The water escaped through an open channel of which the defendant had no prior knowledge, flooding a neighbour's mine. The court held that the defendant was liable for the ensuing damages, even though the defendant was reasonably prudent in the manner in which he had stored the water. The rule then emerged that, in situations where an inherently dangerous substance or animal is kept on a party's property, that party will be strictly liable for the consequences if the substance or animal escapes and does injury to another. This is so, even in the case where no negligence has led to the escape and injury. *Rylands v. Fletcher* is therefore the source of the rule that, for example, where a homeowner keeps a dog in a fenced backyard, the homeowner will be strictly liable for injuries suffered by others if the dog somehow escapes and does damage, whether the likelihood of the dog's escape was foreseeable or not.[15]

Through the doctrines of vicarious liability and strict liability, we find at least partial answers to the policy difficulties inherent in particular situations either where a person is injured through no fault of their own, where no other party is clearly responsible according to the traditional model by which liability follows fault, or perhaps where the obvious defendant suffers from impecuniosity. But these doctrines are very tightly

---

13 The law of vicarious liability is much more complicated than can be summarized in a few short lines, and has been considered time and again by the highest courts in the common law world. Many situations present particularly difficult policy challenges, including for example the case where the employer is a not-for-profit or charitable organization, as opposed to a commercial endeavour. See a series of cases in the Supreme Court of Canada on this question, beginning with *Bazley v. Curry*, [1999] S.C.J. No. 35, [1999] 2 S.C.R. 534 (S.C.C.), and continuing with *Jacobi v. Griffiths*, [1999] S.C.J. No. 36, [1999] 2 S.C.R. 570 (S.C.C.) and *John Doe v. Bennett*, [2004] S.C.J. No. 17, [2004] 1 S.C.R. 436 (S.C.C.).

14 (1868), L.R. 3 H.L. 330.

15 In Ontario, this rule is captured in the statute called the *Dog Owners' Liability Act*, R.S.O. 1990, c. D.16. Note that the statute imposes liability on the dog owner whether the owner knew or not of a propensity in the dog to bite. This is a heightened standard of strict liability when compared to the old common law rule, under which the owner would be liable only if he or she knew of the dangerous character of the dog. In the case of wild animals, the rule of strict liability has always applied, irrespective of the knowledge of the owner.

circumscribed and therefore rarely available. While compensation and deterrence remain central justifications of our tort law system, it remains true that many, many injured parties are unable to recover damages due to one or another of these difficult policy challenges. Whether or not a community-wide obligation exists to compensate such parties as a product of our morality is a debatable question, but it is clear that the law has developed at least some modest exceptions to the model of fault-based liability that tend to address such an obligation, at least obliquely and in part. The extent to which the oblique and partial solution will become the direct and complete response remains unclear.

Chapter 5

Private Law Relations Mediated by Property

I. THE NATURE OF PROPERTY RELATIONS

Consider the following examples. First, researchers at Harvard University apply to the Federal Patent tribunal seeking patent rights over the genetic code of a mouse (the Oncomouse) that they have bred in the laboratory for specialized research purposes. Opposition to the University's claim for patent rights to the genetically modified mouse comes from various groups and organizations concerned about the potential implications of this claim by the University. Among other concerns, these groups argue that it is fundamentally unethical to claim private property rights over the process of life itself. The researchers argue that their research is critical to the development of cancer resistant genes in complex life forms, and as such should be protected by the legal system through the recognition of patent protection for their research.[1]

Secondly, an Indian band whose traditional territories lie in the province of British Columbia applies to the courts for a declaration recognizing the Band's common law aboriginal title to the lands traditionally occupied by the Band. The provincial government defends the claim arguing that the traditional occupation of the predecessors to the present day band over these territories does not give the band any right or title to the land that is enforceable against the provincial government. Moreover, the provincial government argues in addition that any right to traditional occupation or possession of the lands by the band has been legislatively extinguished by provincial legislation that is inconsistent with such a right.[2]

Thirdly, two individuals who have been cohabiting for over ten years without being married to each other decide to separate. One has worked in a largely unpaid capacity in the other's business during most of this period. On separating, the party who contributed the unpaid labour claims

---

1 See *Harvard College v. Canada (Commissioner of Patents)*, [2002] S.C.J. No. 77, [2002] 4 S.C.R. 45 (S.C.C.), discussed further below.

2 See *Delgamuukw v. British Columbia*, [1997] S.C.J. No. 108, [1997] 3 S.C.R. 1010 (S.C.C.), for a fact situation very similar to this.

a half share in the value of the other's business. The two former cohabitants are unable to reach a separation agreement recognizing the value of this contribution, so the party who contributed the unpaid labour sues for a share of the business. Would it make any difference to the issues that the courts have to decide if the ex-cohabitants were both of the same sex?[3]

Fourthly, a property owner whose lands lie adjacent to commercially harvested forest lands seeks an injunction preventing certain forms of chemical spraying over the forest lands, on the grounds that the chemicals used in the spraying operation are a potential health hazard. The forestry company involved in operating the forest lands insists that the chemicals used in the spraying operation are not dangerous when used in these quantities, and that the spraying is necessary to commercially harvest the forest. How should this dispute between neighbouring property owners be resolved?[4]

What do each of these different fact situations have in common? They are all situations in which the legal relationships between the various parties to the dispute are mediated by property rights. As such they all form part of the subject matter of the present chapter. These fact situations also reveal the complexity of the different kinds of interests that may be protected by property rights. Two of these situations deal with property rights in land, or "real property", although in very different contexts. One situation deals with property rights in a business, which may include as part of its assets both real property (for example the title to the premises where the business is conducted), and personal property (such as the value of shares in the company if the business is incorporated). The remaining situation is concerned not so much with tangible things, but with "intellectual property" rights in an idea or a process, and these are essentially intangible forms of property.

So at the very outset of our discussion of property relationships we confront the need to categorize, to make distinctions between different forms of property rights. Perhaps the most traditional categorization of property rights in Anglo-Canadian law is the distinction between real property and personal property, or what civil lawyers refer to as the distinction between moveables and immoveables. As we have seen, real property refers to interests in land. By its very nature, land is immoveable. Consequently, possession of land cannot be transferred physically from one person to another in the same way that possession of moveable personal

---

3 *Pettkus v. Becker*, [1980] S.C.J. No. 103, 117 D.L.R. (3d) 257 (S.C.C.). See also the decision of the Supreme Court of Canada in the case of *M. v. H.*, [1999] S.C.J. No. 23, 171 D.L.R. (4th) 577 (S.C.C.), although the decision deals with support claims as between same sex partners, rather than with a claim to a property entitlement to a share in the business.

4 *Palmer v. Nova Scotia Forest Industries*, [1983] N.S.J. No. 534, 2 D.L.R. (4th) 397 (N.S.S.C. (T.D.)).

property can be transferred physically from one person to another. Possession of land is therefore generally transferred by deed, or by will, or by lease, or by other legal document that creates a record of the transfer of the right to possession of a particular parcel of land from one person to another. Possession of land can also be claimed symbolically, for example, by the ceremonial act of a European explorer in planting a flag on newly discovered lands in the Americas and claiming possession of the newly discovered territories on behalf of the English, Spanish, or French Crown.

By contrast, possession of moveable items of personal property can be physically transferred from one person to another in a way that land cannot be. Consequently, the legal system is able to infer the legal right to possession from the physical fact of possession in relation to moveable personal property without always requiring a documentary record of the transfer of legal possession. If I make a gift of a book to you on your birthday, I may inscribe your name inside the cover of the book. But I rarely consider the need for a formal legal document recording the transfer of possession of the book to you. Simply handing you the book with my best wishes as a birthday gift is normally sufficient to transfer legal possession of the book at the same time.

A second way of categorizing property rights is the distinction between tangible and intangible forms of property. As the name suggests, tangible forms of property have a physical existence, such as a parcel of land, a herd of cattle, an oil tanker, an automobile, or a small item of personal property such as a watch, comb or a painting. Intangible forms of property have no separate physical existence; they cannot be touched, smelt, heard, seen or tasted. Nevertheless, intangible forms of property may have very significant legal and commercial value. Examples of intangible forms of property include intellectual property rights such as trademarks, patents, copyrights, domain names, software codes, or even trade secrets such as the recipe for Coca Cola (itself a commercially valuable trade name), or the secret ingredients of Caramilk! In what many futurists have called the "information age" or the "knowledge economy" intellectual property rights such as these may come to be regarded as the most economically significant forms of property of all.[5]

Having looked briefly at two traditional categorizations of property rights, we need to step back for a moment and ask what we mean by the term "property"? This is not such a straightforward question as it first appears. In ordinary speech, we tend to equate the idea of property with the idea of ownership. My property is that which I own. What you own is

[5] Alexander I. Poltorak and Paul J. Lerner, *Essentials of Intellectual Property* (New York: John Wiley and Sons, 2002), at xiii, xiv. Poltorak and Lerner refer to intellectual property as the currency of the new economy.

your property, and so on. This simple equation of "property" with "ownership" seems to imply that for each article or object of property that can be owned, we can identify one legal person who can claim ownership rights over it. In legal theory, however, things are rarely so simple. For one thing, any particular object of property may be subject to multiple claims of ownership. My grandmother may have recently died, and left the family cottage which she owned in her own name to her five grandchildren. In this situation, each of the grandchildren hold a one fifth ownership share in the cottage. To put this into more technical legal terminology, each of the five grandchildren are now co-owners of the cottage. In addition, my spouse and I recently purchased our first house. Title to the house was put into our two names as joint tenants, with right of survivorship, so that whichever of us dies before the other, the surviving spouse will become the sole owner of the house. Finally, I am also a partner in a firm of architects. The partnership owns its own office building in downtown Ottawa. As one of the partners, I am also a co-owner with my other partners of the title to the office building. Remember that a partnership is different from a corporation in that the partnership is not a separate legal person from the partners. All partnership property is therefore owned in common by all the partners, in proportion to their share in the partnership.

Very quickly, then, we have identified three relatively common situations in which property may be co-owned by two or more persons. We could add to our list of situations of co-ownership of property very easily by using examples of co-owned personal property. Instead of a cottage, grandmother may have left her five grandchildren her shares in Bell Canada; my wife and I may have purchased a car together; and the partnership property may also include a partnership bank account, the funds in which are co-owned by the partners.

Despite the apparent similarity between each of these situations of co-ownership, not all of them are alike. Just ask yourself, for a moment, what would happen if one of the grandchildren who are now co-owners of the cottage were to die? Would that co-owner's share of the cottage be divided among the other grandchildren? Or would each grandchild's share in the cottage be inherited by that grandchild's own family? The answer to this question may depend on the wording of the grandmother's will. If the cottage were left to each of the five named grandchildren in equal and undivided shares, each share is considered to be a distinct parcel of ownership, which can in turn be transferred or sold or left by will to a third party. My share of the cottage would therefore go to my spouse and our two children according to my will, if I were to die. And my brother's share of the cottage could be left to the University of New Brunswick in accordance with the terms of his will, if he were to die. Each of our shares in the cottage is thus considered to be distinct from the shares of the other co-owners in the same property. This is referred to as co-ownership by *tenancy in common*.

When my wife and I purchased our house, however, we purchased it as *joint tenants, with right of survivorship*. This means that if either of us were to die, our share of the property would automatically transfer, or revert, to the other. If three people were to purchase property as joint tenants with right of survivorship, and one were to die, that person's share would revert to the other two remaining joint tenants. The size of each joint tenant's share thus increases as each of the other joint tenants dies, until the last surviving joint tenant will hold title to the entire property — hence the legal term, *joint tenancy with right of survivorship*. In a family context, it may make sense to purchase property in joint tenancy with right of survivorship, because my wife and I expect to live together for our lifetimes, and each probably expects to leave their property to the other on death. Moreover, if the property automatically transfers to my wife on my death, she will not have to pay any taxes on the transaction, as she would have to do in certain circumstances if I left her my share in the property by will. Joint tenancy with right of survivorship therefore corresponds with our presumed intentions in purchasing the property in co-ownership.

With my partners in the firm of architects, however, my intentions are probably very different. If I die, I presumably want my family to inherit the value of my share in the partnership assets. Consequently, it makes sense for partnership assets to be held, like the example of the family cottage, in equal and undivided shares in tenancy in common.

We can see from these simple examples that the concept of co-ownership is not as straightforward as it appears. The law permits us to utilize different forms of co-ownership in organizing our affairs with others. A third form of co-ownership is *condominium*, in which each 'owner' of a condominium unit purchases title to his or her unit, along with an equal and undivided share in tenancy in common with all the other unit owners in all of the common areas of the building or condominium complex. This means that each unit owner is also responsible, as co-owner with all the other condominium unit owners, for all repairs and maintenance to the commonly owned areas of the building or complex.

Co-ownership allows us to subdivide different ownership interests in the property horizontally, so to speak. But the law allows us even more flexibility than this in subdividing ownership interests in property. Let us say that my wife and I, having purchased our home, now intend to spend two years overseas, on a government or company posting. While we are away from Canada we decide to rent the house for two years to a young family who are just moving to Ottawa, and need to find a place to stay while they also look for a house to buy. What is the nature of our relationship with the young family who are renting our house? In legal terms, the relationship between us is one of a lease. My wife and I are the landlords, who hold the legal title to the property, while the young family are the tenants, who hold a leasehold interest in the property during the term of the lease. What the leasehold relationship allows us to do is to separate our *ownership* interest in the property from the right to *possession* of the property. The tenants are currently in possession of the property, while we retain the legal title to the property, what lawyers call the reversionary interest in the property, since the right to possession will revert to us as the landlords, or legal title holders, when the term of the lease is over.

Note that the right to possession is also regarded as a property interest in law. If someone were to trespass unlawfully on the property, it is not only my wife and I, as the owners of the property, who would be able to bring an action in trespass against the trespasser, but also the tenants, as the persons who are lawfully in possession of the property.[6] Indeed, in legal terms, it is the tenants, rather than the owners, who should bring the legal action against the trespasser, because trespass is considered to be an interference with another person's right to possession of property, which in this case, includes the tenants.

Moreover, it is not only against a trespasser, or other unlawful third party, that a tenant can maintain a legal action to protect their right to legal possession of the property. The tenant can also bring a legal action for possession against the landlord, if the landlord seeks to evict the tenant without proper cause during the term of the lease. Suppose that my wife and I spend one year of our two year posting abroad, and then decide to return home to Ottawa a year early, because we think the children will be better off at their old school, for example. Remember that we leased the property to the tenants for a period of two years. Can we give the tenants notice to quit the premises because we are returning to Ottawa after only one year, and need our house back? In law, the tenants have a right to exclusive possession of the property for a continuous term of two years under the term of the lease, provided they pay the rent and comply with the other terms and conditions of the lease. Even if we give the tenants notice of our intention to retake possession of the house, the tenants do not have to leave. Their right to exclusive possession of the property during the two year term of the lease takes priority in law over our need to move back into our house. Our reversionary right to regain possession of the property only applies once the lease has come to an end, or the tenants have given notice of their intention to leave, or the

---

6 See above, Chapter 4, at page 85.

tenants are in breach of the terms of the lease. The law protects the tenants' right to possession as well as the landlord's rights of ownership.

Much the same thing would apply in reverse if this time it was the tenants who wished to move before the two year term of the lease is over. Suppose that the young family who are renting the house find the perfect house at the right price, and decide to buy it. Can they give my wife and me notice that they intend to terminate the lease before the two year term is up? In legal terms, they are obligated to maintain possession of the property for the entire term of the lease. This means that their obligation to pay rent and comply with all the other terms of the lease continues throughout the full two year term of the lease. However, there is nothing to stop the tenants from further subdividing their own right to possession of the property by *subleasing* the property to another subtenant.[7] The subtenant is then a tenant of the head tenant, who is in turn the tenant of the original title holder. In this manner, the original tenant's right to exclusive possession of the property for the remaining term of the lease has been subdivided vertically, to create a new leasehold interest in the property. The diagrammatic relationship between the original landlord of the property, the tenant and the subtenant looks like this:

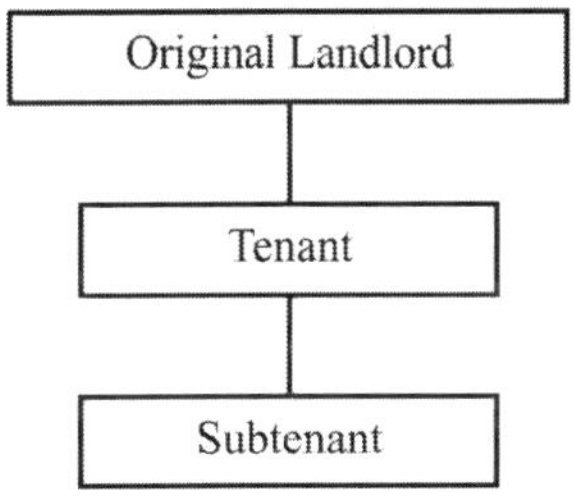

Note that the subtenant's right to exclusive possession under the terms of the sublease can never be greater than the right to possession of the original tenant who created the sublease. This means that if the original tenant fails to pay the rent on the original lease, or is otherwise in breach of any of the covenants in the lease, the original landlord would be legally entitled to bring an action to evict the head tenant from the premises, and thereby regain legal possession of the property, which would in turn have the effect of forcing the eviction of the subtenant. The subtenant's rights to possession of the property are therefore contingent on the rights of the head tenant. When the head tenant's right to possession of the property is

7 Many leases contain a term requiring the consent of the landlord before the tenant can sublease the premises. Otherwise, the landlord would have no control over who actually resides in the premises. Such a clause normally stipulates that the landlord cannot unreasonably refuse the request of the tenant to sublease the property.

extinguished, either because of non-payment of rent or because the original term of the lease has come to an end, the rights of the subtenant to possession of the property are also legally extinguished.

The use of leasehold agreements as a legal mechanism for subdividing the ownership interest in land from the right to possession of land is not restricted to residential tenancies such as the example given above. Many commercial properties are held under long term or short term leases, with consequences very similar to those already discussed. In England, much of the urban development which occurred in the nineteenth and twentieth centuries was based on ninety-nine year leases, under which the original title holder leased land to a developer for a period of ninety-nine years, who then built houses on the land and subleased the houses to individual subtenants. The subtenants paid rent (or a purchase price which amounted to a commuted rental payment) to the developer, who in turn paid rent to the head landlord, the underlying title holder of the land on which the houses were built. Similar long term leases of land for development purposes can be found in places in many cities in Canada. Once the ninety-nine year term of the lease is over, the reversionary interest of the developer in the land reverts back to the original title holder, as occurred in 1999 in Hong Kong, when the former British Colony reverted to the sovereignty of the Chinese Government. The original British colony in Hong Kong was founded on a long term lease from the Chinese Government which expired in 1999, forcing a legal reversion of the title and political control over the colony from the British Government back to China.

Another situation in which long term leases are used for development purposes occurs with oil and gas leases of Crown land. Companies bid on the right to explore for oil on certain segments of crown land. If successful, they can enter into a limited term lease from the Crown to drill for oil and gas on the leased premises, in return for payments of royalties and taxes to the federal or provincial government which has jurisdiction over the Crown land. When the term of the lease expires, the company can enter into negotiations with the federal or provincial (or territorial) government for renewal of the lease. If no agreement follows from the negotiations, the land can then be leased to a new tenant, or left as undeveloped Crown lands.

This illustration of the leasing of Crown lands for development purposes also points to another defining feature of Canadian property law, which is borrowed from English law. It has long been a feature of English property law, since the time of the Norman Conquest in 1066, that the underlying title to all the land in the realm is vested in the Crown, from whom all other titles to real property are derived. This legal doctrine is known as *the doctrine of tenures*, since its consequence is that all titles to real property are ultimately held from the Crown.[8] This means that there is no concept of absolute ownership of land in English or Canadian law. The largest claim to title in land which any individual or corporation can acquire is known as a title in fee simple. When my wife and I purchased our house in our joint names, therefore, we purchased the house as joint tenants in fee simple. Likewise, when the members of the partnership of architects purchased their office building, they purchased it as tenants in common in fee simple.

What we have seen so far, then, is that property rights in real property can be subdivided horizontally, through various forms of co-ownership. They can also be subdivided vertically, through entering into a leasehold or a sublease agreement, which separates the right to possession from the reversionary interest of the landlord to reclaim possession after the expiry of the lease. Another way of subdividing property interests in land or other assets vertically, is by creating what are known as future interests in the property. Let us say that a person might want to make a will leaving certain property for a limited period of time to one person, perhaps for their lifetime, and then transferring the property after that person's death, to another person or corporation. Perhaps I become very wealthy through my career as an architect. I purchase a restored heritage building in Kingston. My daughter lives in the house. But I would like to leave the heritage building to my *alma mater* after I die. Rather than evict my daughter from a beautiful house which she loves but could not afford to buy, I make a will leaving the house to my daughter for her lifetime, and then after her death to Queen's University. I have now created what is called a life interest in the property for my daughter, and a future interest in the property to the University, which is contingent on the death of my daughter. I could do much the same thing with my share of the family cottage inherited from my grandmother. I could leave my wife a life interest in my share of the family cottage during her lifetime (provided she survives my death, of course), with that share of the cottage then vesting in my two daughters (again as tenants in common, rather than as joint tenants with right of survivorship) after her death.

Future interests are also often created by means of a trust.[9] Let us say that my two daughters are still in elementary school, and I have just been diagnosed with cancer. Unless I am very fortunate, I will not survive to see my children finish school, much less go on to university, or begin their careers. But I would like to arrange my future financial affairs so that the children will have enough money available for them to go to college, or buy a house. So I set up a trust fund in their two names, under which

[8] *Tenire* is the Latin verb meaning 'to hold'.

[9] We will discuss the requirements of a trust in Chapter 6.

legal power to invest and manage the trust property is given to a trustee, to manage the property for the benefit of my two daughters (who are therefore called the beneficiaries of the trust), until they reach the age of twenty five. At that point, the trust terminates, and my two daughters will be entitled to full control over their share of the assets that have accumulated inside the trust. By means of a trust, therefore, I have effectively created a future interest for my two children. Their future legal entitlement to the funds contained within the trust is safeguarded by the terms of the trust itself, which provides that the funds invested within the trust shall be distributed in equal shares to my two daughters when they reach the age of twenty five.

It is clear from these examples that the simple equation of the concept of "property" with that of "ownership" is not flexible enough to encompass all the different types of property interests that the legal system may recognize in any one piece of real property, such as my house in Kingston, or even in the funds which I use to set up the trust fund in favour of my daughters. Legal theory recognizes a whole range of enforceable property rights that may amount to less than full ownership, but which nevertheless will be recognized and protected in the courts. This means that anything which is capable of being the subject of property rights may not only have more than one owner, as we have seen, but may also be subject to a variety of different, sometimes competing, property interests, held by different persons, at one and the same time.

In practice this means that we need to think about property rights not so much in terms of the ownership relationship between a person and a thing that may be owned by that person, but more in terms of the various types of relationships that may exist between different rights holders in relation to the same object of property. In other words, property rights under Anglo-Canadian law need to be understood in terms of relationships between different rights holders, rather than as absolute legal entitlements that are enforceable in any circumstances against all other claimants.[10]

Again, we will try to illustrate this point by using a relatively straightforward example, such as the purchase of a course textbook from the university bookstore. A book is an article of moveable personal property, and for the most part, identifying the range of possible property rights in such an article is relatively straightforward. Since the book I purchase costs less than fifty dollars, I pay cash for it, or else use a debit card or a credit card to finance the purchase. In either event, my title to the book is not qualified by any financing arrangement made with the bookstore or with any other third party. Even if I paid for the book by credit card, my obligation is to repay the amount of money borrowed from the bank on

---

[10] See the discussion in Bruce Ziff, *Principles of Property Law* (Toronto: Carswell, 1993), at 1-6.

my credit card at the end of the billing month. The fact that I used my credit card to pay for the book does not affect my legal title to the book. Nor did I purchase the book with another person, so my rights as the owner of the book are not shared with any co-owners.

Despite this, however, my property rights as the purchaser of the book are still qualified in a significant way by the rights of the person who holds the copyright over the contents of the book. Inside the title page of the book there is likely to be an indication as to who holds copyright over the material contained in the book, as well as a statement to this effect: "All rights reserved. No part of this publication may be reproduced, stored in any material form (including photocopying or storing it in any medium by electronic means) ... without the written consent of the copyright holder except in accordance with the provisions of the *Copyright Act*."[11] In effect, this means that my proprietary rights as the owner of the book are limited by the rights of the copyright holder over the contents of the book. I am not entitled to reproduce or copy the material contained in my book other than for the very limited purposes outlined in the federal Copyright Act. If I make a copy of a chapter in the book and try to sell it to another friend in the same course, I may be violating the intellectual property rights of another person in my own book!

What this means is that in legal terms the book cannot be thought of as a single object of property, with a single owner, myself. Instead, it is more accurate to think of the book as a nexus of various types of property interests, which co-exist in the hands of different rights holders.[12] For most purposes, my legal title to the book, and the copyright holder's rights to copyright in the contents of the book are not likely to be in conflict. It is only if I seek to duplicate or to publish the contents of the book without the copyright holder's permission, that my claim to property rights is likely to conflict with the legally enforceable claims of the copyright holder. In short, my purchase of the book does not give me exclusive rights to exercise unlimited control over the contents of the book. My rights as the legal owner of the book are limited by the legally protected rights of the copyright holder. And if we think about this for a minute, we will find that this is equally true of our rights as property owners of a music CD, a

---

[11] This statement is a modified form of the copyright statement found inside many commercially published books in Canada. The reference to the *Copyright Act* is to the *Copyright Act of Canada*, R.S.C. 1985, c. C-42, as amended.

[12] So, for example, the copyright holder might sell the copyright over the contents of the book to another person, or the copyright over the work might be transferred to the author's heirs, after the copyright holder dies. In other words, all the various kinds of interests in property which we have seen with respect to real property are equally applicable to forms of intangible personal property such as copyrights.

software program purchased from a computer store or downloaded from the internet, or even a farmer purchasing seed from a seed company.[13]

II. THE FUNCTIONS OF PROPERTY RIGHTS

This illustration of the use of copyright in published materials leads us into a discussion of the functions of property law. In his book, *Principles of Property Law*,[14] Bruce Ziff identifies two main functions of the law of property. One is concerned with resolving novel claims, such as the claim by the Harvard researchers at the beginning of this chapter to patent a mouse that they had bred in their laboratories for research purposes. The other is to allocate entitlements to scarce resources. Indeed, it may be useful for us to think of property rights as legal entitlements — that is, entitlements that the legal system will protect in a court of law. In this respect, property rules differ from the rules of criminal law, for example, or even the private law rules governing the formation of a contract, or the existence of a duty of care under the tort of negligence, that we have discussed in earlier chapters. The primary function of criminal law rules is to prohibit certain forms of socially undesirable behaviour, such as theft, or fraud or manslaughter; and to specify the sanctions that the law will impose upon those who commit such offences. In other words, criminal law rules regulate social behaviour. In a somewhat similar fashion, the private law rules of contract and tort are designed to regulate social behaviour, by specifying the legal requirements for entering into a contract, or the standard of care that one person is expected to exercise towards another in order to avoid being held liable in negligence. Once again, these private law rules establish a standard of behaviour (although in these instances the standard of behaviour is established by civil law rather than by criminal law), and specify the legal consequences that may follow as a result of failing to act in accordance with these legal standards.

Property law rules, however, are not so much concerned with regulating individuals' behaviour, as with regulating their access to or control over different types of resources. In the case of tangible resources such as land, or water, or moveable personal property, the rules governing access to and control over these resources are reasonably well settled (if not always uncontested). However, in the case of new or unfamiliar types of resources, courts and legislatures are often called upon to establish legal entitlements through property rules that may have far-reaching implications.

---

13 See *Monsanto Canada Inc. v. Schmeiser*, [2004] S.C.J. No. 29, [2004] 1 S.C.R. 902 (S.C.C.).

14 *Supra*, note 10, at 27-32.

In the case of the patent application for the Harvard Oncomouse,[15] for example, the researchers were claiming more than just a property entitlement to the mice they had bred in their laboratories as a tangible form of personal property, together with any offspring of those mice. Such a claim would be consistent with already existing property rules governing property entitlements over domesticated plants and animals. A farmer is entitled to the ownership of the crop that is harvested from the fields she sows; just as a cattle rancher has an enforceable property right not only to the animals in the herd as it exists at present, but also to the future offspring of that herd (including the product of cows that may have been artificially inseminated by the semen of another owner's bull).

The basis of the Harvard researchers' claim to a patent over the Oncomouse, however, was that they had genetically altered the cell structure of the Oncomouse to such an extent that they had "manufactured" or "invented" a new kind of "transgenic" mouse, one that had no origin in nature, and was entirely the product of their intellectual labour. The implications of this claim go far beyond that of the rancher to his cattle herd, or the farmer to her crop. The consequence of this claim, if accepted by the federal patent office, would be that the university and its researchers would be recognized as holding intellectual property rights not only in the process by which the genetic structure of the Oncomouse was transformed in the laboratory, but also over the product of this intellectual process, the transgenically altered DNA of the mouse itself.

It was this issue of the patentability of the mouse as an invention that was litigated all the way up to the Supreme Court of Canada. To its developers, the Oncomouse is just as much a mechanical invention of man as a mousetrap, and thus should be entitled to legal protection in the same way. To some observers, however, this claim amounts to nothing less than the right to play God — except that God was never so greedy, and did not claim any royalties from mankind after having created all the beasts of the field, the birds of the air, and all the fishes in the sea for man's benefit, as indicated in, say, the Bible! More significantly, to many ethicists, the nature of the Harvard researchers' claim to a patent over the Oncomouse implies that there is no longer any distinction between a mousetrap and a mouse, or between the works of nature and the works of man.

In a judgment delivered by Justice Bastarache, a slim majority of the Supreme Court of Canada ruled that the Oncomouse should not be included within the meaning of the words "art, process, machine, manufacture or composition of matter" under s. 2 of the *Patent Act*.[16] While the wording

15 *Supra*, note 1.

16 R.S.C. 1985, c. P-4.

of the *Patent Act* itself does not explicitly refer to the patenting of life forms, and thus does not expressly prohibit the patentability of transgenic material such as the Oncomouse, the majority held that the wording of the *Patent Act* should be interpreted in the light of Parliament's presumed intention not to permit the patenting of higher life forms, and thus refused the claim to a patent made by the Harvard researchers.[17]

The majority argued from the premise that the patenting of higher life forms gives rise to special concerns that do not arise in respect of the patenting of non-living inventions. So it should not be presumed that Parliament intended to permit the patenting of higher life forms when it enacted the wording of the present *Patent Act*. Moreover, higher life forms have unique qualities that transcend their physical composition, and this makes it difficult to conceptualize them as mere "compositions of matter" within the wording of s. 2 of the Act.[18] Any such legislative change should require explicit legislative approval by Parliament, not by the courts, whose role is to interpret the wording of the existing legislation in the context of its entire structure, and not to engage in a constructive lawmaking role by expanding the presumed reach of the legislation in the manner argued for by the respondent researchers.

A strong minority of the Court, however, reached the opposite conclusion, reasoning that as there was nothing in the wording of the legislation to indicate Parliament's intention to prohibit the patenting of life forms as new forms of invention, there was no basis for restrictively interpreting Parliament's intention to prevent the issuing of the patent. Indeed, the minority pointed out that the legislation does not permit the Director of Patents to refuse to grant a patent to a new invention on moral or ethical grounds, or other public policy concerns.[19] The only question to be considered by the Patent Office before issuing a patent is whether the invention or process with respect to which the application for a patent is made technically complies with the Act. If so, a patent should be issued, regardless of whether on ethical grounds the Director considers the requested patent to be in the public interest.

It is up to Parliament, therefore, to legislate as to whether the patenting of life forms should be restricted under the *Patent Act*. In the absence of any express legislative prohibition it should be presumed that Parliament intended to permit the patenting of new inventions of whatever kind, provided only that they satisfy the technical requirements of the *Patent Act*. The four judges in the minority on the Supreme Court of Canada therefore adopted a very different stance towards interpreting Parliament's intention

---

17 *Supra*, note 1.

18 *Ibid.*, *per* Justice Bastarache at 127.

19 *Ibid.*, *per* Justice Binnie, at 63.

than did the five judges in the majority. Instead of asking whether Parliament, in enacting the legislation, would have intended the provisions of the Act to apply to the patenting of higher life forms, the minority suggested that in the nature of things, Parliament could not have foreseen all the new forms of technological developments that could result in patent applications being brought under the Act. Consequently, the four judges in the minority started from the assumption that Parliament's intention in enacting the legislation was to encourage and promote new forms of technological innovation and inventions, without attempting to specify the kinds of uses to which such inventions might be put.

According to the minority, the scientific accomplishment in altering the genetic structure of the Oncomouse such that it is genetically programmed to develop cancerous tumours for research purposes is of considerable value in itself, and deserves patent protection. The purpose of the legislation is to promote private sector investment in new technological processes by rewarding the inventor with an exclusive legal entitlement to control the use of the patented invention, and to claim royalties from other users, for a limited period of time under the *Patent Act*. To refuse to grant patent protection to a valuable invention on the grounds of public policy should be the task of Parliament rather than the courts. Moreover, although this point was not expressly made in the minority decision, to refuse patent protection under these circumstances is to effectively grant the right to other researchers to benefit from the fruits of someone else's research and investment, without having shared in any part of the risk.[20]

It is apparent from this brief discussion that the legal issues raised by the application of existing property rules to new forms of technology are often complex and contentious. Underlying many of these technical legal questions it is possible to see a more fundamental debate over what should be the role of the courts in allocating rights to new forms of intellectual property. Should the courts apply a public policy test to screen new claims to property entitlements to determine whether they are in the public interest, as was the implicit approach of the majority of the Supreme Court of Canada in the recent Oncomouse decision? Or should the courts rely instead on the assumption that investment in technological innovation is inherently useful, and thus deserves the protection of intellectual property rights, as the minority of the Supreme Court seemed to imply?

Another of the underlying policy issues embedded in this ongoing legal debate has to do with the question of what is the most appropriate system of property entitlements for regulating access to new technological

---

[20] On this argument, see the article by Morris Cohen, "Property and Sovereignty", 13 *Cornell Law Quarterly* 8-30, which examines four main justifications for allocating property rights. See also B. Ziff, *supra*, note 10, at 6-26.

developments? Thus far, most of our discussion has focussed around the assumption that private property rules represent the most economically efficient and socially productive system for allocating entitlements to resources.[21] Yet a moment's reflection will show that this is not always the case. Many kinds of publicly owned resources such as Crown lands and forests, fisheries, provincial parks, public highways, even Indian reserves, are administered through different systems of property rules, which regulate access to and use of the resource on the basis of common or collective property entitlements.

The starting point of any system of private property is that the legal right to control access to the resource is allocated to private individuals through property rules.[22] The individual rights holder is thereby entitled to grant access to the resource to other potential users on terms stipulated by the rights holder; or to refuse access to other users at the will of the rights holder. In the case of private property rights over land, for example, the tort of trespass reflects the legal right of the person lawfully in possession of the land to refuse access to any unauthorized user, subject only to the interests of other property rights holders, such as a licensee, mortgagee, or the holder of an easement, for example, as we have seen earlier in this chapter.

By contrast, a system of common property rules does not seek to restrict access to or use of a resource to one privileged rights holder, as does a system of private property, but instead, starts from the premise that access to and use of the resource should be freely open to all members of the community.[23] In some respects, a system of common property can also be described as a system of no property, in the sense that no one person or rights holder is entitled to claim exclusive rights of access to or control over the resource that is communally owned.[24] In international law, for example, access to international waters is governed by the principle of freedom of the seas, which recognizes the rights of all maritime users to make use of international waterways without requiring the permission of any other state. Within a certain territorial limit, those waters that are adjacent to the territorial boundaries of a state are regarded as being within that state's exclusive territorial jurisdiction. Consequently, a state such as Canada has the right under international law to exert control over access to and use of its territorial waters by both Canadian and other maritime users. But outside the limits of any one state's exclusive territorial

---

[21] See Richard Posner, *Economic Analysis of Law (*Boston: Little Brown and Co., 1973), at 10-15; Ziff, *ibid.*; Cohen, *ibid.*

[22] See Jeremy Waldron, "What is Private Property?" (1985), *Oxford Journal of Legal Studies*, 318-44.

[23] *Ibid.*

[24] Ziff, *supra*, note 10, at 6.

(or economic) jurisdiction, international waters are governed as a common property regime, similar to public highways under domestic law, that are freely available to all members of the international maritime community. In other words, the international law of the sea is governed both by private property rules regulating uses of and access to territorial waters, and common property rules governing access to and use of international waterways. The system of private property rules and common property rules coexist within international law, in much the same way that private property rules and common property rules may co-exist within domestic Canadian law.

Interestingly, a patent is a form of intellectual property right that contains elements of both private property and common property systems at one and the same time. In essence, a patent gives the patent holder an exclusive right for a limited period of time to exercise control over the uses to which the patent may be made, and to require any licensees of the patent to pay a royalty to the patent holder. Once the patent expires, however, the exclusive private property right of the patent holder to claim a royalty from other users of the patent also expires, and the invention or process then becomes effectively the common property of all, in that any other user is now entitled to make use of the invention or process without requiring payment of any royalty to the original patent holder.

In the United States the developers of the Oncomouse were granted patent protection over both the process by which they succeeded in introducing a carcinogenic gene into the DNA structure of the Oncomouse, and also over the product of their research, the Oncomouse itself, on the basis of the precedent-setting United States Supreme Court decision in the case of *Diamond v. Chakrabarty*.[25] The Chakrabarty case involved an application to patent a genetically engineered bacterium that could be used to break down the chemical composition of oil, thus helping with the cleaning up of oil spills. The United States patent office originally accepted the patent application over the process for producing the bacterium, while rejecting the patent over the bacterium itself, expressing a similar concern about the patentability of living organisms as that reflected in the majority ruling by the Canadian Supreme Court in the Oncomouse decision. However, by a five to four majority, the United States Supreme Court ruled that the creation of genetically engineered living organisms was consistent with the policy of promoting useful inventions that underpins the patent

---

[25] *Diamond v. Chakrabarty*, 447 U.S. 303 (1980). The Oncomouse has also been held to be patentable in a number of other jurisdictions such as Austria, Belgium, Denmark, France, Germany, Greece, Italy, the Netherlands, Spain, Sweden and the United Kingdom.

legislation, and thereby opened the doors to the widespread patenting of genetically altered material by the biotechnology industry.[26]

In another related case, *Moore v. The Regents of the University of California*,[27] the issue was not so much the patentability of a new biotechnological process or product, but rather who had the better claim to a commercially valuable patent over a cell line that had been developed from a diseased human spleen? The case pitted the rights of a patient (Moore) whose spleen had been removed as part of a course of treatment against cancer, against those of the doctor who had surgically removed the diseased spleen with the patient's consent, and then used the organ in further research that led to the development of the cell line. The release form giving the patient's consent to the extraction of the diseased organ contained no express provision as to what should be done with the diseased spleen after extraction. In particular, the form gave no express consent for the use of the spleen in research after its extraction.

The patient subsequently learned that the university and the physician had obtained a patent on the cell line extracted from his tissue, and sued the university and the physician in damages, claiming breach of fiduciary duty and conversion. The basis of Moore's claim was that every person has a natural property right in their own body, and thus by extension over their own tissue. In signing the release form he had not consented to the use of his tissue for research purposes; nor had he expressly assigned or transferred his property rights in his spleen to the university or the doctor at the time of the operation. Consequently, he argued that the physician and the university were in breach of their fiduciary duty to Moore as their patient in using his spleen for research purposes without obtaining his prior consent. In addition, Moore argued that in using his spleen for research and extracting the cell line from his tissue, the physician and the university were making unauthorized use of his property for their own profit. Perhaps the best analogy to Moore's claim of conversion is that of a farmer sowing on someone else's field, and then claiming the resulting crop as their own. If anyone had a right to the crop (or the patented cell line), it should be he who owned the field, not they who sowed the seed.

In response, the university argued that by consenting to the organ removal, the patient implicitly surrendered or abandoned any property right he or she may have had to their organs prior to the removal. Consequently, there was nothing to prevent the doctor undertaking research on the

---

26 For a discussion of the *Chakrabarty* case and its impact on the development of the biotechnology industry see Fred Warshofsky, *The Patent Wars: The Battle to Own the World's Technology* (New York: John Wiley and Sons, 1994), at 207-09; also Gale R. Peterson, ed., *Understanding Biotechnology Law* (New York: Marcel Dekker Inc., 1993), at 7, 69.

27 *Moore v. The Regents of the University of California*, 271 Cal.Rptr. 146, 793 P.2d. 479 (1990).

medically removed tissue, or in applying for a patent on the cell line that was developed from Moore's spleen. Effectively, the university argued that the spleen, once removed from Moore's body with his consent, had no owner, and thus became the common property of all to use for whatever legitimate purpose they may choose. Moreover, the physician and the university also argued that in developing the cell line they had effectively created something new, that did not already exist in nature in this form, and thus was entirely the product of their own intellectual labour. On the basis of this argument, the physician and the university would be the sole claimants to intellectual property rights over the cell line, and Moore, the erstwhile possessor of the spleen, would be entitled to nothing.

In the event, it was this aspect of the university's legal argument that proved most persuasive to the California Supreme Court. By a five to two majority the Court ruled that Moore had no enforceable property right to any part of the defendants' "invention", and thus could not profit from the cell line. Part of the Court's reasoning was that to hold otherwise might have a negative effect on the supply of available tissue for medical research purposes. However, the Court did accept Moore's argument that a physician has a fiduciary obligation to obtain a patient's consent before using any tissue removed for research purposes. In this way the Court was able to balance the patient's right to privacy and autonomy by requiring consent for the use of tissue for research purposes, while still recognizing the intellectual property rights of the "inventors" of the cell line.

One of the judges who concurred with the majority was less concerned with protecting the rights of the biotechnology industry to make use of human tissue in research than with the moral or ethical concerns raised by the plaintiff's claim that he should be entitled to private property rights in his own organs, even after removal from his body. To Justice Arabian, this claim amounted to no less than the right to sell one's own body tissue for profit, a claim that opened up the spectre of a market in human body parts, with all of the likely negative societal and moral ramifications this would have. The ethical arguments against the commodification of human body parts thus weighed heavily against Moore's claim. Better that human tissue, once removed from the body, should be subject to a no-property rule, as claimed by the defendants, than that a market in human body parts be permitted by ruling in favour of the plaintiff's claim.[28]

[28] 271 Cal.Rptr. 146, at 164-65, *per* Justice Arabian.

III. PROPERTY RIGHTS AND PUBLIC INTEREST

Thus far we have looked briefly at the nature of property rights under Anglo-Canadian law, as well as the functions of property rights in allocating entitlements to resources. We have said little, however, about the related question of what limits should be placed on the rights of a property holder to make whatever uses he or she might choose with their own property? As we have seen, the nature of a system of private property entitlements is to give exclusive rights to the individual rights-holder to make whatever use he or she decides in relation to their own property, within the limits prescribed by law, or the rights of other individuals under contract, tort or property law.

The traditional common law conception of property was concerned with the protection of private rights, to the exclusion of public interests. Over the course of the past century, however, the traditional common law view of property rights as giving the holder absolute dominion over things, subject only to the rights of other property holders, has given way to increasing legislative encroachment on the rights of the private property holder to do what they will with their property. Thus, for example, public regulatory legislation such as municipal planning and zoning bylaws place significant restrictions on the types of uses any given property-holder can make of his or her land. A parcel of land outside a city that is zoned for agricultural purposes, for example, cannot be sold for development uses, even if the market price for the land if sold for development may be three or four times the price the land would fetch if sold for agricultural purposes. Zoning bylaws therefore place significant limitations on the economic uses to which the land may be put. Similarly, if I am the owner of a parcel of land in a city that is adjacent to a highway in need of widening, or which abuts onto land needed to expand the runways of a municipal airport, the city or the airport authority may have legal authority to expropriate my land for public purposes, if I do not agree to sell the land voluntarily.

The state's right to expropriate privately owned land for public purposes amounts to a power of forced confiscation, since the right to expropriate does not depend on the consent of the private owner. In terms of public law, the power to expropriate is subject only to the obligation to proceed for a legitimate public purpose as outlined in the enabling legislation; to act in accordance with the procedures laid down in the legislation; and the obligation to pay compensation to the individual or corporate property owners concerned. Moreover, if the power to expropriate is exercised consistently with the requirements of the relevant legislation, the former owner would have no legal recourse against the municipality or the airport authority even if the land is not immediately used for the purpose for which it was expropriated, and instead is left vacant for a number of years.

Alongside these explicit legislative powers of state intervention into the economic uses I can make of my land, there may be many other forms of regulatory controls on the uses to which the land may be put. If I have a building on my land that is well insured, and which I no longer need, I am not entitled to burn my building down in order to collect the insurance money. Nor am I allowed to set fire to my own building just for the pleasure of watching it burn, or to change its use, if I no longer have a use for the building in its present form. Deliberately setting fire to my own property under these circumstances could result in my being charged with the criminal offences of arson or fraud. Likewise, building codes and environmental laws may require me to keep my building in repair, or impose limits on my ability to use my land as a landfill site, or to emit noxious gases into the atmosphere. Failure to comply with these regulatory obligations may result in prosecution, or even seizure and sale of the land itself if, for example, I fail to pay my property taxes on the land as required by law. (And as with the case of the power of expropriation referred to earlier, I have no right at law to withhold my property taxes on the grounds that I do not concur with the uses to which my property taxes may be put.)

In addition to these public regulatory controls over land use, the rules of private law may also require me to act in such a way as not to injure the rights of my neighbours. Thus, if I am a householder, I have an obligation to take reasonable care to avoid any foreseeable risk of injury to others that may result from any state of disrepair of the premises. If, for example, I knowingly fail to repair a loose tile on my roof, which then falls and injures a passer-by, or even another member of my own family, I could be held liable in damages to that person in negligence. Likewise, if I have a dangerous dog on my premises that bites someone who comes on to the property, I may be held liable in damages to the person who suffers the injury, even if that person comes on the land without my permission. The law does not allow me to take whatever measures I may choose to deter others from coming unlawfully onto my land. Consequently, I could be held liable under civil law for creating a foreseeable risk that results in injury to a trespasser on my land, such as a snowmobiler who is injured as a result of driving through an invisible wire fence.[29] Moreover, my use of a weapon against an intruder could also result in my being charged with a criminal offence, notwithstanding any criminal intention on the part of the person who unlawfully breaks into my property. There is no right to self-defence of property under criminal law as there is to self-defence of the person.

29 *Veinot v. Kerr-Addison Mines Ltd.*, [1974] S.C.J. No. 99, [1975] 2 S.C.R. 311 (S.C.C.).

The legal system, therefore, not only gives rights to a property-holder, but also imposes obligations on the property-holder, both under private law and under public law. One case which addressed the obligations that a private property owner may owe towards his or her neighbours under the law of nuisance is the case of *Palmer v. Nova Scotia Forest Industries.*[30] In this case the plaintiffs sought an injunction to prevent the defendant forestry company from spraying herbicides on a number of forest properties, which were partly Crown-owned and partly owned by the defendant corporation. The plaintiffs were neighbouring property owners who were concerned about the possible health risks posed by the defendant's proposed spraying programme, which was intended to remove hardwood groundcover that would impede the growth of more commercially valuable coniferous trees. The plaintiffs framed their legal claim in private nuisance, alleging that the risks of water and soil contamination from the chemical defoliants used by the defendant amounted to an interference with their own use and enjoyment of their land.

The case, therefore, pitted the rights of one set of property holders (the plaintiff) against the rights of another set of property holders (the defendants). As we saw in Chapter 4, the tort of nuisance is applicable in a situation where one property owner uses their own land in such a way as to interfere with the reasonable enjoyment of another neighbour's property. If I own a garden plot next to your residential property I cannot dump a load of pig manure on my lot where it would interfere with your access to your front door. Even though the pig manure is on my property, so there is no trespass involved, my dumping of pig manure may interfere with your reasonable enjoyment of your property, and so may amount to a nuisance. Nor should you respond by deliberately placing the outdoor speakers on your stereo facing over my property, so you can annoy me by playing loud rap music whenever I come to weed my garden and escape the hustle and bustle of everyday life. Each action involves a private nuisance for which a legal remedy in damages or the equitable remedy of injunction may lie.

The herbicide case involved an application for an anticipatory, *quia timet* injunction to prevent the defendants from acting in such a way as to interfere with the plaintiffs' rights to enjoyment of their property. Such a claim requires the plaintiffs to establish a sufficient probability of damage to the plaintiffs by the defendant's proposed action to justify the court in issuing the injunction. The objective of the injunction, therefore, is to prevent the anticipated damage or injury from occurring. In evidentiary terms, the onus of proof rests on the plaintiffs to establish to the satisfaction of the court that the anticipated damage will occur, since the effect of the

---

[30] *Palmer v. Nova Scotia Forest Industries*, [1983] N.S.J. No. 534, 2 D.L.R. (4th) 397 (N.S.S.C. (T.D.)).

injunction is to prevent the defendant from doing that which he or she would otherwise be legally entitled to do on their land. In the present case, the defendants had obtained the necessary licences to spray from the provincial government for the herbicides in question, and thus were doing nothing illegal by spraying the herbicides on the forest properties that were the subject of the lawsuit.

The case involved 23 days of oral evidence and arguments, as well as reams of documentary evidence from experts on both sides. The defendants' position was that the spraying programme was approved by the Ministry of the Environment, the herbicides were not prohibited, and the herbicides were used in such low concentrations as to pose no significant health risks to humans or animals. In other words, the defendants argued that they were in full compliance with the applicable public law regulations governing the management of forest properties. The plaintiffs argued, on the other hand, that the scientific evidence relied on by the defendants to show no health risks to humans was inconclusive and largely sponsored by industry. Some studies had shown a link between uses of the herbicides and increased risk of birth abnormalities in children delivered by women who had been exposed to the herbicides during their pregnancy, or earlier. And there was nothing to show that the herbicides could not accumulate in sufficient levels of toxicity over time to result in significantly increased risks of cancer and other health problems. In view of these concerns, the plaintiffs argued that the herbicides should be banned from use by the issuance of an injunction, especially since there were other less environmentally damaging ways of managing hardwood growth that were available to the defendants.

After reviewing all the evidence on both sides, the judge ruled in favour of the defendants' position. The judge ruled that the plaintiffs had not satisfied the evidentiary onus to demonstrate a strong probability of serious health risks resulting from the spraying programme, not simply a possibility of harm. In contrast to the plaintiff's argument that in cases of doubt, the better approach is to prevent the potential risk from occurring until it can be proven to be free of risk, the court found that this would be impracticable and an undue interference with the defendant's rights. Unless a strong probability of harm can be shown to result from the defendant's activities, the defendant should not be inhibited from making whatever use of their property they consider to be most beneficial. Moreover, the judge observed that it was not the function of the court in a private nuisance case to effectively oversee the decisions of public regulators who had approved the spraying programme.[31] In the event, therefore, the court's ruling protected the privacy and autonomy of individual property holders

---

[31] *Ibid.*, at 500, *per* Justice Nunn.

(including the holders of crown leases to cut wood on crown lands) to make their own decisions regarding the use or exploitation of their property, unless there is a clear interference with the rights of other individuals, or a violation of public laws designed to protect the environment.

In the Palmer case, the judge adopted a relatively traditional view of the conceptual boundary between public and private law. By contrast, the question of where to draw the line between the private rights and the public obligations of a property owner was at the centre of the Supreme Court of Canada decision in the case of *Harrison v. Carswell.*[32] The case involved an application by the commercial owner of a shopping mall to remove some picketers from the public space of the mall, where they were picketing as part of a labour dispute with their employer, the tenant of one of the stores in the mall. The employees claimed the right to picket outside the door of the store operated by their employer, which was within the mall premises. Under provincial labour law, employees involved in a lawful strike or lockout have the right to picket the employer's premises in order to inform the public about the nature of the labour dispute. The objective of the picketers is to bring economic pressure to bear on the employer by seeking to encourage other customers or persons doing business with the employer to take their business elsewhere. Provided the picketers act in a non-violent manner, and confine their activities to providing information to other persons, rather than trying to restrict their right of entry onto the employer's premises, there is no cause for interference with the picketers' rights under labour law.

As a result, the tenant who operated the store had no right to call the police to ask the picketers to cease their picket and move. However, the owner of the shopping mall was under no such restriction under labour law, since the owner was not a party to the employment relationship. The owner therefore gave notice to the picketers, requiring them to leave the premises of the shopping mall, and sought an application to have them removed under the provisions of the Manitoba *Petty Trespasses Act.*[33] The defendant picketer sought to challenge the right of the owner of the shopping mall to evict the picketers, arguing that this amounted to a violation of their right to picket peacefully, under provincial labour law.

The case proceeded all the way to the Supreme Court of Canada, which had recently heard a similar case involving the rights of a public advocacy group to maintain a consumer boycott outside the premises of a grocery store in a commercial shopping mall.[34] The majority of the Supreme Court handed down a decision consistent with the Court's previous ruling in

---

32 *Harrison v. Carswell*, [1975] S.C.J. No. 73, 62 D.L.R. (3d) 68 (S.C.C.).

33 R.S.M. 1970, c. P-50.

34 *R. v. Peters* (1971), 17 D.L.R. (3d) 128n (S.C.C.).

R. v. Peters, which upheld the right of the mall owner to evict the picketing workers. According to the majority judgment of Justice Dickson, the rights of a private property holder to exercise control over who is entitled to enter onto or remain on the property should take priority over the defendant's rights under labour law. The plaintiff's right to maintain control over its property was enacted into law in the form of the Manitoba *Petty Trespasses Act*, which made no special exception for public access to commercial shopping malls. Consequently the owners were within their rights to evict the picketers, despite the fact that the picketers were not interfering with the rights of other mall users. It was not up to the court to engage in any exercise of balancing the rights of a property owner against the right of picketers. Such a task should be left to Parliament, rather than the courts, according to the majority decision in the case.

In his dissenting judgment, however, Justice Laskin took a very different approach to the facts of the case. Instead of categorizing the mall as a form of private property, akin to a private house or a farm, Justice Laskin suggested that a modern shopping mall was more akin in functional terms to the medieval idea of a public market.[35] At common law, a public market or inn was governed by a different set of property rules than a privately occupied dwelling, to which access was typically restricted and controlled by the property-owner. In a market or an inn, the right of common access took priority over the right to private control. In other words, a market was regarded as a form of "common" or quasi-public property to which the public had a right of access, even if the land occupied by the market was privately owned. The owner or occupier of the land on which the market was held therefore did not have an unfettered right to restrict access to the public, but would have to show good cause before removing any member of the public from the market.

Justice Laskin viewed a modern shopping mall as functionally equivalent to these old common law exceptions to the law of trespass. A shopping mall functions by inviting entry to all members of the public. This may include small children, entertainers, or other persons who have no intention to shop in the stores in the mall. Therefore, the public's implicit license to enter onto the mall premises should be subject only to a corresponding obligation not to cause a breach of the peace or injure or interfere with the rights of other mall users.

From this perspective, the actions of the picketers represented a legitimate use of the mall premises. The picketers were not accused of any breach of the peace or interfering with the rights of others. The person most affected by the employees' actions, their employer, had no legal right to complain about the picketers' behaviour. So why should the owner of the

---

[35] *Harrison v. Carswell*, *supra*, note 32, at 75.

mall have any right to complain about their behaviour? Provided the picketers stay within the law, the owner's right to evict them should be limited. According to Justice Laskin, using the law of trespass to control access to a shopping mall is inconsistent with the very nature of a shopping mall, which is based on inviting entry to the public, rather than restricting entry only to authorized users.[36]

The effect of this analysis was to place the relative rights and obligations of the shopping mall owner and the picketers onto a very different footing. Instead of implicitly privileging the property rights of the owner over and above the legitimate interests of all other users of the mall, Justice Laskin's approach required a balancing of the rights of the owner with the interests of others. An owner of a shopping mall needs the power to exercise control over the mall premises, in everyone's interest. But that power should not be untrammeled. Indeed, the implication of this analysis is that the mall owner is under a quasi-public obligation to promote public access to the mall, rather than the majority's more traditional view that the public is only invited onto the premises at the will or consent of the owner.

The irony of this decision is that while Justice Laskin's view did not prevail in the Court, it did prevail in the legislature. Very soon after the Supreme Court decision was handed down, the Manitoba legislature amended the *Petty Trespasses Act* to preclude its application to certain types of commercial space such as a shopping mall or an industrial park, where similar types of concerns may apply with equal, if not more, force.

Moreover, Justice Laskin's view of the relative rights and obligations of property owners and users of a shopping mall has come to exemplify the relationship between many owners and users of privately owned property. Under provincial human rights law, for example, a shopping mall owner would not be entitled to deny access to the mall to any person by reason of their race, or their gender, or religious affiliation, or sexual orientation, or other similar prohibited grounds of discrimination. The rights of a private owner to do as he or she wills with his or her own property in such circumstances are clearly subordinate to legislation protecting employees or other members of the public from prohibited forms of discrimination. Similarly, a landlord of a privately owned residential building does not have the right to refuse to rent to an individual or family on the basis of their race, their creed, their family status, or sexual orientation, etc. Nor can a landlord evict a tenant at will, even where the tenant is in breach of their obligations under the lease, without giving sufficient notice and showing good cause. Otherwise the eviction will be unlawful. The enactment of human rights laws, therefore, along with other legislation such as tenant protection laws, does impose obligations on an

---

[36] *Ibid.*, at 73, 75.

owner or occupier of private property that are almost in the nature of quasi-public obligations, alongside the rights that are allocated by the law of property.

The implications of Justice Laskin's view about the need to balance competing rights claims in relation to access to private property were further explored in the case of *Ontario (Attorney General) v. Dieleman.*[37] This case involved an application by the Attorney General of Ontario for an injunction to restrain the activities of anti-abortion protestors outside a number of privately operated clinics and publicly funded hospitals providing abortion services in Ontario. The Attorney General sought an injunction to prevent any public anti-abortion protests within 500 feet of the clinic locations. It was claimed that the activities of the anti-abortion protestors, in carrying placards and handing out leaflets with graphic pictures of aborted fetuses, and seeking to provide sidewalk "counseling" to women seeking to enter the facility in order to have an abortion, constituted a public nuisance that interfered with the legal right of access to abortion services guaranteed by the Supreme Court decision in *R. v. Morgentaler.*[38]

Unlike the *Harrison v. Carswell* case, the activities of the anti-abortion protestors did not take place on private property, but on publicly owned sidewalks adjacent to the entrance to the abortion facilities.[39] Anyone working at one of the clinics, or entering the clinic in order to have an abortion procedure, would be confronted with the chants, placards and leaflets of the anti-abortion protestors close to the entrance to the clinic. It was argued on behalf of the anti-abortion groups that they were simply exercising their constitutionally protected rights to freedom of expression and to freedom of assembly on public property. While abortion may have been legalized by the decision of the Supreme Court in *R. v. Morgentaler*, the legal right of those groups opposed to abortion to articulate their moral objections in public should be equally protected by the Charter of Rights and Freedoms.

While recognizing the constitutionally protected right to freedom of expression in any public forum such as sidewalks or public parks, the court observed that this right is not absolute, but must be exercised in a manner that is compatible with the rights of other citizens, and with the function of the location in which the message is presented. In particular, the right to freedom of expression in a public forum necessarily implies the right of other citizens *not* to listen to the message being presented. For this reason, courts have been more prepared to restrain public protestors

---

[37] *Ontario (Attorney General) v. Dieleman*, [1994] O.J. No. 1864, 20 O.R. (3d) 229 (Ont. Gen. Div.).

[38] *Supra*, Chapter 1 at notes 3-4, [1988] S.C.J. No. 1, 44 D.L.R. (4th) 385 (S.C.C.).

[39] As a result, the case was brought as an action in public nuisance, rather than in private nuisance or trespass.

from using forms of public transport such as buses or subway trains as a forum for presenting their political ideas, since the passengers on buses or subways or railway carriages provide a "captive audience" who do not have the opportunity to not listen to the message presented. In the context of the access to private abortion clinics in particular, the court felt that protesters were targeting women using the clinics, as well as physicians and nurses working in the clinics, as a "captive audience" who had no opportunity not to listen to the anti-abortion protesters' message. By contrast, users of publicly funded, multi-use hospital facilities, with several entrances, often set back from public streets, were unlikely to be targeted or held "captive" in the same way as the users of single-use private clinics. In this context, the court felt that the privacy interests of citizens in pursuing their own lawfully protected activities, such as the emotionally and psychologically sensitive decision to have an abortion, were also constitutive aspects of the freedoms and liberties of the citizen within a liberal democratic society. Consequently, targeting the users of privately operated and single use abortion clinics with free sidewalk "counseling" services offered to women prior to entering the clinics was viewed by the court as *prima facie* evidence of an unlawful interference with the rights of the women using the clinic's services, at a time, and in a location in which they were likely to be extremely vulnerable.

In the event, the court granted limited injunctive relief over the activities of the anti-abortion groups. The court ruled that publicly funded hospital facilities with multiple uses and multiple entrances did not require additional legal protections which would interfere with the lawful rights of the protestors to present their side of the emotionally charged abortion debate. For the privately operated, single purpose abortion clinics, however, the court ruled that there should be a protective privacy zone, some 30 to 60 feet in width from the entrance to the facility, in which anti-abortion protesters could not picket or offer counseling services to users of the clinics, or to workers at the clinics; and a further 100 foot buffer zone in which anti-abortion protesters could not voluntarily approach any user of the clinic, or clinic worker, where that person had made it clear that they did not want to hear the message of the anti-abortion protesters. In this way, the court protected the rights to freedom from harassment of those people using and working in the clinics in a way that arguably extended the traditional boundaries of the privacy sphere of private property. In a curious inversion from Justice Laskin's dissenting opinion in *Harrison v. Carswell*, which held that the common spaces in a privately owned shopping mall should be viewed as quasi-public property, the effect of the court's decision in *Ontario (Attorney General) v. Dieleman* was that the public space surrounding the boundaries of a privately owned abortion clinic should be viewed as quasi-private property.

Chapter 6

Relations Based on Trust and Confidence

I. THE ROLE OF EQUITY

In considering relationships based on trust and confidence as a separate category of private law relationships we first need to know something about the historical role of equity in English law, and how the courts of equity ameliorated the harshness of the common law. In medieval England there arose not one but two systems of royal justice. One was administered in the King's courts, and came to be known as the common law, while the other was developed in the Lord Chancellor's court, the court of Chancery, and came to be known as equity.

The equitable jurisdiction of the Chancery court derived from the Lord Chancellor's official role as the keeper of the King's "conscience". Where the King's courts could not give justice to a petitioner, the petitioner might bring his case before the Lord Chancellor and ask for a remedy in equity. Suppose, for example, that the Lord of a manor needed to borrow a sum of money which he could not immediately repay. The lender of the money might demand that the title to the lands be transferred to the lender as a security for the money lent. In this way, if the value of the lands was greater than the amount of the loan, the lender was assured of receiving the land even if the debt could not be repaid. The problem for the borrower was how to ensure that the title to the lands that was conveyed to the lender as security for the loan would be reconveyed back to the borrower when the loan was repaid.

In strict legal terms, once the title to the land had been conveyed to the lender, the lender was now the owner of the land, or the estate holder, as the common law would see it. In the eyes of the common law, however, the lender's obligation to reconvey the lands back to the borrower once the loan had been repaid was viewed only as a *moral* obligation, or an obligation of conscience, rather than a formal legal obligation that the common law would enforce. Consequently, the borrower could not sue in the King's courts for the return of his lands, since the common law did not recognize his legal right to redeem his title to the land. The borrower might then present a petition to the Lord Chancellor, on the grounds that the lender's conduct, in refusing to reconvey title to the lands after the debt had been repaid, went against conscience. If the Chancery court believed the evidence of the petitioner, the court would order the lender to reconvey the lands back to the borrower, or else face imprisonment for contempt of court.

In this manner, courts of equity began to create new equitable remedies based on relationships of trust and conscience that went beyond the purview of the common law courts.

The illustration we have just discussed, for example, involves the creation of a mortgage relationship between lender and borrower. Mortgages were unknown to the common law, and were only enforceable in equity. To this day we still use the language which the courts of equity developed in the middle ages to describe the equitable interest which the borrower, or mortgagor, retains in the land conveyed by the mortgage. It is called the borrower's "equity of redemption" — that is, the right of the borrower to redeem the land conveyed by way of security for the loan once the principal and interest outstanding on the loan have been fully paid off. We even use this same language to describe the value of a borrower's residual financial interest in a house or other piece of real estate which is subject to a mortgage — we call it the value of the homeowner's "equity" in the property.

Until the second half of the nineteenth century, courts of equity were physically separated from courts of common law, so that a claim for an equitable remedy had to be made in a court of equity, while a claim recognized at common law had to be brought before the common law courts. This resulted in procedural difficulties where a common law claim involved a defence recognized by a court of equity but not by a court of common law. This situation endured until 1875 in England, and 1881 in Ontario, when the separate courts of common law and equity were replaced by a unified high court which had jurisdiction both at common law and in equity. Moreover, in the case of any conflict between the two systems of law, the statutes which provided for the merger of the two courts (known as the Judicature Acts)[1] also provided that equity should prevail.

We can see instances of the courts' equitable jurisdiction in many areas of private law. In the law of contract, for example, the remedies of specific performance and injunction were originally remedies that could only be granted by courts of equity. The common law courts would only give a remedy in damages in the event of a breach of contract, and could not force the party in breach to comply with their obligations under the contract. But the courts of equity were under no such constraint, and could require a defendant in breach of contract to perform the specific terms of

---

[1] In Ontario, for example, the relevant statute is the *Courts of Justice Act*, R.S.O. 1990, c. C.43, s. 96(1). Each jurisdiction in Canada has legislation to like effect.

the contract in circumstances where an award of financial damages alone would be inadequate.

Likewise, the remedy of rescission for misrepresentation is an equitable remedy. The courts of equity would permit rescission of a contract that had otherwise lawfully been entered into between two parties where one party had made a material misrepresentation to the other, which induced that person to enter into the contract. Because of the misrepresentation, the courts of equity would not allow the party making the misrepresentation to benefit from their full contractual rights. For example, if a person selling a car alters the odometer to make a buyer think that the car has a lower mileage than in fact it has, this will be viewed as a fraudulent misrepresentation that allows the buyer of the car to rescind the contract and obtain his or her money back.[2] Moreover, the courts have held that the buyer's remedy of rescission for misrepresentation may still be available even if the contract itself contains a term which states that the buyer has read all the terms of the contract and fully understands that there were no legal representations, warranties, or guarantees made by the seller with regard to the condition or the mileage of the car. If this were not the case, the buyer would have no legal remedy against the seller even though he or she had been deliberately misled by the seller's actions into buying a car that he or she would not otherwise have bought.

In this simple illustration we can see an example of the court's jurisdiction in equity taking precedence over the strict legal rights of the parties at common law. As we have seen, the underlying assumption behind the common law view of contractual relationships is that both parties are regarded as autonomous, self-determining actors who are capable of looking after their own legal interests when entering into a contract. From this perspective, when one party signs a contract that contains a clause stating that he or she has read the contract and understands its terms, and accepts that there are no legal representations, statements or warranties made by the other party with respect to the contract terms, then the wording of the contract itself would seem to prevent the "innocent" party from suing the party making the misrepresentation. However, equity does not always view contractual relations through the same liberal individualist prism as the common law. Instead, equity may sometimes view the relationship between the two parties to the contract in very different terms, as a relationship in which one party seeks to take advantage of, or exploit, a legal position of power at the expense of the other party, in circumstances in which this would be unconscionable to the court.

---

[2] See above, Chapter 3, "Private Law Relations Established by Agreement", and below, Chapter 7, "Private Law Remedies".

Clearly it would be unconscionable for the seller of a car to deliberately mislead the buyer by rolling back the vehicle's odometer, and then to rely on the terms of the contract itself in order to prevent the innocent buyer from complaining about the fraud! So in these circumstances, equity permits the innocent purchaser to rescind the contract, notwithstanding anything to the contrary in the wording of the contract itself. Similarly, where one party induces the other to enter into a one-sided contract through the exercise of undue influence or where there is clear evidence of inequality of bargaining power between the two contracting parties, equity will intervene to prevent the stronger party from exercising an "unconscionable" legal advantage over the weaker party.[3]

In each of these different legal contexts, the equitable jurisdiction of the court fulfils a kind of watchdog or supervisory function to ensure that one party does not take advantage of their position of legal power or authority to benefit themselves unlawfully, or "unconscionably", at the expense of the other party. To this extent, equity provides a form of restraint on the exercise of private legal power within many kinds of private law relationships based on exchange, or duty, or property relations. In addition to this general equitable jurisdiction in the field of private law, however, the courts also recognize a number of special equitable relationships based on trust and confidence in which a positive legal duty is placed on the person in a position of trust to account for the manner in which they exercise that trust.

II. PROPERTY RELATIONSHIPS BASED ON TRUST

One such situation is the relationship that exists between a trustee and a beneficiary under a trust. The concept of a trust is a very old concept in English law. As with the development of the mortgage, discussed at the beginning of this chapter, the idea of a trust does not originate from English common law, but was developed by courts of equity. In essence, a trust can be defined as a property relationship in which one person (the *trustee*) is granted legal powers to manage, invest or dispose of property (the *trust property*) on behalf of, or for the *benefit* of, another person or persons (the *beneficiary or beneficiaries*, of whom, curiously enough, the trustee may also be one!).[4]

---

3 See, for example, *Lloyd's Bank v. Bundy*, [1974] 3 All E.R. 757, discussed in Chapter 3, notes 5 and 6 and accompanying text.

4 See generally D.W.M. Waters, *Law of Trusts in Canada*, 2nd ed. (Toronto: Carswell, 1984); Mark R. Gillen and Faye Woodman, eds., *The Law of Trusts: A Contextual Approach.* (Toronto: Emond Montgomery, 2000).

The chief characteristic of a trust relationship is the fact that the legal power to manage or dispose of the trust property is vested in the trustee, while the underlying *equitable or beneficial* interest in the trust property is held by the beneficiaries of the trust. The trustee is then under a legal duty to exercise his or her powers of management or disposal of the trust property exclusively in the *best interests* of the beneficiary or beneficiaries of the trust.

A simple example of a trust relationship might be a grandparent who sets up an investment account in trust for his or her young grandchildren, as a way of setting aside enough money to pay for their college education. While the children are still at school, the amounts in the trust fund are invested on their behalf by the trust company that is given the powers of trustee over the funds in the account. The grandparent (the *settlor* of the trust) may have given specific instructions to the trustee as to how the trust funds should be invested (for example, only in low-risk government bonds, or in secure, dividend-paying stocks like banks and telephone companies; but not in speculative, high-risk technology shares). The trustee is then empowered to invest the funds in the account in accordance with these instructions, but may not disregard the settlor's specific instructions, or use the funds for the trustee's own benefit. The accumulated funds in the trust account constitute the trust property, while the beneficiaries of the trust are the two minor grandchildren for whose benefit the trust has been created.

The above example is an instance of a trust that is created through the express intention of the settlor (the person who creates the trust, and settles money or other property in the form of a trust). For this reason such a trust is referred to as an *express trust*. One of the benefits of creating an express trust is that the terms of the trust, and the obligations of the trustee, will be clearly expressed in a formal declaration of trust. In most situations, therefore, there is likely to be little doubt over the intentions of the settlor, the extent of the property that is subject to the trust, or the identification of the beneficiaries when setting up such an express trust. Many financial institutions use standard form declarations of trust for just this purpose.

Another situation in which a trust-like relationship comes into existence as a result of the express instructions of an individual occurs when a person leaves a will naming another person as the executor of the will. Let us suppose that a parent has made a will naming her eldest daughter as the executor of the will, and leaving the estate (that is all the assets owned by the parent at the time of her death, after all outstanding debts and taxes have been paid by the executor) to be divided equally among her four adult children. In these circumstances, following the death of the parent who made the will, the eldest daughter, as executor, is required to manage the estate on behalf of all four beneficiaries (herself and her three siblings) to ensure that all assets are accounted for, and all debts and taxes paid, before the remaining assets are paid out to the four beneficiaries, under the supervision of the probate court. The executor thus acts as a trustee of the estate, and must act in the best interests of all four beneficiaries of the will. She cannot use her powers as executor to transfer the most valuable assets to her own children, or to hide them in a separate account under her own or an assumed name. If she attempts to do so, she will be held liable to account for the missing or misappropriated funds to the other beneficiaries of the will. In effect, she will have acted in breach of trust.

Once again, the above example is a situation in which the powers of the executor to manage the estate in the best interests of the beneficiaries of the will has been expressly created by a specific clause in the will appointing the eldest daughter as executor. There may be circumstances, however, in which a trust relationship is created not through express agreement, but by implied agreement between two or more parties, or where the court presumes the existence of an implied intention to create a trust relationship on the part of a settlor. This type of trust is referred to as an *implied* or *resulting trust* since the trust relationship comes about as a result of the implied intention of the settlor. An example of a resulting trust would be a situation in which two persons involved in a business relationship both invest money in the purchase of a commercial building, but title to the property is held in the name of only one of the investors. In these circumstances, the courts presume that the "silent investor" in the commercial investment intended to retain a beneficial interest in the investment, even if their name does not appear on the title deeds to the property. Consequently, the court will infer the existence of a resulting trust between the parties, even where there is no evidence of a formal trust agreement between them.

What this means in practice is that the investor in whose name the title to the property is registered cannot act as if he is the sole owner of the property. Even though to the outside world the property is registered in the name of Evans, for example, a court of equity will require Evans to exercise his legal powers as title holder of the property on behalf of both himself and Singhal, the other silent investor. While in law Evans may be entitled to sell or mortgage the property to a third party without requiring the consent of Singhal; in equity this action by Evans may amount to a breach of trust (depending on the terms of his prior agreement with Singhal), for which Evans may be held liable to account to Singhal for any losses suffered by Singhal as a result of the unauthorized transaction. Most obviously, Evans would be prohibited by a court of equity from selling or mortgaging the property to a third party, and then absconding with the money without accounting to Singhal for his share of the proceeds of the sale or mortgage.

In this situation we can see that courts of equity view the relationship between a trustee and the beneficiary of a trust in quite different terms than the way in which the common law normally views the relationship between two autonomous legal actors entering into a business or exchange relationship. Instead of viewing the two parties to the business relationship as if they are autonomous, self-interested, rational actors, each of whom is presumed to be motivated to look after their own self-interests over the interests of others, equity imposes what we might call an *obligation of altruism* on the trustee to act in the best interests of the beneficiary. The obligation of altruism imposes a positive legal duty on the trustee to place the interests of the beneficiary above his or her own self-interest. Failure to place his or her own self-interest aside and to act in the best interests of the beneficiary, will leave the trustee liable in equity to the beneficiary for breach of trust.

We have already encountered a number of other situations in which equity imposes an obligation of altruism on one legal person to act in the best interests of another. Perhaps the most common situation occurs in the context of family relations, particularly the relation between parent and child, or between legal guardian and ward.[5] As with the relationship between trustee and beneficiary, in a parent-child or guardian-ward relationship, one party to the relationship is accorded the legal authority to act or to make decisions on the other party's behalf. Equity therefore imposes a positive legal duty on the part of the parent or the guardian to set aside their own self-interest and to exercise their legal authority over the child or ward in a manner which is consistent with the best interests of the child or the ward.

The structure of the relationship between parent and child is thus curiously similar to that which exists between trustee and beneficiary. In both cases, the essence of the legal relationship between the two parties is based on expectations of trust and reciprocity, rather than autonomy and rational self-interest. In addition, in both situations, one party to the relationship is placed in a position in which they have a considerable amount of power over the other. In the case of the trustee-beneficiary relationship, the power of the trustee to control the trust assets derives from the creation of the trust, and is subject to the consent or the instructions of the trust settlor, or the person making the will. In the case of the parent-child or guardian-ward relationship, on the other hand, the legal authority of the parent over the child, or the guardian over the ward, is accorded by law, and is not dependent on the consent of any third party. As we have seen in Chapter 2, however, the legal authority that a parent

---

5 This would also include a situation in which the state acts as guardian of a child in child protection hearings. See above, Chapter 2, note 19 and accompanying text.

can exercise over a child is not absolute; and the child can be removed from parental control, either permanently or temporarily, in circumstances in which child welfare authorities view the child as being at risk of neglect or abuse from the parent or legal guardian.[6]

III. UNJUST ENRICHMENT AND THE DOCTRINE OF CONSTRUCTIVE TRUST

Thus far we have been considering situations in which a trust relationship is created either by express declaration, or as a result of an implied agreement between the parties. In both instances, the trust relationship results from the voluntary action and intentions of the settlor(s). However, there may also be situations in which a court will find that a trust relationship has come into being without requiring any evidence of an intention to create a trust on the part of the settlor. In these circumstances, the trust relationship is said to arise by operation of law, rather than through the intention of the parties, and is referred to as a *constructive trust*, to differentiate it from both an express trust and an implied or resulting trust.

Typically, a court will be prepared to recognize the existence of a constructive trust relationship in order to avoid a situation of unjust enrichment in which one party would otherwise be able to obtain an unwarranted benefit at the expense of the other party. In effect, through the creation of a constructive trust, the courts impose the obligations of a constructive trustee on the person who would otherwise be unjustly enriched. As we have seen, the duties of a trustee towards a beneficiary in equity differ significantly from the legal obligations owed towards each other by two parties in an ordinary commercial relationship, or by two persons who would not otherwise be viewed as being in a legal relationship with each other at common law.

Suppose, for example, that I go to take some money out of my bank account at an automated teller machine; and in looking at the amount in my account, I discover that it is much higher than I had expected. Instead of only $1,500 in the account, there seems to be more than $10,000 in the account. I check my recent transactions, and discover that a sum of $8,500 was deposited into my account during the past week. This surprises me, as I have no idea where such a large amount could have come from. Not wanting to look a gift horse in the mouth, however, I immediately take out my daily maximum amount of $1,000 per day for the next seven days,

[6] *Ibid.*

and use the money to put a down payment on a new car I had been wanting to buy. Two weeks later, I receive a letter from the bank informing me that the $8,500 had been deposited into my account by mistake. Apparently, I had deposited a cheque for $85 into my account, and put in two extra zeros by mistake. The bank has now cancelled the deposit for $8,500 and replaced it with my original deposit for $85, and informs me that my account is now substantially in arrears.

In this situation, it is clear that the mistake which led to the additional funds being deposited in my account was caused by me. If I were entitled to keep the funds mistakenly deposited into my account, I would be unjustly enriched at the expense of the bank. In these circumstances, equity will hold me liable to account for the funds mistakenly deposited into my account as a constructive trustee for the bank, on the principle that I should not be able to profit from my own wrongdoing.

But what if the mistake which the bank made in depositing funds into my account was not caused by me? Would equity hold me liable as a constructive trustee to return the funds mistakenly deposited into my account if I am in no way responsible for the mistake which the bank made? Do I have any obligation to inform the bank of its mistake? Or can I act as a self-interested actor and take advantage of the bank's mistake, while being fully aware that the bank would not have deposited the funds in my account had it been aware of its own mistake?

Consider the following example. I am waiting behind you in line at a convenience store, and I observe you purchase a lottery ticket and put it into your wallet. However, as you are walking out of the store the wallet falls on the ground and I retrieve it, intending to return it to you when I can. That evening, before returning the wallet, I turn on the TV and discover that the lottery ticket you purchased is the winning ticket. As far as the lottery corporation responsible for paying out lottery winnings is concerned, I am the person in legal possession of the winning ticket and am entitled at law to receive the $1,000,000 payable on the ticket. In equity, however, I will be considered to be a constructive trustee of the lottery winnings on your behalf, since I must have known that you had no intention of abandoning your ticket.

Notice that in these circumstances, I did not act wrongfully in law in picking up the wallet with the ticket in it. Nor was I responsible in any way for your act in dropping the wallet. My wrongful act, or if you like, my breach of trust, lay in claiming for myself that which I must have known was rightfully yours. In these circumstances, a court of equity will not allow me to be unjustly enriched at your expense, and so will impose the duties of a constructive trustee on me to pay the lottery winnings to you, even though there was no prior relationship between us, and *no intention* to create a trust relationship on your part.

Another situation in which equity will seek to avoid one person being unjustly enriched at the expense of another occurred in the case of *Canadian Aero-Service v. O'Malley*.[7] In this case, O'Malley had previously been the president and chief executive officer of Canadian Aero-Service, an aerial surveying company, until August 19, 1966, when he resigned his position with the company, and took up another position with Terra Surveys Ltd., a newly formed aerial surveying company in which O'Malley was one of the leading shareholders. While still employed with Canadian Aero-Service, O'Malley had been involved in the development of a proposal for an extensive topographical survey and mapping contract with the government of Guyana, to be financed by a grant or a loan by the Canadian government. As chief executive officer of Canadian Aero-Service, O'Malley was one of the persons most closely involved in the negotiations with both the government of Guyana and the Canadian government with respect to the financing and specifications for the contract.

In July 1966, O'Malley learned that the financing for the proposed mapping and surveying contract would be approved by the Canadian government. Companies were then invited to bid on the contract, and provide detailed specifications to be reviewed by senior bureaucrats. In August, O'Malley and a number of other executives from Canadian Aero-Service resigned from their positions with the company, and formed their own aerial mapping company, Terra Surveys, which then sought permission to be added to the bidding process, and emerged as the eventual winner, with the most detailed and lowest cost bid.

After the award of the contract to Terra Surveys, Canadian Aero-Service sued O'Malley, Terra Surveys, and the other former executives and officers from Canadian Aero-Service who had together created Terra Surveys with the intention of bidding on the proposed contract. Canadian Aero-Service argued that O'Malley and the other executives who had been involved in developing the specifications for the winning bid by Terra Surveys had only obtained the necessary information required for preparing such a complex bid as a result of the work they had done for Canadian Aero-Service in negotiations with the Canadian and Guyanese governments in anticipation of the award of the contract. As such, Canadian Aero-Service argued that the former employees had effectively taken advantage of a corporate opportunity that properly belonged to Canadian Aero-Service, not to O'Malley and the other former executives, and had appropriated it for their own benefit.

The Supreme Court of Canada upheld Canadian Aero-Service's argument, holding that as executives and officers of Canadian Aero-Service, O'Malley and the other executives owed a fiduciary duty to Canadian Aero-Service

---

7 *Canadian Aero-Service v. O'Malley*, [1974] S.C.J. No. 97, [1974] 1 S.C.R. 592 (S.C.C.).

to act in its best interests, and could not put their own self-interest in bidding on the contract through a new company they had created especially for this purpose, over their obligation to the Canadian Aero-Service. Their fiduciary obligation to the company even lasted after they had resigned from Canadian Aero-Service, provided that the confidential information they utilized in developing the winning bid on behalf of Terra Surveys had come to them as a result of their positions of trust at Canadian Aero-Service. In effect, therefore, the Supreme Court of Canada held that the executives who left Canadian Aero-Service to form their own company would have been unjustly enriched at their former company's expense, had they been allowed to profit from the information they obtained as executives of Canadian Aero-Service to outbid their former employer.

Because both a resulting trust and a constructive trust may come into existence without any express declaration of trust by a settlor, it may sometimes be hard to determine whether or not a trust relationship has been created between two parties. Such a situation occurred in the 1973 decision of the Supreme Court of Canada in *Murdoch v. Murdoch.*[8] The case involved a dispute over the division of marital assets between two spouses who had been married for over twenty years. During that time they had accumulated a great deal of property, including a valuable ranch. The dispute involved a question of the ownership of the ranch property at the time of the divorce. According to the "separate property regime" which governed the division of family assets on divorce in the province of Alberta at the time the parties separated (in 1968), each spouse would be entitled to take out of the marriage any assets which he or she separately owned during the marriage. If any properties were held in the joint names of the two spouses, each spouse would be entitled to half the value of the jointly held properties on divorce. However, any property that was held in one spouse's name alone was presumed to be the separate property of that spouse, and thus not subject to division if the spouses divorced.

During the marriage, all the properties which the couple had owned had been placed in the husband's name alone, so that only his name appeared on the title deeds to the property. However, the wife's evidence, which was not contradicted by the husband, was that both spouses had jointly contributed to the running of the ranch throughout their married life together. Indeed, during several winters the husband worked away from the ranch, leaving the wife to manage the ranch alone while he was away. Moreover, in the early years of the marriage, the wife's parents had provided $3000 towards the purchase of their first property, which, like all of the other properties they subsequently acquired, was registered in the husband's name alone.

---

8 *Murdoch v. Murdoch*, [1973] S.C.J. No. 150, 41 D.L.R. (3d) 367 (S.C.C.).

In these circumstances, Mrs. Murdoch claimed that even though the ranch properties were legally registered in her husband's name, she should be entitled to a half share in the value of the ranch in equity as the beneficiary of an implied or resulting trust. In effect, her argument was that since they had always worked together as partners in building up the ranch property, she should be entitled to a half share in the value of the property, just as any other partner would be entitled to claim their share of partnership assets on dissolution of the partnership. Mrs. Murdoch therefore asked the court to presume the existence of an implied or resulting trust to prevent Mr. Murdoch from retaining all the benefits from their joint contribution to the partnership property.

The trial court judge, however, rejected this argument, and ruled in favour of the husband's claim to the property. The judge held that the wife did not make any direct financial contribution to the purchase of the ranch property, sufficient to entitle her to a beneficial half interest in the property as a "silent investor". (The $3000 from the wife's parents was regarded as a loan to the husband by the trial judge, rather than as a loan to the wife.) Nor did the judge find that her contribution of labour to the ranch was sufficient to create a presumption that they jointly farmed the land as partners. Instead, the judge found that the wife's contribution to building up the ranch was typical of that made by any other Alberta ranch wife, and thus should simply be viewed as part of the contribution which each spouse made to the marriage!

In dismissing the wife's claim, the trial judge sought to make a distinction between a partnership, which he viewed as primarily in the nature of a business relationship, and a marriage, which he viewed in traditional terms as a compact based on mutual love and support, rather than on economic or exchange relations. The consequence of this assumption, however, was that Mrs. Murdoch was not entitled to claim any share of the property they had built up together during the course of their marriage. She could only sue for ongoing spousal support after the marriage had ended.

The wife appealed this decision to the Alberta Court of Appeal, and then to the Supreme Court of Canada, which, by a majority, upheld the trial judge's ruling and dismissed the appeal. The majority of the Supreme Court accepted the trial court's finding of fact about the nature of the wife's contribution to the ranch, and dismissed her claim to a half share of the property on the basis of a resulting trust. In the absence of a direct financial contribution by the wife, the majority ruled there was insufficient evidence of any common intention by the husband and wife that the wife's contribution of labour should give rise to a resulting trust in her favour. Implicitly, therefore, the majority of the Supreme Court also accepted the distinction that the trial court judge sought to make between a marriage and a business partnership.

In what turned out to be a very influential dissenting opinion, however, Justice Laskin adopted a very different approach to determining whether or not a trust relationship had been created between the spouses. Instead of concentrating exclusively on the question of *intention* to create a trust or a partnership, Justice Laskin asked whether the fact situation could give rise to a *constructive trust* between the parties? As we have seen, the purpose of a constructive trust is to prevent one person from being unjustly enriched at the expense of another. Moreover, a constructive trust does not require evidence of intention to create a trust, but will be imposed by the court in appropriate circumstances. Following this logic, Justice Laskin suggested that the husband had been unjustly enriched by the value of his wife's contributions to the ranch (which also included the $3000 contributed by her parents for their first property), and thus should be regarded in equity as a trustee of the wife's half beneficial interest in the property under a constructive trust.[9]

One of the consequences of the Supreme Court decision in *Murdoch v. Murdoch* was that within a very few years after the decision was handed down, all the common law provinces of Canada passed new legislation to ensure that on marriage breakdown, both spouses would thereafter be entitled to share in the division of family assets, regardless of who paid for the assets, or in whose name title to the family assets is held.[10] Ironically, perhaps, the legislative reforms to provincial family property laws now explicitly state that marriage is to be regarded as a *partnership* to which both spouses contribute equally, whether that contribution be in financial terms, or child care, or other forms of contribution to the marriage. In addition, the approach outlined by Justice Laskin in his dissenting opinion in *Murdoch v. Murdoch* to determine whether a constructive trust should be imposed where one spouse contributes unpaid labour to another spouse's business, was subsequently adopted by a majority of the Supreme Court in two later cases, *Rathwell v. Rathwell*[11], and *Pettkus v. Becker*[12], which turned on very similar facts. In the event, therefore, although Mrs. Murdoch did not win her case, the eventual impact of the decision in *Murdoch v. Murdoch* was to provoke significant changes not only in the law of

---

9 *Ibid.*, at 388-89.

10 See, for example, *Family Law Act*, R.S.O. 1990, c. F.3, Part I. Under Ontario's legislation, which is similar to that of most other common law provinces, the spouses can also decide on their own division of family assets by entering into a domestic contract in accordance with the provisions of Part IV of the Act.

11 *Rathwell v. Rathwell*, [1978] S.C.J. No. 14, [1978] 2 S.C.R. 436, [1978] 2 W.W.R. 101 (S.C.C.).

12 *Pettkus v. Becker*, [1980] S.C.J. No. 103, [1980] 2 S.C.R. 834, 117 D.L.R. (3d) 257 (S.C.C.).

constructive trusts, but also in the legislative assumptions regarding marriage that underpin the division of assets on divorce.[13]

IV. THE NATURE OF FIDUCIARY DUTIES

So far we have been looking at a number of different kinds of trust relationship in which equity imposes an obligation on a trustee to act in the best interests of the beneficiary of the trust. The nature of the trustee's legal obligation to the beneficiary is referred to as a *fiduciary duty*. As Professor Waters puts it in his textbook *The Law of Trusts in Canada*:

> The hallmark of a trust is the fiduciary relationship which it creates between the trustee and the beneficiary. The whole purpose of a trustee's existence is to administer property on behalf of another, to hold it exclusively for the other's enjoyment. The ... trustee is expected to put the interests of the trust and the beneficiaries first in his thinking whenever he is exercising the powers or performing the duties of his office. His duty is one of selfless service.[14]

The essence of a fiduciary relationship, therefore, is that equity regards one person (the *trustee* or *fiduciary*) as being under a personal obligation to act in the best interests of another person (the *beneficiary*). In the context of a trust relationship, the trustee's fiduciary obligation is to exercise the trustee's legal powers of disposition over the trust property exclusively for the benefit of the beneficiaries and in accordance with the terms of the trust. If a trustee acts outside the powers granted in the trust, the trustee can be held personally accountable to the beneficiaries of the trust. Thus, if an investment trust were set up, with explicit terms of trust indicating that the funds were only to be invested in certain types of secure investments such as bonds issued by the federal or provincial governments, or in shares of blue chip, dividend paying corporations, the trustee has no legal authority to invest the trust funds in real estate, or to speculate in an initial public offering of shares in a new biotechnology company, for example. If the trustee oversteps his or her authority under the terms of the trust, he or she may be held personally liable for any loss or diminution of the trust property resulting from the breach of trust.

Likewise, the trustee owes a fiduciary obligation to the beneficiaries to exercise his or her powers and authority over the trust property exclusively in their best interests. This means that the trustee is required as a matter of law to place the interests of the beneficiaries over his or

---

13 See the section "Legal Dependency and the Family" above in Chapter 2.

14 D.W.M. Waters, *Law of Trusts in Canada*, *supra*, note 4, at 31.

her own, and to avoid any situations in which there may be any potential or actual conflict of interest. Thus, in the example discussed above, perhaps the trustee believes that speculating in the shares of a new biotechnology company will result in a far greater financial return than can be obtained by staying within the terms of the trust. The trustee is aware that under the terms of the trust he or she is prohibited from investing the trust funds in the biotechnology company. What can be the harm, however, if, instead of investing on behalf of the beneficiaries, the trustee decides to use some of the trust property to invest in shares of the biotechnology company in his or her own name? The trustee's intention is not to steal from the beneficiaries, but simply to make use of the funds temporarily, for his or her own use, and then to replace the trust property after the fact.

In this situation, the trustee will still be guilty of a violation of trust, even if the plan is successful. The trustee will have misappropriated trust property for his or her own personal benefit, even if the trust funds were ultimately replaced. Clearly, if the trustee's unauthorized investment reduces the trust property the trustee will be personally liable to the beneficiaries to make good the loss. What is less obvious, at first glance, is that even if the unauthorized investment turns out to be successful, the trustee will still be liable to account to the beneficiaries for any personal benefits which he or she obtained by unauthorized use of the trust property. The point is that the trustee has made use of trust property to obtain a personal benefit for him or herself. As such, this action amounts to a breach of the trustee's fiduciary obligation to act only in the best interest of the beneficiaries, and to avoid any personal conflict of interest. In short, the benefit still belongs to the beneficiaries of the trust in equity, even though that financial benefit could not have been realised by staying within the terms of the trust itself.[15]

The above discussion illustrates the nature of a trustee's fiduciary obligation which arises through the creation of a trust. However, a trust is not the only context in which a fiduciary duty may come into existence. A fiduciary relationship may also be created, outside of a formal trust context, in any situation in which one person is in a special position of trust and confidence vis-à-vis another. For example, the very nature of a doctor/patient relationship is that the patient places his or her trust and confidence in the doctor's professional skill and discretion. The doctor is under a corresponding duty to exercise his or her professional skill in the best interest of the patient, and to preserve the confidentiality of any information that may be disclosed to the doctor in the course of the relationship. The same is true of the relationship between a lawyer and a client, a principal and an agent, and between many other professionals

---

[15] *Boardman v. Phipps*, [1967] 2 A.C. 46, [1966] 3 All E.R. 721 (H.L.).

and their clients. In each of these situations, the professional advisor is regarded as being under a fiduciary duty to act in the best interests of their patient or client, and to avoid any situation in which their personal interest and their duty to the patient or client may conflict.

It is not only in situations involving professional/client relationships that equity imposes the duties of a fiduciary on a person in a position of trust. In many respects, the relationship between a minister and a member of his or her congregation is similar to that between a physician and his patient or between a lawyer and her client. Indeed, it may well be that a layperson may place even more trust in a minister to give them guidance in both spiritual and everyday matters than they would give to their lawyer or doctor. Likewise, a teacher is often in a position to exercise a considerable degree of influence over her students, and clearly occupies a position of trust in relation to them. Perhaps most obvious of all, family relationships, especially those between adults and children within a family context, are necessarily built upon trust, and involve an implicit obligation on the part of a parent and other significant adults in a child's life to exercise their influence and authority in the child's best interest.[16]

Equity recognizes the existence of a fiduciary relationship in these situations because they share a number of characteristics that make the relationship different from that between two parties involved in an ordinary commercial exchange. For one thing, the person seeking advice from a lawyer, or a doctor, or other professional advisor may frequently disclose personal or confidential information which he or she might not wish to have known by other individuals (for example, the highest price that a buyer may be prepared to pay at an auction). Equity therefore imposes a duty of confidentiality on the fiduciary, not to disclose or otherwise make use of confidential information which comes to them by virtue of their position of trust.

In addition to obtaining access to confidential information, the fiduciary is frequently also in a position to exert a considerable degree of influence or authority over the more vulnerable party to the relationship. Consequently, there is often a significant power differential between the two parties to the relationship, and this again tends to make fiduciary relationships qualitatively different from most ordinary commercial exchanges between two parties who are "at arms length" with each other. Within most exchange relationships, the parties are viewed as self-reliant actors, responsible in law for their own actions but not for those of the other party. In a fiduciary relationship, however, the opposite is true, since the fiduciary explicitly undertakes to act, or to give advice and counsel, for the benefit of the

---

16 See *e.g. M.(K.) v. M.(H.)*, [1992] S.C.J. No. 85, [1992] 3 S.C.R. 6 (S.C.C.), in which a father was held liable in damages for sexually abusing his daughter on the basis of a breach of fiduciary duty.

other party. This places the beneficiary in a uniquely vulnerable position vis-à-vis the fiduciary. A client seeking advice from a lawyer, a patient seeking medical advice from a doctor, even a member of a congregation looking for guidance from a minister, all implicitly rely on the good faith and integrity of the person in whom they place their confidence and trust. Equity therefore places the fiduciary under an obligation not to abuse that trust, and to exercise any power or authority the fiduciary may have solely in the best interests of the beneficiary.

We have seen already that this includes the obligation to avoid any situation in which the financial interests of the fiduciary and the beneficiary may conflict. However, the duty to act in the best interest of a beneficiary is not necessarily concerned only with financial conflicts of interest. In recent years, courts have held that a person owing a fiduciary duty to another may be in breach of their fiduciary duty if they seek to take personal advantage of their position of trust and confidence even in non-financial matters. Thus a doctor who uses his or her position of influence and authority over a patient to initiate a sexual relationship with the patient may be held to be in breach of a fiduciary duty to act in the patient's best interest.

In a situation such as this, equity presumes that the patient who is subject to the doctor's influence is particularly vulnerable. As such, the patient may not be in a position to make their own free choice about whether to enter into the sexual relationship. Consequently, the fact that the sexual relationship may appear consensual does not automatically relieve the doctor from the accusation of breach of professional and fiduciary responsibility. A fiduciary responsibility places the fiduciary under a higher sense of duty or obligation than that between two persons in an exchange relationship, or in a relationship where there is no clear power or authority differential between them.

In the case of *Norberg v. Wynrib*,[17] for example, the plaintiff, a young female patient, alleged that the defendant doctor had taken advantage of her addiction to a prescription painkiller, by demanding sexual services from her in return for access to the drug. The plaintiff brought an action against the doctor for damages for sexual assault and breach of fiduciary duty. One of the issues argued before the Supreme Court of Canada was whether the fiduciary duty of a doctor extended only to those matters which were within the professional competence of the doctor. In prescribing drugs for the patient which she did not medically need the doctor was arguably in breach of his professional responsibility to the patient. But the defendant argued that there could be no breach of a fiduciary duty where

---

17 *Norberg v. Wynrib*, [1992] S.C.J. No. 60, [1992] 2 S.C.R. 226 (S.C.C.).

the patient willingly consented to the sexual relations between herself and the doctor.

This argument was rejected by Justice McLachlin. She held that the doctor's fiduciary duty should not be limited to uses of confidential medical information or giving medical advice. The nature of a fiduciary relationship is that it is a relationship in which one party puts their trust in another. The entrustor thereby places themselves in a position of dependency vis-à-vis the party in a position of trust. In short, the relationship between entrustor and fiduciary is generally one in which there is an unequal relation of power and dependency between the parties. As Justice McLachlin put it:

> The essence of trust and all fiduciary relationships is that the trustee, the person in power, assumes responsibility for the welfare of the *cestui qui trust* for matters falling within the scope of the trust relationship. Having assumed that responsibility, the fiduciary cannot rely on the other party's weakness or infirmity as a defence to an action grounded on his failure to discharge his fiduciary duty properly.[18]

In the present case, the doctor was in a position of power over the patient not only by virtue of his professional status, but also by virtue of his knowledge that the patient had a chemical dependency on the drug. The court held that there could be no true consent by the patient in a situation where the doctor held over her the implicit threat of cutting off her access to the drug. In these circumstances, the doctor explicitly used his position of power over the plaintiff to coerce her consent to enter into sexual relations with him. The court therefore held that the appearance of consent could not be relied on as a defence to an action brought by the plaintiff against the doctor either in tort (per Justice La Forest), or for breach of fiduciary duty (per Justice McLachlin), or breach of professional duty (per Justice Sopinka).

From a legal perspective, the question whether a particular relationship gives rise to the creation of a fiduciary duty is regarded as a question of fact, to be decided on all the circumstances of the case.[19] As the courts are fond of saying, the categories of fiduciary relationships are not closed. Consequently, the fact that a particular type of relationship has not traditionally been regarded as a fiduciary relationship does not preclude a court from recognizing the existence of a fiduciary obligation where this would be appropriate. In this context, the courts have often looked for general principles to guide them in determining whether or not a fiduciary relationship has been created.

---

18 *Ibid.*, at 288.

19 See *Lac Minerals Ltd. v. International Corona Resources Ltd.*, [1989] S.C.J. No. 83, [1989] 2 S.C.R. 574 (S.C.C.).

In one such case, *Frame v. Smith*,[20] the question whether a fiduciary obligation existed between the parties arose out of a custody dispute between two ex-spouses following the breakdown of their marriage. The plaintiff was the estranged father of two children who, at the time of the hearing, were teenagers. The father had been granted access and visitation rights with regard to the children after the divorce. The defendant was his ex-wife, who had been awarded sole custody over the children at the time of the divorce. The plaintiff alleged that the defendant had deliberately prevented him from maintaining any ongoing relationship with his children in violation of his court-ordered rights of access, and in so doing had acted not only contrary to the children's welfare, but also in breach of a fiduciary obligation owed to him as the access, or non-custodial, parent.

The facts of the case did seem to indicate a consistent pattern of behaviour by the ex-wife to prevent the children from maintaining contact with the father after the divorce. This included moving several times in breach of court orders to provide access to the ex-husband and without informing the ex-husband of the children's new address. Nevertheless, the issue before the court was not the factual issue of whether the mother had acted in such a way as to interfere with the father maintaining a meaningful ongoing relationship with the children, but whether, as a question of law, she was in breach of any legal duty owed to him not to interfere with his relationship with the children.

According to the minority judgement of Justice Wilson, the facts of the case were such as to demonstrate all the required elements of a fiduciary duty. First, the mother, as the parent with sole custody of the children, was in a position to exercise considerable power or discretion over the circumstances in which the father as a non-custodial parent was able to see his children. Moreover, the mother could, and did, exercise this power unilaterally to prevent the father from maintaining an ongoing relationship with the children. The father, as a non-custodial parent, was thus in a special position of vulnerability or dependency vis-à-vis his ex-wife, since, despite any court orders to the contrary, she could effectively dictate both the manner and the circumstances in which he was able to maintain access to his children.[21]

Nevertheless, a majority of the Supreme Court of Canada rejected the ex-husband's claim, and held that the circumstances of the case gave rise to no cause of action for breach of a fiduciary duty. Part of the majority's reasoning was that Parliament had legislated a comprehensive statutory scheme for enforcing custody and access determinations under federal and provincial family law legislation. Consequently, there was no need to

---

[20] *Frame v. Smith*, [1987] S.C.J. No. 89, 42 D.L.R. (4th) 81 (S.C.C.).

[21] *Ibid.*, *per* Justice Wilson, at 101-02.

permit additional private law actions, whether in contract, or tort, or for breach of fiduciary duty, in order to prevent interference with access or visitation rights. Indeed, speaking for the majority, Justice La Forest expressed concern about the potential consequences of allowing ex-spouses to sue each other for alleged infringements of custody or visitation rights following divorce. As well as the financial costs of ongoing litigation, which would likely drain the resources of both parents, there are also the indirect costs of litigation to the children.[22] If the non-custodial parent were to sue successfully for damages against the custodial parent in a similar case, the consequences could be financially disastrous for the custodial parent, and therefore also for the children. Moreover, obtaining an award of financial damages would not be likely to bring about an improvement in the relationship between the estranged parent and his or her children, but rather to reinforce their estrangement. While expressing sympathy for the estranged father in *Frame v. Smith*, the majority held that to permit further litigation between the parents in high conflict divorce cases was likely to be contrary to the court's overriding concern with protecting the best interest of the children.

The final context in which we will discuss the elaboration of new categories of fiduciary relationships has to do with the Crown's special historical responsibilities towards aboriginal peoples. Historically, Indian peoples were granted a special protective status under the Constitution, which effectively precluded them from exercising many of the rights and freedoms taken for granted by most other citizens of Canada.[23] In many respects, the legal status of Indian peoples under the constitution was regarded as akin to that of infants or minors before they reach the age of majority. Legislation and judicial interpretation referred to Indian peoples as "wards" of the Crown, a special legal status which had its origins in the feudal rights of a lord to dispose of the estates of an heir or an heiress who was orphaned and under the age of consent. According to the medieval origins of the status of wardship, the feudal lord, whose legal powers were ultimately vested in the Crown, was given wide discretion over the affairs of the ward. This discretion included the power to manage the estates of the ward until he or she came of age or was married, to decide where the ward should reside, and to determine what education if any was appropriate to the ward's condition in life. Generally, the lord had the power to exercise temporal authority over and to provide spiritual

---

22 *Ibid.*, at 118-19.

23 For a discussion of the historical relationship between the Crown and Aboriginal peoples, and the restrictive provisions of successive federal Indian Acts, see *Report of the Royal Commission on Aboriginal Peoples, Vol. I.* (Ottawa: Minister of Supply and Services, 1996), especially Part 2, at 245-319.

guidance to the ward, in much the same manner that a parent was granted legal power to exercise discipline and authority over a child.

As we have seen in relation to the family, over time the absolute authority that a parent could exercise over a child has been significantly modified by the courts and by legislation.[24] Likewise, the absolute discretion that the Crown could claim to exercise on behalf of its Indian subjects has also become qualified by the courts and the *Charter*.[25] Perhaps the major shift in the Crown's legal responsibilities towards Indian peoples is the recognition that the legal powers and authority of the Crown are no longer unlimited, but must be exercised in the best interest of the Indian peoples themselves. In short, the courts have come to recognize that the relationship between the Crown and aboriginal peoples, like that between a parent and a child, is a fiduciary relationship, in which the Crown as fiduciary owes an obligation to exercise its discretionary powers with the utmost integrity and in the best interest of its aboriginal subjects.[26]

One of the first cases in which this new characterization of the fiduciary nature of the relationship between the Crown and aboriginal peoples was considered was that of *Guerin v. Canada*.[27] The case involved a proposal to lease part of an urban reserve occupied by the Musqueam band within the municipal boundaries of the city of Vancouver for use as a recreational golf club. The golf club was looking for new premises after its former lease of Canadian Pacific lands was due to expire. The reserve contained some of the most desirable undeveloped land remaining within the city limits. Negotiations began between the golf club, Musqueam band councillors and the local federal Indian agent, with a view to arranging a lease of part of the band's "surplus" reserve lands for the golf club. In order to finalize any lease agreement with the golf club, however, there first had to be a formal surrender of the band's interest in and right to occupy the reserve lands in question to the federal government, in accordance with the provisions of s. 18(1) of the *Indian Act*.[28] Only then could a final lease agreement be entered into between the club and the Crown, which under the terms of s. 18 of the *Indian Act* was required to act in the band's best interest.

The original legislative purpose behind these restrictions on the legal capacity of a band to convey its aboriginal title to anyone other than the

---

24 See the section "Legal Dependency and the Family" above in Chapter 2.

25 Part I of the *Constitution Act, 1982*, being Schedule B to the *Canada Act, 1982* (U.K.), 1982, c. 11, s. 35.

26 See *R. v. Sparrow*, [1990] S.C.J. No. 49, [1990] 1 S.C.R. 1075 (S.C.C.); Kent MacNeil, "Fiduciary Obligations and Aboriginal Peoples", in M.R. Gillen and F. Woodman, eds., *The Law of Trusts: A Contextual Approach*, *supra*, note 4, at 807-65.

27 *Guerin v. Canada*, [1984] S.C.J. No. 45, [1984] 2 S.C.R. 335 (S.C.C.).

28 The version of the statute under consideration was the *Indian Act*, R.S.C. 1952, c. 149.

Crown was to prevent exploitation of Indians by third parties such as mining companies, or even by colonial administrators intent on opening up reserve lands for settlement. The effect of this legislative scheme, however, was that Indian bands occupying reserve lands with potential for economic development, such as in or near urban centres, or where valuable mineral or forestry resources were located on or under the land, were denied the legal capacity to make development decisions on behalf of the band itself. The only mechanism for developing the land base or conveying lands to third parties was through a formal surrender of the band's title to the reserve lands to the federal government under s. 18, and then trusting that the federal government Indian agent responsible for the surrender would negotiate a development deal that was beneficial to the band.

The Indian agent was aware that certain terms which the golf club were insistent on were not acceptable to the band council, such as the right of the golf club to remove any building or capital improvements after termination of the lease, and a term capping any increases in rent for future renewal periods under the lease to 15 per cent of the previous rental period's rent. Notwithstanding this, the Indian agent indicated to the band council that the council's terms would be met in the lease negotiations with the golf club. On this understanding the band council agreed to execute a surrender of the band's aboriginal title to the land in question to the Crown, so that it could be leased to the golf club. The Indian agent subsequently negotiated a lease with the golf club which contained many of the terms expressly rejected by the band council. The effect of the agreement negotiated by the Indian agent was to give the golf club a very preferential lease of prime development lands within Vancouver at a rental rate that was far below market value, and at a rate that was effectively capped for the entire 75 year term of the lease.

The band subsequently brought an action for breach of trust against the federal government, arguing that the Indian agent had breached his duties as a trustee in negotiating a lease that he knew to be unacceptable to the band council. The trial judge upheld the band's claim of breach of trust, and assessed the difference between the present value of the lease and the potential loss of economic opportunity to the band as a result of the lease at $10,000,000. The Federal Court of Appeal overturned the trial court's judgement, and the case finally came before the Supreme Court of Canada.

The main issue that the Supreme Court had to decide was the nature of the relationship between the Indian agent (and therefore the federal government which appointed him) and the Musqueam band. The band argued that the relationship was in the nature of a trust, or at the very least that a fiduciary obligation was owed by the Indian agent to act in the best interests of the band. The Crown, however, argued that the Indian agent's responsibility did not amount to an enforceable trust; nor did it fall into any of the traditional private law categories of fiduciary relationships. Instead, the Crown asserted that its responsibility under s. 18(1) of the *Indian Act* in receiving surrenders of aboriginal title to reserve lands was more in the nature of a political obligation than a private law obligation that is enforceable in the courts.

The best analogy to the Crown's argument might be the political obligation that an elected member of Parliament owes to his or her constituents to represent their interests in the House of Commons. If the MP fails to respect his or her campaign promises, or otherwise fails to represent the interests of his or her constituents in Parliament, the MP will be accountable to the voters through the democratic political process at the next election. But the MP will not be legally accountable to the voters in a court of law for breach of contract, or for any other breach of duty owed to them. The MP's obligation to his or her constituents is thus a political obligation, rather than an enforceable legal obligation.

The Supreme Court rejected the Crown's argument and held that the nature of the Crown's obligation was that of an enforceable fiduciary duty. Unlike the political analogy mentioned above, the Crown is not in the position of a Member of Parliament who makes election promises to voters. Instead, under s. 18(1) of the *Indian Act*, the Crown is legally empowered to receive surrenders of aboriginal property rights to specific reserve lands. Those reserve lands frequently represent the primary assets or resource base of the Indian band concerned. The Crown is therefore under an obligation to deal with the surrender of reserve lands under s. 18 in much the same way that a trustee must deal with trust property under a trust, or a lawyer is required to deal with any funds transferred into his or her keeping in a real estate transaction, or an investment broker must deal with the investment funds of a client. The broker has discretion with regard to the use of the investment funds, as does the trustee, and (to a lesser extent) the lawyer. But in each case that discretion must be exercised in the interests of the client, or the beneficiary under the trust. No conflict of interest is permitted of the fiduciary in dealing with the beneficiary's property.

In the same manner, the Supreme Court held that the federal government was in the position of a fiduciary when it accepted the surrender of the band's title to the reserve lands for the purpose of entering into the lease. The Indian agent was aware that the band would not have agreed to surrender its aboriginal title to the reserve land if it had known the terms that were to be incorporated into the lease agreement. The Indian agent therefore acted in breach of the Crown's fiduciary duty in accepting the surrender and negotiating with the golf club on terms that were contrary to the band's expressed intentions. To put this decision in the context of the introductory discussion of equitable principles at the beginning of this chapter, the Supreme Court found that the Indian agent's conduct was unconscionable. And as a court of equity the Supreme Court would not permit the Crown or its agents to act in an unconscionable manner towards an Indian band that was placed in a position of vulnerability by the very provisions of s. 18(1) of the *Indian Act*. In this example, therefore, we can still see the capacity of the principles of equity to modify the strictness of the common law and legislation, and to extend the categories of situations in which the courts are prepared to intervene into private law relationships to prevent unconscionable transactions by those in a position of power and trust.

Chapter 7

Private Law Remedies

I. INTRODUCTION

Throughout this book, we have discussed the role of law as a classifier of ordinary inter-personal relationships, whether those relationships are between natural persons (human beings), artificial persons (corporations, trade unions), or some combination of those. It must be emphasized that law's role as classifier is central to the themes of this book. The performance of this function allows the law to direct a great deal of our behaviour as we go about our day-to-day lives, sometimes without our even being aware of the presence of law. For example, it is because the law has responded in a particular way to the circumstances of ordinary transactions of sale that we experience those transactions in the way that we do. The labelling of merchandise with price stickers, one relatively small aspect of the exchange, performs a particular function in sale transactions, actually directing the way in which the relationship between seller and buyer unfolds. The same is true for almost every aspect of these apparently simple, routine relationships, not just in the world of retail sales, but in most of what we do as we carry out ordinary activities. The result is an experience of law that, for the most part, we do not recognize as such until something goes wrong.

But when something does go wrong, we experience another of the principal functions of law. That is, we look to the law to prescribe the consequences of broken relationships, whether those relationships arose out of a formal exchange in contract law, the imposition of a duty in tort law, a violation of property interests, or the particular circumstances giving rise to fiduciary duties. The prescriptive function of law generates a large group of rules collectively known as the law of remedies. This group of rules directs the way in which fractured private law relationships might be resolved. Now, to resolve a broken private law relationship is not to repair it necessarily. It is rare (though not impossible) in private law that the relationship will actually be restored through relying on law's prescriptive function. Rather, in one of a number of fundamental ways, the law attempts to compensate the individual complaining of having been injured through the breach of a private law relationship. Each of these ways involves an award of money to the injured party, and such an award is known as "damages" in the law of remedies. A short description of the various ways in which damages might be considered for breach of private law relationships is one of the principal purposes of this chapter.

Damages is a legal remedy, meaning it emerged from the legal side of the law and equity heritage that ultimately merged to give us the English tradition we experience today. In equity, however, judges devised a collection of remedies that are often awarded as alternatives to damages. As is always the case when equitable considerations have explicit influence on the way in which litigation unfolds, judges are very cautious about the award of equitable remedies. The litigant seeking an equitable remedy must demonstrate to the judge that the situation is well suited for the judge's intervention through the exercise of equitable jurisdiction, that the situation is not suitable for the ordinary legal remedy of damages, and that the claimant has done nothing to render the judge's intervention unsavoury from an equitable perspective. The range of equitable remedies is particularly adapted for breaches of contract, and for certain breaches of duty resulting in damage to property interests. The principal examples are injunction, specific performance, rescission and rectification. We will consider each of these remedies later in this chapter.

Of course, if a party complaining of having been injured through breach of a private law relationship is to receive an award of damages, or perhaps a remedy in equity, that party must sue the other party to the relationship. Remedies are awarded by judges, and judges are not able to make an award unless the parties come to the judge asking for adjudication of their dispute. It is well known that litigation is very expensive, and often inordinately time consuming, meaning that the remedies available to some injured parties are not available to others. Some injured parties simply cannot wait for the litigation process to unfold, and some parties are unable to afford expensive lawyers and other experts. The injustice of this situation is obvious to all of us, but while steps were taken during the 1980's and 1990's to expedite the litigation process, and while legal aid is available to qualified persons for many private law problems in Canada, the fact remains that litigation is beyond the realistic contemplation of many people suffering private law wrongs.

In thinking about these problems, however, we cannot lose sight of the idea that there are alternatives to litigation when private law relationships are breached. The vast majority of private law disputes are settled through negotiation rather than litigation, either privately between the parties themselves, or with the assistance of legal counsel or other representatives. Further, there are additional well recognized alternatives to litigation that have a real impact on the way in which a large number of disputes are resolved. Many family disputes, for example, are particularly well suited to mediation rather than litigation. In mediation, a professional person, experienced and expert in techniques of compromise and negotiation, will assist the parties to the broken relationship in reaching a solution that is palatable to all concerned. In several provinces of Canada, mediation is becoming an attractive and popular alternative to litigation for many types of private law disputes, including complex commercial law matters. In addition to providing, in almost every case, a quicker and less expensive alternative to litigation, mediation can tend to focus on the wider significance of the relationship at stake in the dispute, recognizing the individuals involved as members of both an immediate relationship and a wider set of community relationships that work together to foster a healthy, fulfilling environment. Such considerations are rarely at the forefront in litigation, where the adversarial model of warring individuals continues to prevail.

Arbitration is another way in which private law disputes might be resolved, although its use is generally limited to conflicts between union locals and the employer, and between parties to relatively sophisticated commercial transactions. This alternative provides that the dispute will be referred to a single arbitrator, or perhaps a panel of three, who will listen to the parties' representations, review the evidence and the terms of the relationship, and then render a decision. The rules by which arbitration is conducted are often much more relaxed than the rules of litigation, and that tends to allow the matter to be concluded more quickly. In almost every case, the choice of arbitration as an alternative to litigation is directed by the terms of the contract between the parties. Collective agreements in the labour law field invariably provide for the resolution of disputes through arbitration, and commercial contracts often contain a clause giving the parties the freedom to refer their disputes to arbitration. Contracts containing an arbitration clause will direct the way in which the parties will appoint the arbitrator or establish the panel, and will also direct the extent to which the decision rendered through arbitration will be binding on the parties.

It is interesting to note that, in the case of a non-binding arbitration award, the parties have no alternative to litigation in the event that one party refuses to comply with the arbitrator's decision. There is no formal procedure to compel compliance, and short of litigation, the parties must rely on good faith, and maybe ordinary business ethics, to see justice done. Further, even in the case of binding arbitration, if one party refuses to comply with the decision, there is still no method of compulsion. If the successful party wishes to see the arbitrator's decision implemented over the unwillingness of the other party, then the only alternative is litigation. Finally, arbitration in complex matters can be expensive. The arbitrators themselves must be paid, and the parties must retain experts to assist in the presentation of their positions.

Reliance on one of the alternatives to litigation, of course, means that the legal remedy of damages and the various equitable remedies are not strictly available to the injured party. Through negotiation, mediation or arbitration, it may be that a decision will be reached where one party will be entitled to receive a payment of money from the other as compensation for their loss. Superficially, such an entitlement looks much like an award of damages. Or it may be that one party will be required to do something to make amends, or refrain from doing something that contributed to the injury of which the other party complained, and such a requirement looks much like one or another of the equitable remedies we will consider as this chapter progresses. But one of the interesting differences between litigation and its alternatives is that the state will assist the successful litigant in seeing to the collection of an award of damages, or in ensuring that an equitable remedy is performed in the way that the judge directs. The office of the sheriff, for example, can be conscripted by a successful litigant to assist in the enforcement of the judge's decision, often for a very small fee. Further, the penalties for failure to comply with an order of a judge, even in private law matters, can be very severe indeed, meaning there is added incentive for an unsuccessful litigant to fulfill the terms of a judgment. It is only rarely, however, that the state might be called upon to intervene on behalf of a party to a dispute which has been resolved outside of litigation, and then only when the parties agree or the law otherwise provides that the court's approval of the settlement of the dispute must be obtained.

II. REMEDIES AT LAW — DAMAGES

By far the most common remedy sought and awarded in litigation emerging from private law disputes is an award of money as compensation for a loss or injury. This is the situation both in suits in tort and in claims for breach of contract. Money is a convenient (albeit imperfect) medium by which a judge can translate injuries and losses into an apparently objective standard or valuation for purposes of compensation, and in most cases it serves its purpose very well. There are situations, of course, especially where injured parties have been permanently disabled or otherwise severely adversely affected through another's tortious act, where an award of damages can never fully compensate for what has been lost. In such circumstances, judges are nevertheless confined to the use of money in the attempt to satisfy the injured party's claim.

In our consideration of damages as a remedy for breach of private law relationships, it is helpful to recall that much of private law is organized around the various interests of the parties to the relationship. From this point of view, and in large measure at least, private law is constructed so as to protect those interests from violation. This is so, it could be argued, to the extent that, from the perspective of private law, individuals are fundamentally considered as a composite of their interests, whether in bodily security, in reputation, in the exercise of dominion over property, in seeing to the performance of contracts to which they are party, or perhaps in preserving their dignity in relationships of radical imbalance of power. In turn, the identification of these interests emerges from basic assumptions about the nature of individuality, about the human individual as an essentially self-interested individual, about the requirement of respect for individual autonomy and freedom. The law of damages, one of the significant sub-divisions of the law of remedies, is the means by which private law attempts to value those interests following their injury. Therefore, it plays a very significant role in the expression through law of our central assumptions about the nature of human individuality and interaction.

In the law of contract, the calculation of damages for breach of the relationship is ordinarily straightforward. Generally, injured parties point to some easily quantifiable loss consequent on the other party's breach. Perhaps, on the strength of an assumption that the other party would perform their obligation, the injured party has changed his or her position and suffered some expense as a result. Perhaps the injured party has performed their side of the exchange, and ought to be compensated for that performance when the other party defaults. Perhaps the contract has raised a reasonable expectation of profit in the injured party, an expectation that is left unfulfilled when the other party fails to live up to their promise. We will consider these possibilities more deeply later in this section, but it is easy to see that the calculation of a money award to compensate the injured party for these sorts of losses in contract law is not a terribly difficult exercise. In most cases, successful complaints about breach of contract can be compensated quite satisfactorily through a money award.

In the law of tort, however, the question of damages is often the most difficult question in the entire process of negotiation and litigation. This is the case especially where there has been some violation of personal interests, whether in bodily integrity or reputation.[1] It is enormously difficult

[1] Comments in this section on damage awards in tort cases will be limited to situations of injuries to the person, as opposed to injuries to property interests. Ordinarily, injuries to property interests are compensated in one of three ways. First, a claimant might request compensation for a reduction in the value of the property, objectively considered. This would be the situation, for example, where a trespass to land has damaged the market value of the land, or where the escape of water from one property to another has caused damage. Secondly, a claimant might request compensation for loss of use of the property. This might occur in the case of detinue, where a chattel used by the claimant to earn income has been lost to the claimant for a period of time.

to translate an injury such as a broken leg into an award of money, and it is impossible to know precisely how to compensate someone for a slander on their good name. As a result of these difficulties, a complicated body of common law precedents has developed over the years, giving judges guidance on how best to calculate damages in claims for personal injury compensation, and on what level of compensation is appropriate in the widely different circumstances that present themselves to judges in each and every case. To assist judges in this respect, the award of damages in personal injury litigation is broken into two broad categories, known as "special damages" and "general damages". The latter is broken into two further sub-categories, called "general damages — pecuniary loss" and "general damages — non-pecuniary loss".

Special damages function as compensation to the injured party for out-of-pocket expenses suffered by the injured party between the date of the injury and the date of the trial. Obviously, the expenses must be referable to the injury to be compensable. We must not forget that the judge is making a determination as to the amount of money that the injured party will recover from the party at fault, such that the amount claimed must be a consequence of the injury that arose through the activity which is the subject of the complaint. Special damages are easily calculated, once the necessary connection has been established between the amount claimed and the injury. Ordinarily, the injured party will present evidence of lost wages prior to trial, and perhaps receipts for ambulance service, prescriptions, special medical treatments or devices, the cost of care at home, and other like expenses incurred prior to trial.

It is in the case of general damages that the calculation becomes more difficult in tort law. General damages — pecuniary loss relates to actual money losses to be incurred following the trial. Again, the items to be covered in this award must be demonstrated to be the direct result of the injury suffered by the claimant. The most important are the loss of future earnings and the cost of future care. Often, an injured party will suffer a disability that prevents her from working, either for a relatively predictable fixed period of time, or permanently. In either case, the judge must calculate the present value of the injured party's projected earnings over the anticipated period of the disability, a calculation which is necessarily uncertain. Every element of the calculation is a variable, based on assumptions about working life expectancy, the relationship between anticipated earnings and the injured party's education, contingencies such

---

Thirdly, slight trespasses to land or chattels are actionable *per se*, whether or not the thing itself has been adversely affected. Remember that it is the claimant's interest in dominion over the thing that is the subject of the claim, such that any trespass is actionable. In such circumstances, however, modern courts award only nominal damages.

as the likelihood of future layoffs or future illness that would adversely affect the injured party's prospects, and a host of other considerations. Once this calculation is made, the judge must then translate the amount into a present value, even though the interest protected under this category (earning potential) would have been realized only over an extended period of time, had the injury not intervened. Similar difficulties present themselves when judges must calculate the cost of future care for injured parties. How is one to know with certainty the level of care that will be required, the drugs and prosthetic devices that might be needed as the injured party's condition changes, the cost of full time nursing attendance, the duration of physiotherapy? Judges are often assisted in these calculations through expert actuarial and medical evidence, and there is a host of judicial precedents on which judges might rely. But these calculations remain among the most uncertain and difficult in all of private law litigation.

The difficulties are exaggerated when we consider the question of general damages — non-pecuniary loss. This heading covers non-monetary losses suffered by the injured party from the time of the injury through to the time of the trial, and then into the future. Contemplated here are two main items, called "pain and suffering" and "loss of the amenities of life". The former item functions as an attempt to compensate an injured person for the misery and anguish suffered due to their injury, including that which is anticipated to be endured following the award of damages. The latter item is the attempt to identify the impact that the injury has had and will have in the future on the ability of the injured party to enjoy life in the way that they would have had the injury not occurred. Often, for example, an injury will prevent a parent from playing with their children, or will interfere in the practice of hobbies, or will force the suspension of athletic pursuits. All of these matters must be assessed by the judge, and then valued based on the evidence that is tendered, the precedents that are relevant, and the injured party's particular circumstances.

It should be evident from this short description of general damages — pecuniary loss and general damages — non-pecuniary loss that different persons suffering the same injury as a result of tortious conduct may in fact receive widely different monetary awards as damages. Suppose two separate traffic accidents, both of which are caused by the negligence of an automobile operator, and both of which result in a total permanent disability for a pedestrian. In the first case, the injured person is a homeless person, middle aged, unemployed, and with no realistic prospects of employment. In the second case, the injured person is a mother of two small children, she is in her twenties, and a doctoral candidate in computer engineering. The homeless person will receive a very small amount of damages. Under the heading general damages — pecuniary loss, only the cost of future care will be relevant, and then only for a relatively short period of time. The injured party's life expectancy may be only 25 years, likely shorter than the average person of similar age because of the injured person's living conditions. As well, there will likely be no award, or at least a very small award, for lost earning potential. The injured person has no work, and no prospects of work. Further, the award for general damages — non-pecuniary loss, under the heading "loss of amenities of life", will likely be discounted as well. The homeless person's situation does not translate well, as one might predict, into a claim for lost amenities. In the second case, however, the cost of future care will be inflated by virtue of the injured party's youth, and her extended life expectancy. Further, her earning potential was enormous, given her age, education and specialty. Finally, an active mother with two small children will claim a significant amount for lost amenities. Her disability, she will argue, will interfere with much of what she had planned to do, both in her own pursuits and in her relationship with her children. Ultimately, the difference in the damage awards for the two injured parties could amount to hundreds of thousands of dollars, despite the fact that the injuries were identical, and despite the fact that the tortious act giving rise to the injuries was the same in all material respects.

The justice of such widely variant results is not at all clear. Somehow it seems unfair that two negligent parties, committing the same error of judgment in the same community, might be treated so differently by the law. Further, can it be just that the homeless person in our example above receives such a remarkably reduced damage award, when his situation is compared to the young doctoral candidate? As we consider these questions, however, it must be remembered that, while the law by which liability is established focuses almost exclusively on the actions of the wrongdoer, the law of remedies focuses just as completely on the peculiar situation of the injured party, on a case by case basis. In almost every case, the impact of a damage award on the wrongdoer is simply not relevant to the calculation of that award. Further, and to underscore the focus on the injured party's particular predicament, in the law of remedies we have something known as the "thin skull rule", translated into the maxim that a wrongdoer must take the victim as they are found. If a very slight automobile collision causes a total permanent disability because of the injured party's congenital predisposition to neck injuries, then the wrongdoer must compensate the injured party on that basis. If an equally slight collision does no injury to the innocent party, then the wrongdoer will still be liable, but only for nominal damages. Such is the result in the law of tort and the law of remedies.

The courts have made attempts to control some of the parameters by which damages are awarded in tort law, primarily in the area of general damages — non-pecuniary loss. In the famous 1978 Supreme Court of

Canada decision in *Andrews v. Grand & Toy Alberta Ltd.*,[2] the court imposed a limit of $100,000 in claims for pain and suffering and the loss of amenities of life in personal injury cases, a limit which, since 1978, has been adjusted to more than $250,000 to allow for changes in the value of money over time.[3] The court said "that there is no objective yardstick for translating non-pecuniary losses, such as pain and suffering and loss of amenities, into monetary terms. This area is open to widely extravagant claims."[4] The imposition of such a limit does tend to reduce the disparity between claimants based on their life conditions, and that may in turn answer some of the worries about justice that arise when claimants of vastly different circumstances present themselves as injured parties. At the same time, however, the limitation on awards of general damages for pain and suffering and loss of amenities of life may reduce the extent to which the law of damages functions as a deterrent to tortious conduct. We shall consider this difficulty a bit more carefully in the last section of this chapter.

When we focus on damage awards for breach of contract, many of the difficulties encountered in tort cases are absent. The law recognizes an individual interest in seeing to the performance of contracts to which the individual is party, and for violation of that interest the law of remedies prescribes a money award. In virtually every case, however, the calculation of damages for breach of contract is directly referable to some out-of-pocket expense or other money loss, such that the potential extravagance in awards of general damages, and the discretion that must factor into their calculation, is rarely a problem. The broad interest individuals have in seeing to the completion of contracts to which they are party is broken down into three specific categories of interest, primarily for ease of calculation and for isolating particular types of losses we might anticipate when directing our attention to breach of contract cases. Those three specific interests are known as the restitution interest, the reliance interest, and the expectation interest.

The restitution interest emerges when one party, on the faith of the contractual commitment of another party, confers a benefit on that other party which is then lost when the other party defaults in performance of her contractual obligation. Suppose I agree to wash your car on Saturday in return for a payment of $10. On the strength of my commitment, you pay me $5 in advance. Ultimately I fail to wash your car, breaching the

---

2 *Andrews v. Grand & Toy Alberta Ltd.*, [1978] S.C.J. No. 6, [1978] 2 S.C.R. 229 (S.C.C.).

3 See, for example, the decision of the British Columbia Supreme Court in *Williams (Guardian* ad litem *of) v. Low*, [2000] B.C.W.L.D. 956, [2000] B.C.J. No. 408 (B.C.S.C.), in which the upper limit of awards for general damages — non-pecuniary loss was said to be $267,000.

4 *Andrews v. Grand & Toy Alberta Ltd.*, [1978] S.C.J. No. 6, [1978] 2 S.C.R. 229 (S.C.C.), at 261.

contractual obligation that induced the $5 payment. In this situation, the law says that I have been "unjustly enriched", and the law of remedies will order the benefit I have received to be restored to you. As is the case in most areas of private law, this particular sub-category of the law of remedies (known as the "law of restitution" or the "law of unjust enrichment") is much more complicated than this short explanation and simple example reveal. But the key is that the interest of the innocent party in seeing to the performance of contracts to which they are party is captured in part by the idea that benefits conferred pursuant to contract on a party who ultimately fails to honour their obligation ought to be restored to the innocent party.

In the case of the reliance interest, the circumstances might be similar, but instead of conferring a benefit on the party who ultimately breaches the contract, the innocent party changes her position to her detriment on the strength of the contractual commitment. Usually, a party will expend an amount of money, knowing that the expense will be reasonable so long as the other party performs her obligation. Suppose you are interested in improving the landscaping at your home, and you are unable to perform the work yourself. I agree to do the work you require beginning on a stipulated date, in exchange for which you agree to pay me $5000. In reliance on my promise, you purchase a quantity of exotic shrubs at a cost of $1000. However, I fail to live up to my promise to begin work on the date specified, as a result of which the planting of the shrubs is delayed. Despite your best efforts to protect the shrubs, they die because of the delay. The value of the injury to your interest in seeing to the completion of this contract to which you are party is $1000, that is, the extent to which you have detrimentally relied on my broken contractual commitment. That will be the measure of damages in a successful suit for breach of contract. The rule of thumb is that the reliance interest is satisfied through an award of money that would put the innocent party in the same position they would have been in had the contract never been negotiated.

The rationale for an award of damages for injury to the expectation interest is opposite to that of the reliance interest. Here, the court will award damages so as to put the innocent party in the position they would have been in had the contract been performed. In other words, the court is compensating the innocent party for what they might reasonably have expected to attain by virtue of the other party's performance of the contract. Ordinarily, it is not appropriate that the court compensate an innocent party for injuries to both the reliance interest and the expectation interest. After all, a party cannot be restored to their pre-contract position, yet compensated for their anticipated post-performance position, at the same time. Further, compensation for injury to the expectation interest is ordinarily limited to actual, quantifiable, anticipated economic loss, such as loss of profit on re-sale of goods. Suppose you are aware that I am a dealer in fine gemstones. You contract to sell me a quantity of rare stones at a price of $100,000. We agree that the transaction will be completed in four weeks' time. After we agree, I find a further buyer for the gems, and agree with him that he can purchase the gems from me in five weeks' time for $150,000. Ultimately, you default on your commitment to sell the gems to me, as a result of which my anticipated profit of $50,000 has been lost. This type of injury, lost profit, is well recognized in the law of remedies applicable to breach of contract, but it is rare that a court will award damages for injuries to other than economic expectations. Suppose that, instead of re-selling the gems, I plan to display them in my home, and my expectation is that I will gain considerable prestige in the eyes of my neighbours as a result. If you breach your contract to sell the gems to me, such that my expectation of increased prestige is not realized, it is unlikely that a court will compensate me for that loss.[5]

The difficulty modern courts have in extending claims for damages in breach of contract cases outside the parameters of the restitution, reliance and expectation interests is referable to the early English case, *Hadley v. Baxendale*.[6] There, the court developed a two pronged test for the compensability of losses attendant on breach of contract:

> Where two parties have made a contract which one of them has broken, the damages which the other party ought to receive in respect of such breach of contract should be such as may fairly and reasonably be considered either arising naturally, *i.e.* according to the usual course of things, from such breach of contract itself, or such as may reasonably be supposed to have been in the contemplation of both parties, at the time they made the contract, as the probable result of the breach of it.[7]

Losses incurred through injuries to the reliance interest and the restitution interest, for the most part at least, are losses that arise naturally from a breach of contract. To the extent that the expectation interest compensates for the loss of anticipated profits, then that head of damage, too, might be considered to flow naturally from the breach. As well, ordinary expenses incurred by an innocent party in reliance on another party's commitment will be such as are in the reasonable contemplation of both parties at the time the contract is made, and are therefore compensable under the second

---

5 In recent years, courts have become more sympathetic to claims for damage to interests other than economic interests in breach of contract cases. For example, see the discussion of damages for injured reputation in *Francis v. Canadian Imperial Bank of Commerce*, [1994] O.J. No. 2657, 21 O.R. (3d) 75 (Ont. C.A.), a case involving the breach of an employment contract by the employer.

6 *Hadley v. Baxendale* (1854), 156 E.R. 145 (Exch.).

7 *Ibid.*, 151.

branch of the test. The same might also be said for lost profits, so long as the defaulting party is aware that the innocent party intends to re-sell the goods, or that the ordinary business of the innocent party is re-sale. But in the case of demonstrated injuries outside the fairly strict confines of the tests in *Hadley v. Baxendale*, perhaps hurt feelings or lost prestige resulting from the unfulfilled contract, the courts insist that the possibility of such injury be made explicit in the negotiations leading up to the finalization of the terms of the contract. If the damages sought are not such as would have been in the ordinary contemplation of the parties as they negotiated their relationship, then the court will not award those damages unless it can be demonstrated that the defaulting party was made aware of such a possibility in the event of breach. In considering the appropriate level of damages for breach of contract, therefore, we are forced to consider not only the effect of an award on the injured party's situation, but also the justice of the award considered from the perspective of the wrongdoer. This rule distinguishes the law of remedies in contract cases from the situation in the law of tort, where the justice of the award of damages from the wrongdoer's perspective is relevant only rarely.

III. REMEDIES IN EQUITY

It is sometimes the case in private law disputes that an award of damages is inappropriate, or at least ineffectual, for the purposes of fully resolving the issues between the parties and giving both the sense that closure has been accomplished and justice has been done. As mentioned above, many personal injury cases involve suffering and losses that are simply too profound to be compensated by a mere money award, although in such situations judges are constrained both by the law of remedies and by the reality of human inability to relieve every problem of suffering that presents itself. Money is the only available remedy in such situations, inadequate and ineffectual as it may be. In certain other situations, however, judges have an additional series of remedies available that, when appropriate, offer the possibility of alternative solutions to private law disputes. This series of remedies emerged from the equitable side of our heritage, and consists of four major types. They are injunction, specific performance, rescission and rectification.

For the most part, equitable remedies are adapted for use in cases of breach of contract, although an injunction is often an appropriate remedy in torts cases involving actual or threatened injury to property interests. An injunction is an order of a court requiring a party to do something (a "mandatory injunction") or refrain from doing something (a "prohibitory injunction"). In the law of tort, a prohibitory injunction might be issued to force one property owner to stop activities which constitute an actionable nuisance to the neighbouring property owner. Or perhaps a mandatory injunction would issue to compel a party to remove a fence that impedes access to another party's land. Personal interests, too, are sometimes protected through the issue of an injunction. In the law of defamation, a prohibitory injunction may be the appropriate remedy to force the discontinuation of a continuing libel, or to prevent the broadcast of a television programme that contains defamatory material.[8]

As is the case with all equitable remedies, the party seeking an injunction must demonstrate to the Court that their conduct has not been oppressive or unfair to the offending party. This introduces a discretionary element in the grant of an injunction that is a difficult variable in all cases of claims for equitable relief. The judge must weigh the claimant's behaviour against ordinary standards of right conduct, developed by the judge through her own experience, intuition and interpretation of the precedents, before deciding if the court's equitable jurisdiction ought to be invoked. This is a difficult assessment for most judges, and even more difficult for the litigants to predict with certainty. Lawyers refer to this dilemma as the rule that "the party seeking equity must come to the Court with clean hands", although no one is quite sure what that rule really means, objectively considered. Our ideas of fairness are largely a question of our own experience and the circumstances that present themselves to us as we go about our day-to-day lives, such that judges are free to draw on their equitable jurisdiction by subjectively assessing the comparative conduct of the parties, relatively immune from scrutiny on appeal.

Nevertheless, in awarding an injunction judges must observe one very important guideline. An injunction is an inappropriate remedy where an award of damages will suffice. The court will always consider the legal remedy first, and will only invoke equitable jurisdiction where the law is somehow inadequate. Suppose your neighbour plays baseball with his children in his backyard, and negligently hits the ball through your kitchen window. You seek damages for the broken window, and an injunction to prevent the neighbours from playing baseball on their property. In this situation, unless it could be demonstrated that there is a continuing and persistent threat of injury, a judge will award you damages for the broken

---

8 The examples used in the discussion of injunctions in this section of this chapter relate exclusively to situations arising in the law of tort. Injunctions are occasionally issued in cases of breach of contract, but this is quite rare in Canadian law. For example, see *Lindsey v. Le Sueur*, [1913] O.J. No. 168, 29 O.L.R. 648 (Ont. C.A.). There, an author in the course of preparing a biography of William Lyon Mackenzie was enjoined from using in particular ways certain items related to Mackenzie's life, despite a contract allowing the author access to those items. The court decided that the intended use was not in keeping with the spirit of the contract, and issued the injunction.

window, but will not issue a prohibitory injunction to prevent further activity. Damages is an adequate remedy here, even if the event were to recur occasionally. A similar situation often arises in cases of golf courses in residential neighbourhoods, where property owners complain that stray golf balls interfere with the ordinary enjoyment of their homes. In this case, however, the threat of injury is continuing, and no measure of damages can compensate for a continual threat. The owners of the golf course might be ordered to erect netting to protect against injury, or to re-route particular holes to reduce the risk.

The rationale for the rule that an injunction will only issue where damages is an inadequate remedy is based on the underlying principles of individual autonomy and respect that have formed the focus of much of our discussions in this book. An injunction is a positive interference by the court in the activities of one party, requiring that party to do something or to refrain from doing something, removing from that party the freedom to choose their own behaviour and make their own decisions relative to a particular activity. It is overt direction of behaviour that is highly unusual in private law matters. An award of damages, however, focuses virtually exclusively on the injuries of the complaining party and requires the mere payment of money by the wrongdoer, leaving the latter to pursue their self-interest and choose their behaviour without the continuing direction and supervision of the court. In all cases, courts will make an award of damages where damages is an adequate remedy for the injured party, rather than actively interfere in the wrongdoer's activities through the grant of an injunction.

The equitable remedy of specific performance is limited to cases of breach of contract. It is an order of the court by which a party is ordered to do what the party has promised to do by virtue of the contract. As is the case with all equitable remedies, the grant of an order of specific performance is in the discretion of the judge, and the judge must consider the adequacy of an award of damages before deciding to compel performance of contractual obligations through an order of specific performance. In the law of contract, however, the rule against invoking equitable jurisdiction where an award of damages is sufficient is not so strictly observed as it is in the law of tort. In fact, there are many cases where both damages and specific performance might be awarded, depending on the circumstances. For example, in a contract for the sale and purchase of residential property, the seller's failure to complete the transaction on time may cause the purchaser to incur expenses for temporary lodging that are recoverable through an ordinary claim for damages. Further, however, the purchaser may succeed in convincing the court that an order of specific performance ought to issue, compelling the completion of the transaction by the seller at the earliest opportunity. Sometimes an order for specific performance is made after a default has occurred, but it is often the case that a party will seek an order of specific performance prior to breach. This situation occurs where the other party has given a reasonable indication that, when the time for performance arrives, a breach will occur. This is referred to as a situation of "anticipatory breach", and in the appropriate circumstances it will be enough to justify an order of specific performance. Such an order is much like a mandatory injunction in effect.

It is not in every case, however, where a court will consider making an order of specific performance. In the world of private law, it is considered unacceptable to order the performance of a contract for personal services over the objections of one party. A contract for personal services is one in which the knowledge, talents or skill of one party to the contract are integral to the performance of the contract, involving the personal participation of that party to a level not easily performed by someone else. Ordinarily, to be classified as such, personal services contracts must involve some measure of confidence exhibited by one party in the talents of the other. For example, if a symphony orchestra contracts with a maestro to be the orchestra's conductor for the coming concert season, then it is likely that a court will not order specific performance of the conductor's contractual obligation in the event of his breach. This is a personal services contract, dependent for its successful performance on the particular knowledge and talents of the maestro, and on the confidence of the orchestra in his ability to perform.

In our isolation of personal services contracts from other contracts for which specific performance might be ordered, and as is often the case in our discussion of the peculiarities of private law relationships, we turn for our explanation to the idea of the dignified, autonomous individual, choosing their own life's path and acting in their self-interest. This image looms large over the reluctance of the court to specifically enforce personal services contracts. It is considered contrary to the guiding principles of human dignity and respect that a person be forced to serve another against their will, even in the situation where that person has freely chosen to commit contractually to that very service. Such compulsion is undignified and disrespectful, notwithstanding the initial agreement. Remember that the remedy of specific performance is an equitable remedy, and as such is awarded only in the discretion of the court after full consideration of the entire circumstances of the situation. It is hardly equitable to force someone to perform personal services over their objections. Remember too, however, that the unavailability of the equitable remedy does not mean that the non-defaulting party is without recourse. An action for damages continues to lie against the defaulting party for breach of a personal services contract, and a compensatory money award based on the reliance interest and the expectation interest is generally the appropriate result.

Rescission is another equitable remedy available in particular circumstances of breach of contract. Strictly speaking, an order of rescission returns the parties to the position they were in before the contract was negotiated, effectively nullifying their contractual obligations. The term used to describe the effect of an order of rescission is *restitutio in integrum* (meaning "restoration to the original condition" when used in the law). The order of rescission is one of the most direct ways in which the court protects the restitution interest, referred to above in this chapter in the discussion of the legal remedy of damages for breach of contract. The order itself is granted on equitable grounds, and then an award of damages is made so as to make recompense for inappropriately conferred benefits. Often, of course, it will be impossible to restore the parties to their pre-contractual position, as in the case where one party irrevocably changes their position on the strength of the other party's contractual obligation. In such a case, damages calculated on the basis of the reliance interest may be the better alternative.

Normal equitable considerations apply in the award of rescission, meaning that the remedy is discretionary, based in large measure on the conduct of the parties and the entire circumstances of the case. Because of this discretionary element, courts are reluctant to provide any definitive list of situations in which rescission will be granted. A review of the cases, however, suggests that at least one of three possibilities must prevail to support a successful application. First, the applicant might establish that their contractual commitment was induced by fraud, and that the fraud compelled them to make a mistake as to the nature of the contract. Suppose a shareholder in a company fraudulently represents to you that her shares are worth twice as much as their actual value. Despite your being as diligent as possible, you fail to detect the fraud, and therefore agree to buy the shares at the inflated price. Prior to the completion of the transaction, however, you are informed by another shareholder of the actual value of the shares, and as a result you seek rescission of the contract to purchase. In such circumstances equity will intervene to prevent the fraud from generating a windfall for the dishonest shareholder, and to protect you from an unfortunate bargain. Secondly, a mistake as to the true nature of a contract may result from an innocent misrepresentation, and in such circumstances a court may order rescission so as to restore the parties to the position they were in before the misrepresentation was made and the contract was negotiated on mistaken grounds. Thirdly, where there has been some undue influence or unconscionability in the negotiations leading up to the settling of the terms of the contract, a court may order rescission. This is the situation, even where the undue influence or unconscionability is not such as to constitute fraud.[9]

The fourth equitable remedy of note is also one designed exclusively for cases arising out of exchange relationships. An order of rectification is occasionally issued by a court to make some adjustment in the actual terms of the contract. Our understanding of the respect paid by the law to individual autonomy and choice in the negotiation of contractual terms ought to indicate that this remedy is ordered only rarely and in very circumscribed circumstances. The ordinary situation in which rectification is the appropriate remedy arises where a written contract is inconsistent with the agreement it is intended to represent. Suppose two parties negotiate an agreement by which the first party will perform certain landscaping services for the second party, all to be completed by August 31. After the work begins, the parties agree to reduce their contract to writing, and in doing that they mistakenly insert September 30 as the completion date. When it becomes clear that the first party will not finish the job by August 31, the second party tries to enforce the early completion date, and the first party resists. In such a case, a court would feel free to exercise equitable jurisdiction, rectifying the written contract so as to make it consistent with the original agreement. Then, if the first party still refused to complete on time, an order of specific performance or damages for late completion would be appropriate.

At common law, a court was not permitted to change the terms of a written contract. But we must not forget that rectification is a remedy in equity, and in equity judges have a much wider discretion to order the results that they feel are just in the circumstances, even where those results are, strictly speaking, in contravention of formal legal rules. The party seeking such equitable intervention must be absolutely innocent of any wrongdoing in the relationship under review, for otherwise they will be unable to demonstrate to the court that they are seeking equity "with clean hands". In the case of a request for rectification, one of the most difficult strict legal barriers to be overcome is the rule known as the "parol evidence rule". Simply stated, the word "parol" means "given orally", and in the law, evidence given orally in court cannot justify a judge's alteration of the terms of a written agreement. The rule extends to prohibit the introduction of any evidence of the meaning of a written

---

9 Readers will recognize the grounds on which rescission might be appropriate by reference to the section "Excuses for Non-Performance" in Chapter 3 above. If an innocent party to a contract claims relief from performance based on misrepresentation, undue influence, unconscionability and like excuses for non-performance, then the appropriate remedy is ordinarily rescission. The restitution interest is very important here, since the court, when ordering rescission, will also order that any benefits conferred by one party to the other be restored, thereby returning the parties to the position they were in before the contract was negotiated.

contract apart from the terms of the written contract itself, unless there is some ambiguity in the contract's terms. But the strict parameters of the parol evidence rule do not bind a judge in equity. There is more discretion in equity to allow evidence that tends to fully explain the entire circumstances of a case, especially where one party pleads mistake and seeks rectification. Further, courts in equity have distinguished the parol evidence rule by saying that it relates most directly to problems of the interpretation of contracts, rather than to problems of the compatibility of a written agreement with the actual agreement between the parties.[10]

IV. CHALLENGES IN PRIVATE LAW REMEDIES

As was suggested at the beginning of this chapter, it is likely that the majority of individuals experience private law most overtly through the law of remedies. Much of what the law does otherwise is more subtle in its effect, directing the way in which many of our relationships are structured and executed without our ever being aware of law's influence. But when we seek the law's assistance in repairing a broken relationship, or in compensating for the injuries we have suffered through someone's tortious behaviour or breach of contract, the law of remedies has direct, significant influence on our lives. Awards of damages for personal injury, for example, can help ease the suffering of long-term disability, provide funds for future care, replace lost earning capacity, and ease the transition from an active life to a restricted life. Damages are also available to assist in the adjudication of disputes arising through breach of contract, perhaps to help restore an innocent party to the position they occupied before being induced by a fraudulent misrepresentation to make a bad bargain, or to compensate for damage to the expectations that naturally flow from exchange agreements. Equitable remedies, too, are available in appropriate circumstances to assist the court in coming to a just result, notwithstanding that the strict rules of law may purport to impose limits on what a judge is free to do. In total, then, the wide variety of remedies available, combined with the formal attributes of law and the flexibility and discretion characteristic of equity, carries the potential to generate an experience that, for many litigants in private law, is quite satisfactory.

---

[10] Perhaps the clearest statement of this difference in Canadian jurisprudence is found in *Bercovici v. Palmer* (1966), 58 W.W.R. 111 (Sask. C.A.). At page 113, Justice Culliton made it quite explicit that the evidence to be allowed when considering the question of rectification of a written contract may often be significantly different from the evidence to be allowed when merely seeking assistance in interpretation.

But the prescriptive function of law is not performed without difficulty, and those difficulties generate some very interesting challenges in the world of private law. In our introductory discussion of alternatives to litigation earlier in this chapter, we made reference to problems of cost and time in seeking a remedy through litigation. These problems continue to plague the conventional judicial system despite some fairly innovative approaches to quickening the pace of litigation and diverting many matters to alternative mechanisms for solving private law disputes. The challenge, of course, is to offer a procedure by which private law problems might be resolved quickly and inexpensively, both out of a continuing search for greater efficiency in the allocation of human and other resources, and out of the recognition that justice is better served when everyone, regardless of their wealth or circumstances, has an equal opportunity to pursue their private law rights. The problem remains, however, that suffering is often exacerbated because a remedy is not available precisely when it would be most advantageous to an injured party, and it is also true that disputants with limited personal resources are frequently at a significant disadvantage when engaged in a contest with a wealthy opponent.

The problem of the impecunious wrongdoer is another challenge that regularly presents itself to the successful litigant in private law matters. It is one thing to persevere through a difficult pre-trial and trial process, and ultimately to obtain an award of damages that, all things considered, does as much as can be done with money to alleviate the innocent party's suffering or otherwise compensate them for their injury. But it is quite another thing to actually collect those damages from the wrongdoer. The judgment by which an award of damages is made is virtually useless unless the wrongdoer has the means to pay those damages. Although the forces of the state are available to the successful litigant in seeing to the fulfilment of money judgments, there is nothing the state can do in the event that the wrongdoer cannot pay. Many individuals are without assets and without income, and these individuals simply lack the means to satisfy a money judgment. In such circumstances, the successful litigant is without further recourse, and obtaining the judgment becomes a hollow victory. Debtors' prisons were abolished long ago, and seeing the wrongdoer in bankruptcy offers little consolation to the successful litigant.[11]

There are situations, of course, where someone other than the wrongdoer is responsible for payment of the damage award. In cases of injuries caused through automobile accidents, for example, the ultimate responsibility for paying the amount ordered by the judge falls to the wrongdoer's insurer. This is a matter of contract between the wrongdoer and his insurer, such

---

[11] As mentioned in Chapter 4 above, the doctrine of vicarious liability offers some relief for this difficulty in certain limited circumstances.

that when the injured party sues the wrongdoer in tort law, the insurer will step in and defend the action on behalf of the wrongdoer. When an award of damages is made, then the insurer pays. As between the wrongdoer and the insurer, however, the negligent operation of the automobile may cause the wrongdoer's premiums to go up, but this has no impact on the injured party.[12] Insurance also plays a role in cases of medical malpractice and other situations of professional negligence. In situations, then, of impecunious defendants, insurance has the tendency to minimize the problem of the uncollectable judgment.

At the same time, however, insurance may tend to limit the deterrent effect of damage awards, especially in cases of products liability or negligent manufacture. In theory at least, the prospect of being ordered to pay a significant amount of money to an injured party ought to convince most individuals to behave in ways that reduce the likelihood of such an order. The extent to which the law of tort and the law of damages succeed in this respect is fairly uncertain, but in theory the threat of a private law judgment does encourage us to be more careful as we go about our daily routines. However, the knowledge that our insurer stands behind us, ready to pay any award against us that might be made, is just as likely to limit that deterrent effect, to the extent that it exists at all. In many situations, the difficulty resolves itself into measurement of the risk attendant on certain behaviour, consideration of the likelihood that injuries will result if that behaviour is undertaken, security in knowing that liability insurance is ultimately responsible, and the willingness to pay whatever increased insurance premiums may result.

In cases of products liability, it is sometimes the case that pure economic considerations outweigh any threat of private law judgment. Suppose that a manufacturer sells millions of units of a particular product. The manufacturer is aware that its product contains a flaw that, according to the manufacturer's best advice, may result in serious injuries to a very small number of users of the product. To recall the product will cost an enormous amount of money, involving extensive publicity campaigns to warn the public, educating the various dealers on the best way in which to correct the defect, thousands of hours of mechanics' and administrators' time, and unpredictable adverse effects on the manufacturer's goodwill.

---

[12] There are various systems of automobile insurance in place in different jurisdictions. The short summary related in this paragraph refers to a traditional contract of indemnity (by which the insurer agrees to pay the insured person the amount of their loss up to a certain point, equal to the award of damages made to the injured party in our example) and what is known as the principle of subrogation (by which an insurer under a contract of indemnity has the right to defend the action on behalf of the insured person). For a more complete summary of some of the issues at stake in the law of insurance as it relates to automobiles, see Craig Brown, *No-Fault Automobile Insurance in Canada* (Toronto: Carswell, 1988).

On a comparative basis, if the product currently in use by consumers is not recalled, then the damage awards that might ultimately be made against the manufacturer on behalf of the small number of injured parties will be insignificant. Based on strict economic considerations, then, the manufacturer might decide to run the risk of a series of private law damage awards, knowing that, ultimately at least, the manufacturer is better off. It ought to be clear, of course, that decisions made on the strength of pure economic calculation neglect the fact that the suffering endured by the injured parties can never be fully compensated by a mere money award. In other words, while the economics of the situation are attractive to the manufacturer, the plight of the injured party is only partly economic. Pain and suffering, and the disruption to one's life that comes with debilitating injury, can never be fully relieved.[13]

While it is unclear the extent to which deterrence has an impact on behaviour in the world of private law, there are other functions of the law of remedies that have more obvious effect. Throughout this chapter we have discussed the role of damages as compensation to the injured party, and this is the acknowledged principal purpose of tort law remedies. In contract law, too, compensation, together with restitution, is the principal focus. Equitable remedies, especially specific performance and injunction, fulfil special roles where the law of damages is inadequate. We ought to note, however, that compensation and deterrence are not the only functions of the law of remedies. In a small number of cases, damages can be used as punishment for the wrongdoer. As indicated earlier in this chapter, in almost every case the law of remedies considers the impact of the breach of contract or tortious behaviour on the injured party, and calculates the appropriate damage award on that basis alone. The wrongdoer is virtually irrelevant for this purpose. But in some situations the court feels compelled to punish particularly reprehensible conduct by making an award of damages that is disproportionate to the injured party's suffering. Wildly reckless disregard for the consequences of our actions, for example, especially where the wrongdoer knows the conduct is virtually certain to cause injury, may support the court's decision to make an award of punitive damages. This is rare in Canadian jurisprudence, but significant nonetheless. It is another example of the situation referred to in Chapter 1 above, in which criminal law and tort law share certain characteristics,

---

[13] The situation related in this paragraph is similar to what occurred in the infamous case of the Ford Pinto automobile. There are other examples. See Richard L. Abel, "A Critique of American Tort Law" (1981), 8:2 *British Journal of Law and Society* 199, for a comprehensive assessment of the impact of the profit motive on decision-making respecting risk assessment and potential tort liability.

and may function to enhance the possibility of successful deterrence of reckless or particularly malicious behaviour in the law of tort.

As we have seen, the law of remedies often functions quite nicely to compensate parties for their injuries, and in most situations the process by which this occurs is conveniently understood through looking at the interests of the injured party deemed worthy of protection. In other words, the law of tort views bodily integrity, reputation, dominion over property and other interests as valuable to the autonomous, dignified individual. In the law of contract, considerations such as restitution, expectation and reliance are protected so as to address wrongs resulting from breach. In both contract law and tort law, the law of remedies is called upon to give meaning to the protection of these various interests by making a money award as compensation for injury. Now, while this is a convenient model for us to use in our attempt to come to terms with something of the structure of private law, it is nevertheless an incomplete picture. As alluded to in Chapter 4 above, there are some interests that are not fully protected in the law of tort, and this shortcoming in the law of remedies is one of the most perplexing challenges in all of private law.

For the most part, imperfectly protected interests present a problem in tort law. The most significant arise in cases of psychiatric injury of certain types, and in cases of pure economic loss that is not consequent on some other type of injury. The cases of the former type to which legal academics most often refer arise where witnesses to gruesome accidents sue the wrongdoer for negligently inflicting psychiatric harm. In the course of many cases decided over several years, the courts have decided that such injuries are sometimes compensable, perhaps dependent on some close relationship between the physically injured party and the party suffering psychiatric damage. The question of the foreseeability of psychiatric harm is relevant, too. In other words, it may be reasonable, and therefore foreseeable, that a witness responds badly when their own child or life partner is injured through a wrongdoer's negligence, but perhaps such a response is not reasonable, and therefore not foreseeable, if the injured party is a stranger. In any event, however, the claimant must manifest some physical symptoms of emotional damage, or perhaps a recognizable psychiatric illness such as chronic depression, to recover. Ordinary emotional upset is not compensable in any case.[14]

Claims for compensation for pure economic loss in negligence cases have presented an equally difficult challenge. It has never been doubted that the adverse economic consequences of personal injury are fully compensable. This is why lost earning capacity is recovered in a damage

---

14 The standard line of cases on this matter begins with *McLoughlin v. O'Brian*, [1982] 2 All E.R. 298 (H.L.) and *Alcock v. Chief Constable of South Yorkshire Police*, [1991] 3 W.L.R. 1057 (H.L.).

award by a person whose negligently inflicted injury renders them unable to work. But sometimes economic losses occur independently of some other sort of injury, and it is in this situation that the law of remedies hesitates. Suppose you employ a highly skilled carpenter in your furniture manufacturing business. Through the negligence of an automobile operator, the carpenter is injured, and because of that injury your business suffers. Are you entitled to sue the negligent driver directly, claiming damages to compensate you for the losses suffered due to the absence of the carpenter? In the law of tort, such a claim has never been allowed, the argument being that the composition of the class of potential injured parties is rendered too unpredictable and indeterminate. The corollary to this position is that the law of tort ought to strive for certainty, not simply in the manner by which we judge standards of conduct, but also in the limitations we impose on the expanding applicability of the neighbour principle in negligence cases.[15]

We ought not to be surprised that the challenge of imperfectly protected interests, the puzzling problem of deterrence, the nagging difficulties of cost and delay, and a number of other issues continue to influence the way in which the prescriptive function of private law is performed. The law of remedies, like other categories of private law, is imperfect, as are the people who inhabit the system by which the law is administered, and as are the litigants who appear day after day before judges vested with the responsibility of adjudication. The social world, of course, is impossibly complex, comprised of an incalculable number and variety of interpersonal relationships. Yet the law must be flexible enough to respond to each and every one of those relationships if called upon, and then be sage enough to prescribe the remedy that will best satisfy the litigants' search for justice and closure. The process of classification of relationships, the first step in the legal attempt to impose some order on a chaotic network of activity, results in an abstraction, of course. That abstraction, for our purposes captured in the principal private law categories, is then relied upon to generate real, valuable, efficacious solutions to disputes that have

---

15 For a helpful example of the court's reasoning in this respect, and a concise statement of the policy behind the rule against the recovery of pure economic loss in negligence cases, see *Electrohome Ltd. v. Welsh Plastics Ltd.*, [1968] 2 All E.R. 205 (Q.B.). There, a fire hydrant was negligently damaged, causing an interruption to the water supply and forcing a factory owner to close its plant for a day. The losses arising in consequence of the closure were not recoverable against the wrongdoer. At page 208 Justice Geoffrey Lane said:

> In the case of water being cut off in this manner one can imagine a whole series, maybe hundreds, of actions being brought against the defendants based on this type of negligence and ... the complexity of society would mean in effect that there might be no end to the concatenation of resulting damage.

On the neighbour principle generally, see above, Chapter 4, notes 10-12 and accompanying text.

immediate, often profound, impact on the ordinary lives of ordinary people. On occasion, the transition from abstract categorization to concrete remedy is an awkward one that taxes the ingenuity of judges and the creativity of academic lawyers. In many ways, however, and in most cases, the intersection of private law and social life is as natural and seamless as the complexity of human endeavour will allow.

Index

A

B

C

E

F

G

H

I

R

S

T

U

V

W

Z